BECOMING
BULLETPROOF

PRAISE FOR
BECOMING BULLETPROOF

"Evy's insight into safety and self-defense is second to none. In addition to her incredible knowledge, training, and experience she is battle-tested and proven having stood tall for our country when so many lives were on the line including her own. For anyone concerned over personal safety in these challenging times, this book is a must-read."

—Maria Menounos, *New York Times* bestselling author

"Evy takes readers on a powerful journey from being vulnerable and afraid to being prepared. Not only would I trust her with my life, I would go through any door with her."

—John (Buck) Smith, Chief Inspector/Fugitive Task Force Commander, United States Marshals Service (Ret.)

"Poumpouras's wise direction and actionable lessons will be relevant to audiences of all ages. Those looking for a shot of confidence will love this."

—*Publishers Weekly*, Starred Review

"In a world that seems to be getting more violent, less safe, and crazier year after year, Evy is the much-needed voice of calm, humor, and sanity."

—Jenny Hutt, Sirius XM radio host

"Evy brings her experienced and persuasive voice to one of the most important issues we face personally and globally: safety."

—Gavin de Becker, bestselling author of *The Gift of Fear*

"San Bernardino, Paris, Las Vegas . . . for years I have turned to Evy to advise, guide, and empower in times of crisis. When it comes to security and safety, I find myself asking, 'What would Evy do?'"

—Dr. Drew Pinsky

"Evy offers us a new narrative about what strength, determination, and grit sound like, act like, and look like. Her book shows us where our true power and fearlessness come from: the mind. In the midst of the current political, social, and cultural climate, she introduces a new way for us to empower and protect ourselves."

—Iman Oubou, founder and CEO of Swaay Media

BECOMING
BULLETPROOF

LIFE LESSONS
FROM A
SECRET SERVICE AGENT

EVY POUMPOURAS

ILLUSTRATIONS BY REMIE GEOFFROI

ATRIA PAPERBACK

New York London Toronto Sydney New Delhi

ATRIA
PAPERBACK

An Imprint of Simon & Schuster, LLC
1230 Avenue of the Americas
New York, NY 10020

First Atria Paperback edition March 2024

ATRIA PAPERBACK and colophon are trademarks of Simon & Schuster, LLC

Simon & Schuster: Celebrating 100 Years of Publishing in 2024

For information about special discounts for bulk purchases, please contact Simon & Schuster Special Sales at 1-866-506-1949 or business@simonandschuster.com.

The Simon & Schuster Speakers Bureau can bring authors to your live event. For more information, or to book an event, contact the Simon & Schuster Speakers Bureau at 1-866-248-3049 or visit our website at www.simonspeakers.com.

Interior Design by Silverglass

Illustrations by Remie Geoffroi

Manufactured in the United States of America

7 9 10 8

Library of Congress Cataloging-in-Publication Data has been applied for.

ISBN 978-1-9821-0375-0
ISBN 978-1-9821-0376-7 (pbk)
ISBN 978-1-9821-0377-4 (ebook)

For my father, Ioannis Poumpouras
July 11, 1945–September 1, 2019,
for teaching me to embrace the fight rather than fear it.

Contents

BECOMING
BULLETPROOF

Prologue

Nothing is, everything is becoming.
—Heraclitus

September 11, 2001

It sounded like a garbage truck had dropped out of the sky. The rattling of a thousand pieces of metal and glass and concrete reverberated around us, piercing a hole into the quiet September morning. But neither I nor my colleagues in the United States Secret Service's (USSS) New York Field Office had any idea of what was about to happen.

The Secret Service occupied the 9th and 10th floors of the forty-seven-story building that was World Trade Center 7. I had gone into work early that day to meet with our United States Customs Service liaison, Lenny, who I hoped would be able to help me apprehend a Frenchman I was pursuing for a fraud investigation. When the first plane hit the tower, truth be told, I was so focused on getting Lenny to agree to put my suspect on a watch list that I didn't even glance up at the sound. "Hey, Lenny! Focus," I said when his head started to turn toward that distant boom. "This is important."

Then there were gasps. Everyone around us, all the others who had come into the office early that day, slowly stood up or jumped to their feet. When we noticed everyone moving toward the windows, our conversation automatically paused. We got up and followed them.

As we gazed out at the World Trade Center's Twin Towers, the fire was incomprehensibly massive. Its flames poured upward from the gaping hole, engulfing the top of the building entirely. Unable to reconcile the sound we had heard with the destruction confronting us, my mind immediately sought out a mundane explanation. *Maybe it's an electrical fire*, I thought.

A voice came over the building's PA system, calm and authoritative. "We are evacuating the building. Please head toward the nearest exit or stairwell."

No reason was given, no mention of the fire in the adjacent tower or the noise we had heard. As one, we all headed for the stairwell.

An eerie sort of silence hovered over everyone on the walk down. There were no voices, no anxious questions asked—just the sound of hundreds of footsteps descending through the building, and emerging into the crowded lobby on the ground floor. One by one we paused in front of the lobby's floor-to-ceiling windows. The scene that unfolded before us was like a disaster movie playing out in full color, surreal to the point of seeming fake. Car-sized chunks of burning metal rained down from above, detonating like bombs where they crashed into the ground. Toxic smoke and flames poured out of the gaping hole in the tower looming over us. The wreckage falling from the sky made escape through the main entrance of our building impossible, and so the security staff were directing everyone to the emergency exits.

My gun and my badge—the only two things I made sure to take with me—were useless at that moment. I didn't know that a plane had been hijacked and flown into the World Trade Center's North Tower between the 93rd and 99th floors. I didn't know that the second plane would soon strike the second tower, or anything else that would happen that day. I knew only that as a Special Agent, I needed to help, however I could.

As people streamed toward the emergency exits, I immediately started looking around for my fellow agents. I found some of them deliberating in a small group by one of the stairwells and rushed over. "What are we doing?" I asked.

"Let's get the FAT kits," one agent said. FAT kits were the first aid trauma kits we kept in the field office, and which would undoubtedly be needed by anyone trying to escape the fire raging in Tower 1. Without hesitating, we ran back up the ten flights to retrieve them. The kits contained oxygen tanks, bandages, and a vast array of medical supplies and trauma necessities for helping people in the field—essentially, an ambulance in a bag—but at about twenty-six pounds, the kits were *heavy*. I picked up my kit, knowing it would be a challenge to get these supplies to the people who needed them most, and looked at the others. There were six of us total. With more than two hundred agents, we were the largest field office in the country, but I had no idea where everyone else was. We headed back down to the ground floor, the cumbersome kits dragging down our shoulders and cutting into our hands.

Since there was no way to get out through the front doors, we used the side doors and ran as fast as we could toward the main entrance of the North Tower as burning metal relentlessly thundered down from above.

That's when I heard it. A sound distinctly out of place, especially this close to the epicenter of New York with its high-rise office buildings and skyscrapers. Among the cacophony of destruction already unfolding—of twisting steel and shattering glass—came what I only later understood to be the engines of a Boeing 767 revving for maximum impact. A moment later, United Airlines Flight 175 flew into the South Tower.

And then hell got even hotter.

The force of its impact between floors 77 and 85 of Tower 2 instantaneously turned what was already unfathomable into Armageddon. As fire and heat and massive chunks of metal fell toward the earth from hundreds of feet overhead, I felt a strong hand grab my wrist and yank me back. It was my colleague Michael. I hadn't even seen the plane, but he had. We were out in the open and completely exposed. We knew we needed cover, so we broke out into a full sprint back toward our building.

There was confusion everywhere I looked. Some people were running. Others were walking. Some just stood there, frozen in disbelief. As I ran, I saw a man motionless, staring at the destruction above when something large fell on top of him. And then he was gone. Just gone. It still hadn't registered to me that it was now two planes that had flown into two towers, or how that was even possible, or what it meant. All I knew was we had to get to the people who needed help.

When we finally reached World Trade Center 7, Michael slammed me against the brick wall, forcing the breath out of my lungs as he tried to shield me with his body from the fire and fuel and glass and metal crashing to the ground. It felt like an eternity as we waited for the insanity of the massive explosion to slow. Our path now blocked, Michael and I zigzagged our way through the obstacle course of debris, trying to find our other colleagues and another way into the towers. We ran into a group of about fifteen agents and a supervisor huddled together.

"Listen, I'm going in there to help," the supervisor said as the towers blazed behind him. "Obviously this isn't like anything we've ever seen before. You don't have to go. No one's going to think badly of you if you don't. So whoever wants to come, come with me, and whoever wants to turn around and go, please do."

We all fell into silence for a moment. I looked over toward the towers, at all of the people streaming out of them, some shouting or crying, some expressionless with shock, and then I stepped forward, as did several others.

At the same time, someone nearby started screaming, then I heard a sharp gasp. "Oh my God," someone said. "They're jumping!"

I looked up, but at first I couldn't process what I was seeing: It was a man in a white shirt, his tie blowing back behind him as he fell through the air. His tie looked purple, or maybe blue. He had a mustache. His expression was blank when he hit the roof of one of the smaller buildings surrounding the Twin Towers and disappeared.

Countless more followed, maybe even hundreds. It was incomprehensible. It was raining people. Then I understood. All those people were choosing death on their own terms. Instead of burning, they chose to jump.

I looked over at my colleague Keven, who was standing next to me. There was a gash in his arm with blood trailing down. "Keven, we have to do something," I said. "We have to help."

Keven's voice was quiet when he answered me. His eyes remained fixated on the burning towers. "What can we possibly do to stop that?" he asked.

I remember feeling angry at what he said. The idea that we should just stand there while something so horrifying unfolded in front of us was enraging. But the fact is he was right. There was nothing we could do—nothing but witness all of those people falling to their death.

Never in my entire life have I ever felt more helpless than I did in that moment.

"Okay," our supervisor said. "Let's go."

I didn't look to see who chose to leave and who stayed. It didn't matter. All that mattered was helping everyone we could.

By now my hands were cut and blistering from the weight of carrying the FAT kit by its flimsy nylon handles. The barrage of falling destruction made it impossible to make our way in, so we set up a triage by the West Side Highway near the base of Tower 2. Ambulances had begun pulling up to the curb.

"Go to the water," we told the survivors who could walk on their own, pointing them toward the Hudson River. We guided those who needed immediate medical help into the ambulances—treating what injuries we could on our own. There were still so many people trapped in those buildings that we couldn't reach. It was awful, infuriating that we couldn't get to them, but we tried to focus on helping who we could.

One woman who came to us was having trouble breathing. When I tried to use the oxygen tank to give her air, I couldn't get it to work—it had been a long while since I had used one. I knelt next to it, laser-focused and cursing myself for not being able to get it to function. I was so fixated on connecting the tubes that I didn't notice when everything around me went quiet.

It was only when I looked up that I realized everyone had disappeared.

And then, from high above, there was the eerie, unmistakable wail of bending steel.

It happened slowly, just a metallic echo resounding through the air at first, followed by the grinding, groaning sound that precedes total destruction. Something awful was about to happen.

I wasn't afraid, exactly—mostly because I didn't know what I should be afraid of. I had no idea that the tower was going to fall. Based on that terrible rending sound, I guessed that the roof or some other type of massive debris was about to slide off of one of the towers. Whatever the cause, I knew that I needed to find shelter fast.

My mind went into autopilot, every second stretching out endlessly. The 110-story building loomed overhead. There was likely no cover that could shield me from the chunks of steel that were about to come down, and the nearness and sheer magnitude of the tower meant that I couldn't outrun it. So I did what I could to ensure my survival. I spotted a concrete wall at the base of the closest building and sprinted toward it, grabbing one of the bottles of water we had been using to clean out people's eyes and mouths; if I was going to be buried alive, I knew I would need water. I rushed through the patio of an abandoned Au Bon Pain restaurant and paused just long enough to take hold of one of the metal tables crowding the patio space. One thing you learn in explosives training with the Secret Service is that glass can kill you just as easily as bullets can. My adrenaline spiked as I dragged that brutally heavy table over to the building, hoping that it would protect me from falling debris and provide me with a pocket of air to shelter under should I be buried. I pushed it against the wall, crawled underneath, and pulled my knees to my chest to make myself into a smaller target.

The deafening groan of steel bending crescendoed as the tower broke apart, thousands of windows simultaneously shattering as the structure of the building finally failed.

And then the tower fell.

The cataclysm of noise and devastation that swept over me was unlike anything I've ever experienced. It was like sitting in the center of a volcano during an eruption. The heat and toxic dust filled the air so densely that I could hardly breathe. Cement and steel and shards of glass crashed all around me and the ground thundered with the continuous impacts, growing more deafening by the second. It quickly became clear that this was going to be beyond anything I had imagined. Day turned to night. The earth beneath me roared so deeply that I thought it was going to open up and swallow me whole. It seems pointless now, but I began shaking the table as hard as I could, feebly hoping that I could keep it from accumulating debris that would bury me. It was the only thing I could think to do, the only way I could try to fight. I still had no idea what was happening, but as the devastation continued unabated, the realization came to me, both fast and slow, that I was going to die.

I remember that I didn't feel afraid—only sad that I was going to die alone, and that when all was said and done, I'd be pulverized. Annihilated. There would be nothing left of me. No body to send back to my parents. I had been prepared for death, but I had never been prepared for a death such as this. This was the end. My end. The sorts of worries and preoccupations that took up so much attention in my daily life cleared away, leaving me only with this thought: *Had I done enough? Had I helped enough? Had I lived enough?* I thought of my fellow agents and all the people we had been trying to save. I hoped they were safe, or if it were the end for them, too, then I wished them a painless death. As I waited for death to claim me, I hoped that I had been a good enough person, that my family knew how much I loved them. That I had somehow somewhere made a difference in someone's life.

Then I started to pray aloud.

"Our Father who art in Heaven,

Hallowed be thy name . . ."

I prayed in Greek, as I'd been taught growing up in the Greek Orthodox Church. I kept my eyes open as the world around me split apart. I wanted to see death coming for me. I knew I had no choice in my death, but I could choose how I faced it. Even when I could no longer hear the sound of my own voice, even when my face and mouth filled with dust and ash, I kept my eyes open and prayed. As the tower collapsed above me, strange as it might sound, I felt a peculiar peace spreading through me. No longer able to speak, I prayed silently in my mind as the force of the blast slammed me back against the concrete wall of the building. Smoke and metal and cement and grit shot into my throat and into my ears and into my eyes, burning me.

And then, somehow, at some point, it stopped. The destruction fell to stillness. I realized that it was over only when I heard the quiet—the most deafening silence. Now there was nothing but a void of blackness as dense as the dust-choked air in my lungs.

The only indication that I was still alive was the pain. My mouth and throat were on fire. My eyes and nose burned. I didn't know that I was covered in a toxic mix of chemicals and building materials and God knows what else. I raised my hand in front of my face, but I could see nothing. Had I been buried alive after all?

I cautiously probed around me. Nothing. No molten metal or twisted beams of steel encasing me inside a metal tomb. With my arms stretched out, I began to crawl from underneath the table and stood only after feeling the certainty of a brick wall to my left. That terrible stillness was all I could hear. *Oh my God*, I thought. *Everyone must be dead.* Though my eyes were scorched with ash, I forced them to open wider and focused on what I thought was a distant shimmer of light.

I moved toward it. If I was alive, the light was a good thing. If I were dead, I figured the light would still be a good thing. The glow was like the soft haze of a candle, and I followed it until I finally heard a voice. I recognized it at once—my friend and colleague Gabriel, calling out for me.

I don't think I can adequately express the relief of hearing a familiar voice after thinking the world had just ended.

I tried to shout out, but my voice couldn't get through all the chalky debris in my mouth and throat. I spit some of it out and tried again. "Gabriel, is that you? Gabriel, I can't see."

"Stay where you are!" he yelled. "I'm coming to you."

I stopped moving and waited until he found me. As he led me through the wreckage, my eyes slowly began to clear. I faintly watched two firefighters heading in another direction. They looked like they were coming from battle. One was holding up the other, who was still grasping his ax, dragging it across the ground. There was blood streaming down his face. The world looked like the set of an apocalyptic movie, impossible to make sense of.

We continued to stumble through the near-darkness and then practically collided with two other agents.

"Genie?" Michael said (my nickname was Genie at the time, short for Evyenia). "My God, is that you?"

I heard that same relief in his voice—I knew exactly how he felt.

"It's me."

Together we walked into the lobby of a nearby building. Inside there were about a dozen or so people, who had managed to escape the worst of the blast of the first tower falling. I stood there, my eyes shut tight, the burning worsening as I tried to get my bearings. Looking back on it now, I thought that I had been brave by keeping my eyes open and facing death head-on, but in hindsight it probably wasn't the smartest idea, exposing myself to all that heat and ash.

A moment later, I felt someone begin wiping at my eyes with a wet cloth. I flinched at the sudden contact, but gradually relaxed as the burning diminished. "Better now?" asked a man's voice with a thick Spanish accent. I opened my eyes and saw the building super cleaning the ash from my face. I nodded and thanked him.

I looked around the lobby and my gaze fell on a little boy of about seven who was looking back at me. He was holding a bottle of peach Snapple as he and his mother walked over. "For your mouth," said his mother when her son offered the bottle to me. "Rinse your mouth out."

I accepted the bottle, took a big swig, and spat it out. I wanted more, but I didn't want to take any more of the little boy's drink in case he might need it.

I still didn't completely understand what was happening, or what might still be coming.

The one thing we did know was that it wasn't over. We probably had only minutes or seconds before the second tower fell, and we needed to evacuate as quickly as possible. We used our badges to show everyone we were law enforcement agents and convince them, forcefully but calmly, that they needed to get as far away as possible—right now. "Everybody out and head toward the water," we told them. "You all need to get out of the area."

We pushed them as far from the vicinity as we could. When the North Tower started coming down seconds later, everyone began to run. Even when the cloud of dust spread out from Ground Zero and engulfed us, we kept moving, sprinting away from the explosion, grabbing people, pulling them toward safety, carrying people too injured to run. At one point I saw a man in a truck stop in the middle of the street, get out, and gaze up at the mountain of debris where the towers once stood.

I immediately ran over to him. "Hey, you've got to get out of here," I told him. "It isn't safe."

"My cousin, she works there," the man said in a thick Polish accent, still staring up, immobilized and helpless. I knew what he was feeling. I had friends and colleagues in those towers, too.

"Listen," I said. "There's nothing you can do to help her right now. You've got to get yourself to safety."

He started to weep and put his arms around me, the two of us standing there, hugging in the middle of the West Side Highway as people stampeded down the sidewalks on either side of us. Fire trucks were tearing down the road away from the destruction, their sirens screaming, firefighters shouting through their loudspeakers that a gas line had broken and everyone needed to run for their lives. It was pandemonium. The other agents kept yelling my name, calling me back, but I couldn't leave the driver as he sobbed and held on to me. Finally, I helped him back into his truck and watched as he drove off before I returned to my colleagues to help the other survivors.

I spent the next couple of weeks as a part of the search-and-rescue effort. I sifted through the rubble of Tower 7 for sensitive intelligence from the Secret Service as well as the Central Intelligence Agency (CIA), whose office had been in the same building as ours. I canvassed the surrounding area for human remains, which we then sent to the labs so that grieving families could identify their loved ones.

It was three days in when my friend Sofia called me, distraught. "They can't find Joanna," she said. "What do we do?"

Joanna was a friend I had known for many years from the community of Greek girls I'd grown up with. She was kind, bubbly, always laughing. And she had worked at Cantor Fitzgerald, which occupied the 101st through 105th floors of Tower 1, only a few floors above where the first plane hit. With the initial smash of glass and metal we heard that morning, Joanna's life had probably ended, along with so many others.

Later, when Joanna's sister, Effie, called me, I was racked with guilt over the fact that I was alive and Joanna probably wasn't. I told her that I needed Joanna's DNA—hair from a hairbrush—and cheek swabs from family members.

There was a long silence on the line. "Okay," she said.

Seven months later the search team found a small fragment of Joanna's right arm, which meant that her family was finally able to put her to rest. In the aftermath of 9/11, going to Joanna's memorial service was one of the hardest things I had to do. My survivor's guilt became so overwhelming that I left the church midway through. While her family and friends honored her inside, I sat on the front steps of the Greek church, huddled over and heartbroken.

About twelve months later, my supervisor called me into his office to say that the Secret Service was awarding me and the other agents who had stayed to help on September 11 the Valor Award—a medal of the highest honor within the Service. He told me the day of the ceremony and that Jerry Parr, the agent who had saved Ronald Reagan's life after he had been shot, had been given that same honor. But as he spoke, a knot formed in my stomach.

"I'm sorry, sir," I said. "I will be overseas, visiting family. Can someone else accept it on my behalf?"

He agreed, somewhat reluctantly, and I left his office.

That night, I went home and booked my flight to Greece for the date of the ceremony. It's not that I was insensible to the importance of being awarded an honor rarely given, particularly one that so few in the Service have ever received. But I just couldn't bear the thought of being given a medal for living when so many others had perished.

And after all, I'd done only what I was supposed to do—help. The same thing that every police officer, firefighter, paramedic, and first responder had done. The same thing that civilians had done, like the building super who cleaned the ash from my eyes. The little boy who gave me his Snapple to rinse my mouth. The man in the truck who might have run into a collapsed burning building to save someone he loved. They didn't need any specialized training to look out for people who were hurt and scared, nor did they choose to help in the hope of being awarded medals or recognition. They helped because it was the only thing they could do. Because, without being told, they already knew that when it seems like the world is ending, being willing to help others is the antidote to fear.

And that is the first step toward becoming bulletproof.

Introduction: Harder to Stop

To him who is in fear, everything rustles.
—SOPHOCLES

Survival Skills

The will to survive is fundamental to us all. But in a life-or-death situation—when calm, careful planning, and logical thinking are what's needed most—research shows that most of us will lose our shit.

I know fear. I have been trained by the best of the best to recognize when fear is walking through the door like an uninvited houseguest planning to stay awhile. And I know his crazy cousin, *panic*—that guy will wreck your house faster than you can blink. If either of these two take over, things can become very dire very quickly.

Here's what I also know to be true: Fear is relative to the situation you're facing. Whether you find yourself in the middle of a terrorist attack, trying to find the courage to deal with confrontation, or negotiating an important business meeting, your ability to conquer your fear, survive, and even thrive comes down to one thing and one thing only: mental attitude. Survival is about mastering yourself and your fear response, being able to think and act while keeping your panic at bay. Being able to navigate your mental and physical response to fear is your number one survival skill. It can also be the best ally you have in any intimidating situation life throws your way. Managing your fear requires a deliberate act of courage. It is a choice that you make, and it's one that everyone is capable of making.

The Post 9/11 World

The world was a different place before September 11, 2001. Before the towers fell, no one worried about planes being hijacked by terrorists and flown into buildings. Most police departments didn't even have terrorism units prior to 2001. They focused primarily on crime. After 9/11, however, all that changed. As the world watched in horror while New York City filled with smoke, a new era of threats rushed in, and with it, new fears. Things most of us had never heard of began making their way into our conversations, words like *al Qaeda*, *suicide bomber*, and *infidel*.

Fast-forward to today and we find ourselves facing new fears. Mass shootings, school shootings, and cyberattacks filter into our social media and news feeds. The world feels full of fear in a way that can immobilize and overwhelm us at a moment's notice. The fear of going to work in a high-rise building, the fear of going to school, the fear of going to a country music concert, or to the movies—our fears follow us like ominous shadows from home, to work, to wherever we go. Some of us wish we could keep ourselves and our loved ones safely tucked away inside, sheltered against the unstoppable dangers in a world just waiting to prey on us. But the truth is that's not possible. Nor is it a way to live. Instead, as our fears evolve, so too should the way we respond to them.

The best way to manage fear is preparation. It isn't hiding from the things we're afraid of—it's facing them head-on, taking responsibility for our own safety, and giving ourselves the tools and knowledge we need to manage any situation that might come our way. It's about confidence, personal strength, and self-sufficiency.

This book is about teaching you to become your own hero—to not only recognize when fear is rearing its ugly head, but how to control it, reduce it, and even harness it. It's about helping you make empowered choices rather than letting fear run the show.

Our fears are tailor-made for each of us. Some fears are handed to us by our families and culture; some just show up in our minds with no explanation while others are a result of a traumatic situation or experience. If you want to be capable of facing conflict and crisis without falling apart, you must first understand yourself, your fears, and then strategize how best to manage them. This book will teach you to do just that—to prepare you for those life-threatening situations we all hope to never confront, and to gain the confidence to handle whatever adversities you may face.

Throughout this book, I will share with you my own experiences with fear. From going through some of the most intense training academies in the world to interrogating criminals to protecting some of the world's most high-level targets, fear has shown itself to me time and again, in multiple forms and many ways. I have become intimately familiar with each of them—fear of death, fear of danger, fear of public perception, fear of failure, and fear of following your dreams. These fears are familiar to us all at different times and in varying degrees.

One thing I cannot teach you is how to be fearless. Being fearless is bullshit. It isn't possible to live without fear, and it shouldn't be necessary in order for you to live a healthy, successful life. Fear is natural, useful, and it keeps us alive. The reason you don't drive fast is that you fear getting into an accident or getting a speeding ticket. The reason you wait for traffic to pass before crossing the street is that you fear getting hit by a car. The reason you study before an exam is that you fear failing it. The reason you pay your taxes (hopefully) is that you fear the IRS will come knocking on your door. All good reasons to be afraid. I've worked with some of the bravest—and I mean bravest—people in the world. And none of them are void of fear. Neither am I.

Division of Labor

This book is divided into three sections: The first section, PROTECTION, dives deep into the myriad ways in which you can protect yourself, your loved ones, and your property. As an agent assigned to the Presidential Protective Division (PPD), I've learned a thing or two about what it takes to keep the most powerful human being in the world safe. But protection isn't just about jumping in front of a bullet at a moment's notice; it's about planning for the "what-ifs" in life. Here, I'll share some personal stories of how I overcame a childhood spent in fear and how I became a Special Agent for the US Secret Service. More important, I'll offer unconventional advice about how you can protect yourself in practical ways that you can use, from choosing the safest seat at a movie theater to talking to your kids about gun violence and lockdown drills. Protecting yourself and those around you is simply about preparation. We'll also discuss strategies and tips for when you're traveling or away from home and help you create your own personalized protection plan.

Part 1 concludes with the seemingly most difficult, yet most important lesson to learn when overcoming fear: how to take a punch. Whether in the combat stages of Academy training, the mat room of my local jiujitsu school, or nearly causing an international incident with a bully from a foreign delegation, this lesson has helped me through countless personal and professional challenges. I've learned how to take a hit and how to hit back, whenever and wherever necessary. To be clear, I don't advocate violence in any form and my hope is that by reading this book, you'll walk away a wiser and more confident person who doesn't need to fight at the first slung insult. You should try to avoid physical confrontation at all costs. But when you do need to fight . . . I want you to have the conviction and courage to do so.

Part 2 shares the secrets to the art and science of READING PEOPLE. As a former polygraph examiner and interrogator trained by the US Department of Defense, I'll reveal how you can tell what's really going on in the minds and bodies of the people you talk to. From the subtle direction someone's feet are pointing to the hidden meanings behind their words, you'll get a crash course on picking up verbal and nonverbal cues to indicate honesty and deceit.

We'll also explore how not to become overwhelmed when you think you're being lied to. After all, everyone lies, and often we have very good reasons for doing so. By the end of this section, you won't need a polygraph machine to tell if someone's lying—you just need to be willing to truly *listen*.

Part 3, the final section, is about INFLUENCE. Here, I'll teach you strategies to influence others. We'll discuss the often-overlooked value of our voice, our appearance, and the words we use in everyday conversations. You'll sit beside me inside the interrogation room where I use subtle, yet highly effective techniques to influence people into speaking openly and honestly. These persuasion tactics can be employed just as powerfully outside the interview room, with business partners, professional colleagues, longtime friends, and even loved ones. Sometimes all you need to get what you want is the ability to nudge people in the right direction. But watch out! Influence isn't just a one-way street. We are just as susceptible to being influenced—even if we don't realize it. Whether you're negotiating a deal, turning a blind eye to the actions of an unfaithful partner, or somehow always saying "Yes" to your best friend's annoying favors, I'll point out the red flags and white lies that often show up when the influence tables are being turned against you.

At the end of this section, I'll share with you some of my most memorable experiences protecting some of the world's most memorable people. And I'll show you why these leaders were, in fact, *leaders*. I'll describe how their virtues influenced me and can inspire you. From the late president George H. W. Bush's genuine appreciation of people to former president Barack Obama's poise in the face of duplicity, you'll come to understand what it means to be "presidential" in every situation.

Layers Upon Layers

You may be surprised to learn that the modern-day bulletproof vest is not made up of one solid piece of material, such as a molded piece of steel. Rather, it's composed of multiple layers of fabric called *Kevlar*, which are woven together to create a material so strong it can stop the piercing velocity of a bullet or the slash of a knife blade. Bulletproof vests come in a variety of thicknesses based on the level of threat the wearer is likely to face. Police officers, bodyguards, and Special Agents usually wear a softer, more flexible type of bulletproof vest that fits underneath their uniform or suit jacket, while military units and law enforcement tactical response teams typically wear a thicker vest composed of both Kevlar and a type of metal or ceramic—worn on the outside of their clothing. These vests are often bulkier and quite a bit heavier, but offer an extra level of protection against more lethal attacks, like bomb fragments or bullets shot from high-powered rifles.

As a Special Agent, I was issued my first bulletproof vest the day I graduated from the US Secret Service Training Academy. Along with my gun and badge, my vest became a normal part of my wardrobe. It didn't matter if I was standing outside the door of a protectee's hotel room or breaching the door of a fugitive's apartment; my bulletproof vest was always on. Wearing it gave me a sense of confidence, knowing that it could save my life, but it also gave me something else: a physical reminder that I was not completely safe. You see, feeling that bulletproof vest velcroed around my torso kept me mindful of the fact that I was not wholly protected from danger; my arms, legs, and even head were still exposed and susceptible to attack. Even the vest itself couldn't protect me from every type of bullet leaving the barrel of a gun. If someone had a high-powered rifle or was using a specially designed armor-piercing bullet, my vest wouldn't be able to save me. But it could save me from the many other things that I faced in my job. And that's why I wore it. I was not unstoppable, but I was harder to stop.

The lessons, tools, and techniques within the three parts of this book have been written to be applied to your own protection, much like the individual Kevlar layers in a vest. When you put together all of the information shared throughout this book, chapter upon chapter, layer upon layer, you'll come away having created your own piece of armor—a foundation of strategies to help you face the world as a stronger, more resilient human being.

But this book is not only about teaching you what you can use; it's also about teaching you to recognize what you can't. Like the vulnerabilities that still come despite wearing ballistic armor, I want you to remember that you're not completely shielded against the harshness of the outside world. And that's okay. Being keenly aware of what can still harm you actually helps you better prepare, defend, and often avoid threats altogether. You likely have natural strengths and aptitudes that you may not yet know how to tap into. These, too, can become a part of your mental, emotional, and physical armor in the world.

Today, I still value the lessons that issued piece of equipment taught me. Although physically it was about how several individual layers of fabric could work together to protect me, metaphorically it was about something greater. It meant that I was a protector. And to protect others, I had to arm myself with the tools needed to stay safe, strong, and mentally sharp. I want to help you build the mental attitude you need to confront your own unique set of fears and challenges and learn how to become your own protector—as well as the protector for those you love.

Part 1

PROTECTION

Chapter 1

How We Fear

Courage is knowing what not to fear.
—PLATO

Don't Panic!

As the cold water rushed in, I gasped for one final breath before I was completely submerged. I remember the whole cockpit tipping over, the sinking sensation in my stomach, my body straining against the harness strapping me to my seat before I hit the water sideways. My body lit up with adrenaline, ready to panic. And then everything went quiet.

I unclenched my hands and took a mental pause. Panicking would only make it harder to think, wasting valuable seconds I didn't have. Blackness obscured my vision—there was no way to see my way to safety. If I was going to get through this, I knew I would have to feel my way out. I reached down for the release on the seat belt harness to my left . . . or was it my right? Was I completely upside down now? I had to be—I had lost my bearings and couldn't find a reference point.

Don't panic. Find the latch. Pull to release. Swim to safety.

I repeated these words as I fumbled in the dark. Damn it, where the hell was that release? My fingers finally grasped hold of the U-shaped harness lever, yanking it to the open position. As the two-inch nylon straps slowly loosened around me, I wiggled free and pulled myself through the cockpit door. I knew I had to swim clear of the cabin before making my way to the surface. My lungs were burning now, my heart pounding. A few more seconds and I would be free. I finally kicked hard and forced myself upward. As I broke through the water's surface, I gasped for my first breath of air in what seemed like an eternity.

"Good job, Poumpouras. You didn't drown!" shouted the Secret Service instructor. "Now get out of the pool. Next!"

The Academy training scenario for the day was a simulated helicopter crash in the Olympic-size training pool. Each recruit was first blindfolded, then strapped into the seat of a mock helicopter cockpit. The cockpit was then flipped upside down, submerging the agent, who then had to release themselves from the safety harness and swim through an underwater maze before surfacing. The training was designed to teach us how to survive should we ever find ourselves in that exact situation.

But the simulation wasn't just a "what-if" scenario. It became part of our training after a Secret Service agent died in a real-life helicopter crash on May 26, 1973. That evening, twenty-five-year-old Special Agent J. Clifford Dietrich, along with six other agents and three Army crew members, were flying from Key Biscayne, Florida, to the Grand Cay Islands in the Bahamas for their overnight presidential protection assignment for President Nixon. Shortly before landing, the twin-engine Sikorsky VH3A helicopter crashed into the Atlantic Ocean. Although the aircraft initially remained afloat, it soon capsized, causing the cabin to quickly fill with water. While the other passengers climbed to safety on top of the overturned helicopter, Agent Dietrich never made it out.

When his body was recovered, he was found still strapped into his safety harness. According to the medical examiner, Agent Dietrich's cause of death was asphyxia, due to drowning. Our training instructor also told us that both of the agent's thumbs were broken. That meant Agent Dietrich had been alive and conscious when the helicopter hit the water, but ultimately drowned because he was unable to free himself from the seat belt. Under stress, the agent would have reverted to what he knew about seat belts—you push the release button with your thumbs, like in a car. But in a helicopter, the seat belt mechanism is completely different, something the agent most likely couldn't remember in his final moments of panic.

Even though I logically knew that I probably wouldn't die in a simulated helicopter crash, there was no way around the instinctual onset of panic that flooded through me. My mind didn't care that this was a controlled exercise, which meant the fear of drowning was as real as anything I'd ever experienced. This exercise had nothing to do with physical strength or agility. While I was looking for a way to physically Houdini myself out of the contraption and not drown in the process, the simulation was teaching me how to maintain control of my emotions.

Fear is a healthy and natural response to a perceived threat. On the other hand, panic causes us to lose control of our faculties. When we panic, we can't think, can't reason, can't process or plan. And under extreme circumstances, panic is likely to kill you faster than whatever it is you're afraid of. If you've ever experienced a panic attack—heart beating rapidly, hyperventilating, trembling, feeling like you're about to die—then you may understand what that agent felt as he hung upside down in the darkness underwater, one simple click and brief swim to his survival. He probably had minutes to assess his situation, form a plan, and escape to safety, but his panic made that impossible.

Think about car accidents. Most people, when in a car accident, will take their hands off the wheel. At a time when logic says we most need to keep our hands at ten and two, panic causes us to take our hands away from the very thing that might save us. And where do people's hands go? Over their face. In the moments when we most need our steering wheel and our vision, panic causes us to abandon both.

This book is not about never feeling fear. It's about understanding fear and learning to control it. I want to help you master your fear so that it doesn't turn to panic in a moment when you need to be able to think clearly. Fear can also be a limiting influence in our lives. It can prevent us from pursuing goals that we long to go after, from speaking openly and honestly, from being who we're truly meant to be. When we feel threatened or exposed, our fear can confine us and cut us off from the world. If that feels familiar, I'm going to help you change your relationship to fear. I'm going to show you how to get to know your fear, trust your instincts, and make choices that will keep you safe and strong.

Surviving Fear

We are born with two kinds of fears hardwired into our system for survival—two fears that scientists call innate: the fear of falling and the fear of loud sounds. Most of us have had a dream where we're falling and then startle awake. This fear of falling has been with us since birth. Newborns are quickly wrapped in a blanket because they can't immediately distinguish where their body ends and the world begins, which causes them to constantly jerk as if they are falling, a fear that eventually diminishes once their depth perception develops. Beyond their startle reflexes, studies show that infants refuse to crawl over a platform made of clear Plexiglas even when their mothers are at the other end calling to them. They will stop at the edge and cry rather than risk going over the "visual cliff." Their innate fear of falling is strong enough to override even that powerful bond between mother and child.

Loud noises are the other stimulus that humans innately equate with danger. When we hear a loud noise, our acoustic startle reflex kicks in and our bodies instantly react. That's why we jump when a car backfires, why children cry at firework shows, and why we immediately drop to the ground when we hear anything that sounds like a gunshot.

Beyond the fear of falling and the fear of loud noises, all other fears are learned fears. These are the fears that we inherit from our parents or acquire while growing up. If your mother is afraid of dogs, chances are you are going to grow up being afraid of dogs as well. Learned fears come from everywhere—our family, our friends, our culture, the news we watch, the harm we've witnessed or experienced. We are taught to be afraid of failing or afraid of trying at all. There is no limit to the fears we can accumulate in our lifetime.

Every generation seems to grow up with some type of societal fear. In the 1950s, it was the Red Scare and communism. The 1960s became a decade of fearing for personal safety with the Cuban Missile Crisis, and the assassinations of President John F. Kennedy, Dr. Martin Luther King Jr., and presidential candidate Robert F. Kennedy. In the 1970s, it was the foreign oil crisis, the political upheaval with the impeachment of President Nixon, and the skyrocketing of crime throughout the United States. In the 1980s, it was the fear of external threats against the United States, particularly with Iran and the Soviet Union. In the 1990s it was the Y2K scare, fearing that all life and technology would cease once the calendar year hit 2000. The early 2000s ushered in a global threat unlike anything before it—terrorism.

Today we have mass shootings. A 2018 Pew Research Center study found that more than 50 percent of teenagers were concerned that a shooting would happen in their school, with 25 percent of them being "very worried." This fear persists despite the statistical improbability of any one student becoming a school-shooting victim. With more than 50 million American youths attending public K–12 schools for roughly 180 days of the year, the chance of being killed by a school shooter is about 1 in 614 million. By contrast, the likelihood of being struck by lightning in any one year is 1 in 1.2 million. Highlighting this mathematical implausibility, however, usually won't diminish the worry of students or their parents, any more than it would diminish the fear of being attacked and killed by a shark (1 in 3.7 million) or being in an airline crash (1 in 5.4 million).

The debilitating nature of any fear, especially unlikely ones, can drastically limit our ability to simply enjoy life. These fears can make some people too afraid to board a plane or swim in the ocean. Perhaps those people would be willing to drive to the beach, so long as they don't wade into the water past their knees, or take a long road trip rather than take the risk of flying. They might choose these deceptively "safer" options despite the fact that there is a far greater chance of being injured in a car crash than a shark attack or plane crash. In fact, there is a 1 in 102 chance that you could be killed in a car accident in a given year.

So why aren't people more afraid of dangers with a higher statistical probability, like car accidents? Why do we become so preoccupied with threats that have an incredibly low chance of ever occurring? Our fears have to do with several things, the first of which is the sensationalizing nature of the incidents by the media. When things that rarely happen, happen, they become newsworthy. You are more likely to see, and thus remember, the social media post or evening news story about the victim of an unlikely tragedy—a surfer attacked by a great white shark off the coast of California—than you are about the two-vehicle accident that sent one driver to the hospital, something so common it likely won't even make the news. Exposure to those kinds of stories make those unlikely threats feel more real to us, and that fear overrides our ability to logically assess the probability of those things actually happening.

Additionally, we are genetically predisposed to avoid things that can cause instant death—a big fish with teeth, a 1,000-volt bolt of lightning, or falling out of the sky. My intent here is not to make you more afraid of driving, but to get you to reflect on those things that you are most fearful of, to assess why you are afraid of them, and look at them logically, rather than enduring a clouded sense of dread amplified by sensationalized stories.

What Fear Looks Like

When I was sixteen, my family and I moved from Long Island City into a better neighborhood in Queens. Although crime in that part of New York wasn't nonexistent, it wasn't nearly as bad as where we came from. Because money was always tight, my little brother, Theodoros, and I helped our parents clean office buildings on the weekends after they each finished their day jobs. One Sunday night, after finishing early, my mom and I drove back to our house while my father and brother stayed a few minutes longer to lock up.

When we pulled into our driveway, I noticed the vertical blinds in the living room were open and the lights were on.

"Why are the lights on?" I asked my mom. "And the blinds open?"

She looked confused. "I don't know. We always close them."

We didn't completely register that something was amiss until my mom unlocked the front door and we walked in. And that's when I saw him—a man running through our house toward the side entrance.

My mom immediately froze—literally went motionless, as if her feet were cemented into the floor. I, on the other hand, didn't hesitate—I charged inside.

"No!" my mom screamed. "Stop!" But she wasn't yelling at the intruder. She was yelling at me. I was already running after him. When I got to the side door, I saw him leap over the neighbor's fence and into the black of night. Gone.

"Maybe there are others still here!" I shouted back to her and began checking every room in the house.

"No," my mom pleaded. "Stop, just stop."

She was terrified for me, but her cries somehow sounded far off in the distance. I was mad going on furious as I first cleared the basement and then worked my way back upstairs. I was going to protect my mom, protect our home, no matter what. I may have only been a teenager, but God help whoever was still in this house. I didn't know how, but I was not going to let them get away until the police arrived and took them to jail.

Now, at this point in the story you might be thinking *Wow, you've got some balls!*, or maybe *Listen to your mother, you idiot. You're gonna get yourself killed.*

Regardless of what you're thinking about my level of bravery—or stupidity—I share this story with you for an entirely different reason. First, let's go back to the start of the story: we pulled up to the house together in the car and immediately knew something was wrong. Our sense of fear and uncertainty began to build. When we walked inside, we saw a man running through our house. Fear built faster alongside the slightly delayed recognition that we were being burglarized. Now what happened? What did my mom do? What did I do? My mom froze in her tracks. I ran after the guy. Bravery? Hardly.

My mom and I experienced the exact same exposure to a threat, yet we had two completely different reactions. These reactions are called our *Fight, Flight,* or *Freeze responses*, also known as the F3 response. My mom went into Freeze mode, whereas I went into Fight mode. And you could argue that the intruder I was chasing was in Flight mode.

Researchers say our Fight, Flight, or Freeze response activates even before we are aware of it as a way of assessing danger. If it's a threat we think we can overpower, we go into Fight mode. If it's a threat we think we can outrun, we go into Flight mode. If it's a threat where we think we can do neither—we Freeze. People may have a different response to the same stimuli—as my mother and I did—but no matter what your particular response to fear may be, the most important thing is to know and understand it so you can control it.

Fight, Flight, or Freeze

F3 is your body's way of arming itself to help protect you. It is your physiological response to help you deal with the situation at hand. It's you—but a heightened version of you. A more aware and alert version. Your heartbeat increases so as to pump more blood throughout your body, which will make it easier to punch someone (Fight) or run away (Flight).

For people like myself who naturally go into Fight mode when faced with a threat, our natural instinct is to immediately combat whatever is threatening us—whether or not it is safe to do so. If someone hits you, you hit back. If someone yells at you, you yell back. It's a response in which you retaliate with an aggressive behavior to protect yourself. You make the decision to take a defensive stance against the threat, whoever or whatever that may be.

The Flight response occurs when you feel the threat is more than you can handle. People who are predisposed to Flight will run away from danger rather than run toward it. If someone threatens to attack them, they will get the hell out of there (which is often a very good idea). Similarly, if someone verbally confronts them, they will do all they can to avoid or remove themselves from the situation. The Flight response is designed to protect you by getting you out of a volatile situation as quickly as humanly possible.

Freeze occurs when you are so overwhelmed by a perceived threat that you can't respond. It is overstimulation that grips and immobilizes you. Have you ever seen someone go still with that deer-in-headlights expression on their face? They're probably in a Freeze response. Often when this happens, it can feel like your body is turning on you; you can't think, can't plan, can't act. All you can do is remain frozen in place and hope that the threat passes.

Within the body are competing neurological pathways called the sympathetic (SNS) and parasympathetic nervous systems (PSNS). Both the SNS and the PSNS are part of the autonomic nervous system, which means they can't be controlled voluntarily. The sympathetic—or stress—response is what gets activated when we're scared. In that moment, our body attempts to become superhuman by flooding itself with norepinephrine and adrenaline. This chemical dump is what makes our hands sweat, our hearts beat faster, our muscles tense, our pupils dilate, and our breathing increase—everything we physically need to deal with a threat at that particular moment. Your vision becomes laser focused; being sweaty makes you harder to hold on to, and your muscles are full of blood and oxygen, ready to respond to danger at a moment's notice.

The parasympathetic system, on the other hand, is what helps us calm down, relax, and recover. It's what goes to work after we've eaten and what helps us fall asleep. Essentially, it does the opposite of the SNS in an effort to keep the body's constant effort to maintain homeostasis—a physical state where everything is balanced.

Identify Your Fear Response

You may come to find that you have a pattern when it comes to F3—a way you habitually respond to danger or conflict. The way I responded as a teenager to the intruder in our home was characteristic for me. My go-to response has always been Fight. Even now, whenever I feel threatened, my immediate response is to go on the attack.

My mother's F3 response in the above scenario was initially Flight, but after I ran in, she couldn't leave me, so instead she Froze. She was too overwhelmed and confused to know what to do. Her F3 response wouldn't allow her to follow me into the house because it sensed danger and was keenly aware that what I had done was completely stupid, which meant Freeze was the only option. Yet over the years, my mother's natural pattern of dealing with conflict has usually been a Flight response.

It's important to know that no one F3 response is the "correct" response to a threat. There's no such thing. Our F3 response is simply what we're predisposed to, which can help us in some situations and hinder us in others. Knowing that I typically respond to a threat with Fight mode means that I have to be careful, because there are plenty of times when fighting my way out of a situation could be dangerous or dumb. Sometimes fleeing is by far the best thing you can do in a threatening situation. If I could go back and give my sixteen-year-old self some advice about how to respond to a home intruder, I would tell her to get the hell out of that house and help her mom find a safe place to call the police.

At the same time, my mother's pattern isn't a prudent response to every situation, either. She goes to great lengths to avoid conflict. If she needed to fight back, I'm not sure that she would be able to. The idea here isn't to respond to every situation in one way, but to understand how you naturally respond. Before we try to learn how to manage our fear response, we must first identify our patterns.

Understanding my personal F3 response allows me to exert control over myself, to identify what I will do before it happens, and assess the tactical costs and benefits of that response. So take a moment to identify what camp you're in. If you don't know right away, make a list of three times when you felt threatened. What did you do? Did your response vary depending on the kind of situation you faced? Or is your particular pattern pretty consistent across the board? Once you know your instinctive F3 response, you can begin to predict what you will most likely do and come up with ways to manage that response before a volatile situation arises.

If, for instance, Flight is your go-to F3 response, the next time you feel the need to flee, take a moment to consider if that's the best way to handle it. Maybe getting away is indeed the best thing you can do, or maybe staying put to assess the situation or fight back is actually a safer or more practical option. Once you achieve a deeper understanding of yourself and your F3 response, you can create other options to choose from. You can give yourself more choices based on your ability to plan and strategize rather than responding unconsciously to a threat (chapters 3–8 will give you some great ideas as well). The more control you have over your F3 response, the better you'll be able to deal with difficult situations and thrive in the world—a fundamental lesson to becoming bulletproof.

Chapter 2

Harnessing Fear

Difficulties are things that show a person what they are.
—EPICTETUS

Our Possible Selves vs. Our Feared Selves

The more awareness we can gain over our orientation to fear, the more we can claim agency and autonomy over our lives and choices. Fear doesn't have to limit you. And it's not always about overcoming fear—sometimes it's about learning how to use and harness your fear to achieve what you truly want out of life, to become the strongest version of yourself that you can possibly be.

I grew up reading about Alexander the Great, king of Macedonia, the same place my mother was from. I learned about Greek heroes like Odysseus, who spent ten years at sea; warriors like Achilles who fought in the war of Troy; King Leonidas of Sparta and his three hundred men, who stood against an entire army of Persians. I breathed these stories in like air. And the more I learned about these great heroes, the more I began to see myself as one of them. They were the legends of my people. Their courage and valor lived in me, forming how I viewed the world and my place in it. As kids, it's easy to draw inspiration from stories like these, to see ourselves as a hero. We daydream about the qualities we hope to embody—bravery, strength, justice, integrity—and begin shaping our lives around such virtues.

This visualization about our future is called the *theory of possible selves*, a term created by Hazel Markus and Paula Nurius. Possible selves describes how as individuals we self-identify using experiences from our past and project those into our future. We manifest our possible selves in two ways—through our hopes and through our fears.

Our hopes center on who we want to become, a term called *hoped-for selves*. It's who you imagine yourself to be: I hope to be a doctor. I hope to be the president of the United States. I hope to be a Secret Service agent.

Conversely, our fears center on who we want to avoid becoming— a term called *feared selves*. This is where we decide who we don't want to be. I fear becoming homeless. I fear becoming like my father. I fear becoming weak.

It's the combining of these two selves that guides us toward who we strive to ultimately become—both the person we want to be and the person we don't want to be.

But sometimes the trajectory of our lives—the decisions we make, or don't make—lead us to live a filtered or more conservative version of the life we had dreamed of when we were growing up. For me, the world I grew up in didn't mirror the warrior mindset I hoped to one day embody. In fact, my earliest years were a perfect contradiction of who I hoped to become as opposed to who I was becoming—cautious, quiet, encumbered by a constant shroud of fear.

Growing Up in Fear

New York City in the 1980s and '90s was a far different beast than it is now. In 2018 there were 289 homicides in the city. In 1990, when I was thirteen years old, New York City had 2,245 murders. Crack cocaine and gang warfare had turned New York into a war zone. In one five-mile area of Brooklyn, police logged a homicide every sixty-three hours. The news was filled with images of bodies on the streets lying in pools of blood, children caught in drive-by shootings, and random people being pulled from cars and killed because they turned down the wrong block.

My parents, both immigrants from Greece, were no strangers to the dangers of their new land. My uncle was mugged repeatedly. My father robbed at gunpoint while working his first job in America at a coffee shop, and also attacked while driving his taxi. My mother physically assaulted by a neighbor. Our cars were broken into and stolen. Our home burglarized—the money my mother had saved and the few pieces of jewelry I had were all gone.

In their effort to protect us, my parents handed their fears down to my brother and me. They kept us inside—all the time. We were not allowed out of the house except to go to school. We didn't play outside. We rarely went to friends' houses. We didn't trick-or-treat. We didn't take the subway because, according to my parents, it was a graffiti-covered Wild West frontier where anything and everything bad happened.

Fear was everywhere. Growing up, I breathed it in like oxygen—in every word of caution my mother, father, and grandmother said to me.

Watch out.

Be careful.

Hurry inside.

Stay quiet.

Look away.

Be smart.

Stay safe.

They taught us to look over our shoulders every time we walked out the front door of our roach-infested, low-income housing to the bus stop. And to hurry straight back to the apartment once we stepped off the school bus in the afternoon. Something bad was always about to happen. I was taught to fear strangers. To fear my neighbors. To fear friends. To fear the world outside. The people standing on the corner. The people driving by. I walked with fear every time I took a step out of my home.

And I'd be lying if I said it didn't piss me off. Fear took so much away from me—so many opportunities and experiences, even a good education. When I placed into Brooklyn Tech High School, one of the top three high schools in New York City, I wasn't allowed to go. My mother said it was too dangerous to take public transportation to get to school every day. According to her, Brooklyn was an even scarier place than Queens—there was no way I was going to school in Brooklyn. If Queens was a war zone, Brooklyn might as well have been the underworld.

No matter how hard I begged, the answer was always the same. No. The reason?

Fear.

The more I was told to be afraid—told to be careful, to watch out, to stay safe—the more I resented it. And the more it fueled my determination not to allow fear to dictate the course of my life.

I know fear keeps us alive, but I also know that fear can keep us from living.

Rebelling Against Fear

My parents' ambitions for me were in total conflict with what I wanted for myself.

"Find a good man to marry and take care of you," they told me. According to them and the community I grew up in, good Greek girls work safe, sensible jobs until they find a nice Greek man to marry and make babies with.

I, on the other hand, wanted to be strong. Fierce. To do everything and anything I was told I couldn't. If there was anything that came from the victimizations my family had endured, it was a steely resolve that had formed in me not to bow to fear, but defy it. I didn't want to be someone who watched on the sidelines and did nothing; I needed the strength and training to make me and the world I lived in safer.

So at the age of twenty-three, I joined the New York City Police Department (NYPD) Academy.

To call this my parents' worst nightmare is probably an understatement.

"Why are you doing this?" my father asked, peering over my shoulder while I filled out the Police Academy application. "Don't even bother. They're not going to hire someone like you. They're not looking for someone like you."

After I was accepted, he voiced his disapproval even louder and more often.

My mother was in denial. And her typical F3 response—Flight mode—meant that she tried to avoid the problem altogether. And so anytime the topic about her daughter came up, she just told whoever was asking that I had a nice, respectable job—as a secretary working in Manhattan.

They were so disappointed in me that they did the only thing they could think of—they stopped speaking to me. Maybe they thought I would back down in the face of their silence. Maybe they thought it was an inappropriate career for a young girl. Maybe they had a premonition of how hard it would be, how much pain and exhaustion and frustration I would have to endure to meet the standards of the NYPD Academy. I certainly had no idea. But what I did have was a lifetime of experiences growing up in our immigrant community in Queens to help harness my fear and fortify my resolve.

What the Fuck Was I Thinking

"Papadukis! What the hell is this?"

It was my second week at the Academy, and by then I was already used to the NYPD instructors saying my name five different ways in a day. *Pompoukus. Pompadoris. Papadopoulos. Pompadoralakalous.* There was no end to the way they butchered it. They did it on purpose, despite the fact that it was written on the back of my T-shirt in big block letters. Their job was to annoy us, harass us, and break us down in any and every way possible.

I already wanted to quit. I was totally out of my element. During my college years, I worked at a Gold's Gym in Queens and was in pretty good shape, but Academy training was entirely different. My gym went from a 10,000-square-foot air-conditioned training facility to a five-by-two-feet imaginary rectangle around me. No towel, no mat, no insulated water bottles or peppy music to keep me inspired. Three hundred people within arm's length of each other struggling to keep up with the lead instructor's pace. Push-ups, sit-ups, jumping jacks, arm circles, all in sync with him, one after the next after the next.

The female instructor currently butchering my name was screaming in my face so close that I could smell the black coffee and eggs she had for breakfast.

"Answer me, Pompalompus!"

Every *p* and every *s* sent her saliva spraying across my face. I knew not to wipe it off. She reached out her nonmanicured fingers and scraped them across my right eyelash, holding her thumb and forefinger up for me to see the offending black smudge.

"What the hell is this?"

"Cover Girl, ma'am."

So maybe that was a little too specific for her, because she got so close to me that our noses were touching. That close up she almost looked like a cartoon character. I fully expected steam to start pouring out of her ears.

To be fair, wearing mascara isn't a crime. It's not a sign of weakness. But it was against the rules.

"Do we wear makeup in the Academy, Poopopus? Do we?"

"No, ma'am."

"Then why the hell are you wearing makeup?"

I wanted to tell her exactly why I was wearing makeup. I was tired. I was beat-up. I felt a little lost. I was afraid I had made a mistake going into the police academy. My parents hadn't spoken to me since the day I told them I was going to become a police officer. I felt like quitting. And so, staring at my own blurry eyes in the mirror that morning at 5 a.m., I had put on the faintest bit of mascara just for a little confidence boost. A little something to help me get through another grueling day of hell. But I didn't tell her any of this. I had enough people doubting me; I wasn't going to admit that I had doubts of my own.

"I don't know, ma'am."

"Do we need makeup to be a police officer, Poumpouras?"

She always said my name correctly when it would embarrass me more than saying it wrong.

"No, ma'am," I said quietly.

She gritted her teeth and growled at me. "If I see this shit again, you're done. Now drop and give me fifty!"

I dropped to the gym floor, grateful that she didn't make everyone do push-ups for my mascara. When one of us screwed up, usually we all paid the price.

For me, the runs were the worst part. We ran miles around the gym. Circle after circle, running in formation—four across, always within arm's length of the person in front of you and behind. Not only did we have to maintain perfect rank, but we had to run at the speed of the instructor. Up until that point, I had never even run a mile. If you couldn't keep up, the instructors pulled you out of line and ordered you to run suicides in the center of the gym in front of everyone, back and forth from one end of the gym to the other. It was humiliating—definitely not something you wanted to happen.

On one of those runs in my first week, we were going so fast I thought my lungs were going to burst. I was panic-breathing. Stumbling over my feet. Struggling to hold rank. Sure enough, one of the instructors pulled me out with a look of disgust on his face. I made my way to the center of the gym and began running suicides—back and forth, back and forth—my chest now completely on fire.

Another recruit fallout who was running next to me started to heave.

"The garbage can is by the door," the instructor yelled at him.

The recruit ran to it, put his head inside, and began vomiting. When he was done, he crumpled to the floor.

"What are you doing?" the instructor bellowed. "There is no sitting down. You either get back in the run or take yourself to Cabrini." (Cabrini was the hospital down the street.) "You choose."

Facing this choice, the recruit looked like he was going to throw up again, but said nothing and came back in to run suicides with the rest of us.

When physical training (PT) was over, the instructors had the entire gym class—all three hundred cadets—face the center of the gym, where I and the other fallouts stood.

"You see these recruits!" the instructor shouted, gesturing at us. "These recruits need to quit. You should want them to quit. Because when you need help on the street and call for a 10-13—officer needs assistance—they're going to get you killed. You know why? Because they won't be able to run to help you!"

Then the instructor looked at me and the other fallouts, his gaze shaming us into the ground. "Do us all a favor and quit before you get somebody killed."

I was humiliated, mortified. I felt like a failure. But after that day I promised myself, I would never fall out again.

That night, I went home, laced up my shoes, and went for a run. I began running every day on my own after class. Despite how much I hated it and how painful it was, it didn't compare to the pain I felt that day in the middle of the gym. I started praying before every PT session silently by my locker. *Please, God, don't let me fall out. Please.*

The instructor's words had terrified me. I was afraid of putting any of my fellow recruits in danger. I was afraid of failing, of what my family would think, how I would feel if I failed. I was afraid of enduring another humiliation like that again.

And so I used my fear to fuel me; to keep me from becoming my *feared self.* Eventually, my running took on a ferocity and determination that I didn't know I was capable of.

That day was the first and last time I ever fell out of a run.

The Power of Regret

It took a lot of mental effort to not give in to my parents' fears and my own fear that somehow I wasn't enough—tough enough, strong enough, brave enough. I knew my parents were disappointed in me. I was an outcast in our community—an embarrassment. Even my friends thought what I was doing was ridiculous. But I couldn't live my life in a tiny bubble. I wouldn't. Even while every muscle in my body ached, I knew that if I gave in to my fears, something else was going to hurt even worse. Muscles recover. But regret? That shit can be painful for a lifetime.

There are two types of regrets: The regrets we have after *doing* something and those that come from *not doing* something. Although regrets for our actions are often psychologically agonizing at first, their pain tends to diminish over time as we begin to either justify how they happened or find meaning in why they happened.

Inaction, on the other hand, is something we hold on to, wishing we could turn back the clock and do things differently. Research shows that far more people regret actions that they *didn't* take than the ones they did, even if they later come to see a certain past act as a mistake. It's the things we don't do that tend to haunt us long-term—such as choosing not to take a new job, not to pursue a relationship, not to stand up for ourselves, or not to push beyond our comfort zones. We tend to remember the things in life we had the chance to do, but didn't—an opportunity lost, a promise unfulfilled. Failing to act leaves open infinite possibilities of what might have been. Because these scenarios leave us without closure, our minds are left to imagine a life or a circumstance different than the one we're living now.

This can be both a curse and a blessing. Although we may never become as efficient in a certain skill as we would have had we started long ago, we can still begin. There are examples of this everywhere. When you hear of someone quitting their high-paying job to become their own boss, or an accomplished adult returning to school to study a new discipline altogether. Simply put, when looking back, people are more able to deal with the idea that they tried something and failed versus never trying at all.

All that said, I can't deny that my insufficiencies felt so numerous and obvious to me in those early days of training that it took extreme effort to keep going. The mind can be both friend and foe, and just as it can push us to pursue our highest goals, it can also come up with a thousand compelling arguments for why we shouldn't. I didn't grow up in a law enforcement family. No one thought I should be there. But despite some of the hellish days I endured at the NYPD Academy, I noticed something interesting start to happen—I began to fear the consequences of quitting more than the hardship that every day of training had in store for me. I had this glimpse into my new future—one in which I was strong, powerful, capable of helping people in a meaningful way. The clearer this picture became, the more I couldn't bear to let go of it.

So I kept moving forward.

I stopped thinking about the totality of what I was doing. Eight more months of this. Of instructors yelling. My parents ignoring me. Of my body hurting. Of me struggling to survive in a world I knew absolutely nothing about.

Instead, I began to live minute by minute. Hour by hour. I focused on the present. I harnessed my fear of quitting, of the regret I would feel if I didn't give it my all. As my body got stronger, my mind grew tougher, more resolute and resilient. What my family thought started to weigh less heavily on me. My own insecurities got quieter as I proved my ability class after class, day after day. The weakness in my mind and body faded as I built a foundation on which I could continue to strengthen and push myself, which led me to take an even bigger risk than I ever had before.

The Next Challenge

Five months into the Academy, I walked into the offices of the Training Division, where the department's most senior management sat. We recruits referred to this echelon of men and women—lieutenants, captains, inspectors—as "white shirts" because their uniform shirts were, well . . . white. Typically, we all steered clear of them and this office, but I had a life-changing decision to make.

I had been standing at attention for more than fifteen minutes when an NYPD lieutenant finally took his eyes off his paper and looked up. "At ease, Recruit. What do you want?" His tone was gruff and impatient as he swiveled slowly in his chair.

I lowered my salute and nervously cleared my throat, "Sir, I need to speak with someone. I've just been offered a chance to become a Special Agent with the United States Secret Service."

In the months before joining the NYPD Academy, I had quietly applied to the USSS. My interest in the USSS came during my time interning for New York congresswoman Carolyn McCarthy. Her staff had suggested I look into the agency after seeing a female agent protecting then–First Lady Hillary Clinton during a meet and greet with the congresswoman. They also knew I held a degree in political science and international affairs, had studied extensively overseas while in college, and spoke four foreign languages at the time: Greek, Spanish, Italian, and French.

It was a conditional offer of employment, one dependent on my passing the rigorous USSS training academies. I'd like to say I was excited to receive the offer, but I wasn't. I had adjusted well to my new way of life at the NYPD. I knew what to expect, when to expect it, and how to get through it. I made some great friends—in fact, the camaraderie

I felt was unlike anything I'd ever experienced. It turns out that when going through something as intense as the NYPD Academy, you end up creating a close bond with your fellow recruits. A career within the Secret Service meant uprooting myself entirely. Not only would I be sent out of state for training to Georgia and then Maryland, but I could be assigned to any place where the agency had an office, including overseas. And I'd be starting all over again, but this time with one of the most elite agencies in the world. Everything about this choice and its possible ramifications unsettled me.

I went over to the lieutenant and sat down. I explained my dilemma and he listened patiently before responding. His tone had softened from that of a "white shirt" to something that resembled a patient mentor.

"Listen," he said. "It's not often one of our recruits gets accepted into the federal government, especially as a Special Agent for the Secret Service. It's a huge opportunity and one I think you should take. If you end up not liking it, we'll always take you back."

I had a million little reasons to stay right where I was, but deep down I understood this was a risk worth taking. Somehow, even then I knew that I would come to regret not going. If I was able to push my mental and physical limits this far in the Police Academy, what more could I do in the Secret Service? I had no idea, but I wanted to find out. I carried that strength and determination all the way to my first day of training in Glynco, Georgia.

I was soon going to need every bit of it.

The United States Secret Service

Established in 1865, the USSS is one of the oldest US federal agencies. Created by President Abraham Lincoln to combat counterfeit currency—nearly one-third of all US currency at that time was fake—it was placed under the Department of Treasury. In 1894, the Service took on the added responsibility of part-time presidential protection beginning with President Grover Cleveland. Then in 1901, after the assassination of President William McKinley, who was the third US president to be assassinated in thirty-six years—Abraham Lincoln in 1865 and James Garfield in 1881—the agency was assigned to protect the elected position around the clock. Most people don't know this, but the Federal Bureau of Investigation (FBI) was created in 1908 using a handful of Secret Service agents hired by the US attorney general at the time, Charles Joseph Bonaparte. On March 1, 2003, the Secret Service was moved into the Department of Homeland Security, a newly created division within the US government after the terrorist attacks on 9/11.

The USSS is made up of two divisions: the Uniformed Division and Special Agent Division. The Uniformed Division is responsible for protecting the White House grounds and all foreign diplomatic missions within the Washington, DC, area, as well as the president's and vice president's personal residences.

The Special Agent Division has two missions: Investigations and Protection. Investigations involve counterfeit currency, financial crimes, cybercrimes, child pornography, and forgery. Protection includes that of the US president and first family (wife and children), the vice president and family, foreign heads of state who are on US soil, and all former US presidents and their spouses, as well as all major presidential candidates. In 2000, the Secret Service also became responsible for securing sites deemed a National Special Security Event, such as the Republican and Democratic National Conventions, the Super Bowl, and the Olympics.

When I was accepted as a recruit into the Secret Service, I went from a diverse class of 1,500 at the NYPD to a training class of fifty-four. This was the setup: We would train in the blistering Georgia heat at the former Glynco Naval Air Station for three months and then, if we made it through, we would go on to the freezing cold of Beltsville, Maryland, for another three months of the more specialized Secret Service Training Academy.

There are approximately 3,600 Special Agents. The caliber of the men and women who get accepted into the agency are, in essence, the elite of the elite. Its cadre includes former collegiate, professional, and Olympic athletes; Navy SEALs; Army Rangers; and seasoned police officers with years of Special Weapons and Tactics (SWAT) experience. Those who weren't battle-hardened operators often held multiple advanced degrees or spoke different languages, a valuable asset when working alongside foreign heads of state and their security teams. In any given year, it's statistically harder to get into the US Secret Service's Special Agent Division than it is getting into Harvard—one of the world's most exclusive academic institutions. The agency accepts roughly only 1 percent of those who apply compared to nearly 6 percent of Ivy League applicants. And somehow, amazingly, I was one of those applicants.

Having grown up surrounded by legends of Greek heroes and their remarkable feats, I never hesitated to imagine myself as someone capable of that kind of strength and valor. The fact those stories were all about men never dawned on me. And so it also didn't faze me that my recruit class was composed almost entirely of men. At the time, more than 90 percent of Special Agents were male. Given that and the caliber of my peers, I knew I had to earn my place. I wanted to be seen not as a female Special Agent, but as a Special Agent. Period.

Over the following months at Glynco, I trained like a maniac. I worked out with my class during the day, getting my ass kicked with the rest of them, and on my own every night. I ran extra miles, swam additional laps in the pool, and logged more hours at the shooting range. I chose the biggest guys to spar with to force myself to train at their level. The first few weeks were hell. My body ached like it had been beaten with a baseball bat. I was covered in cuts and bruises and was popping Advil on the regular. Yet, I was determined that there wouldn't be any doubt about my abilities—not in the minds of our instructors, in my peers who trained alongside me, or my own mind. I understood my limitations, which meant that often I had to work longer and harder. And I was more than okay with that.

In our sparring lessons, I learned early on that recruits were most often partnered by weight class. In my second week at Glynco, I found myself standing next to Matt, a former Army Ranger more than twice my size and made of solid muscle; before they could partner me with someone closer in size, I asked Matt to be my partner. I wanted to train with someone who would push me. Matt understood why I had picked him, and so he didn't take it easy on me. More important, I didn't want him to. One day, we practiced flipping each other. Matt went first. I might as well have been a rag doll for how far he threw me. It seemed like I weighed nothing to him. Time and again I hit the floor with my back and head thudding heavily to the ground. I could feel my bones vibrating under my skin. My joints hurt from absorbing the shock of falling and my lungs burned from the compression force each time I was slammed into the floor. My body yelled in protest. But I was doing what I set out to do. So I got up.

"Again," I said. "Throw me again."

When it was my turn to throw Matt, I noticed the other recruits took a break from their own sparring matches to watch how this was going to shake down. There was a pause, a suspended hush as I somehow managed to heave Matt over my shoulder and throw him. And then that was it. Everyone turned back to focus on their own partner and the task at hand. We all had our own goals to meet.

It wasn't just the physical requirements that were intense—the academic portion was equally difficult. I studied hard to learn the legal framework we operated under, the investigative policies and procedures, and built a deeper understanding of the scope of our federal jurisdiction. It was a type of academic schooling that was totally unfamiliar to me, and truthfully, it didn't come easy. In fact, I failed my first law exam—which meant I needed to buckle down even more. While many of my classmates would go out and take breaks from the intense curriculum, I'd stay in. I would study, sleep for a few hours, study, and then study some more. I didn't want this once-in-a-lifetime opportunity to go to waste, so I did everything in my power to make sure that didn't happen.

Six months later, I became a Special Agent for the United States Secret Service.

Over the time span of my twelve years as an agent, I learned from the best and worked alongside the best, so I could eventually try to be my best. What makes us the best? I tend to think it's the struggle. It's the choice to face a challenge head-on instead of turning our backs to it. It isn't solely about physical strength or bravado. It's about endurance. And by this, I mean mental endurance—the ability to endure whatever life throws at you, to keep going no matter how hard it gets.

Chapter 3

Mental Armor

For a man to conquer himself is the first and noblest of all victories.
—PLATO

Creating Your Mental Shield

Because the world is interwoven with both good and bad, there will undoubtedly be individuals and events that will cause you harm—and, by consequence, pain. You don't have to like it, but you shouldn't be surprised by it, either. And more important, you shouldn't allow someone's cruelty or negligence to throw you off your game. But how do you do that? How do you keep certain people from messing with your head?

The answer lies in fortifying your mental armor, a protective shield that you put between yourself and the outside world. Mental armor acts as a psychological barrier that insulates against destructive people and situations that might otherwise infringe on you with their toxicity.

When I worked in law enforcement, I was exposed to the worst of humanity. I dealt with people in their lowest moments, when they were the most afraid or angry or hurt, which meant that I was constantly on the receiving end of insults and verbal abuse. And it wasn't just people I had to shield myself from, but also situations—horrible crimes, people suffering from terrible tragedies. If I had taken all that in along with every taunt and aggressive slur thrown my way to heart, I would have been a cowering mess by the end of the day. That wasn't an option, if I wanted to be good at my job—I needed to be impermeable, and that's a skill that has supported me just as much in my personal as in my professional life.

Your mental armor is an internal firewall against the harmful words or actions of others that might otherwise undermine or diminish you. Developing this kind of shield gives you agency; it allows you to choose what you want to take in and what you want to keep out.

The late Maurice Vanderpol, former president of the Boston Psychoanalytic Society and Institute, conducted extensive research on some of the most effective ways of coping with the worst sorts of suffering people have endured, particularly in Holocaust survivors. What he found was that many of the men and women who went on to lead normal lives after their experiences in concentration camps had used what he called a *plastic shield* to protect them from suffering and abuse. This shield comprised several factors, such as mental sovereignty—an inner psychological space that protected the survivors from the intrusions of abusive others—and a sense of humor. Often the humor was black, but nonetheless it provided a critical sense of perspective that made it possible for them to withstand the relentless fear and violence they endured.

Think of a mental shield as bubble wrap around a piece of china. If wrapped well, it can withstand a great deal. If poorly protected, however, it becomes more vulnerable to developing cracks or breaks.

A mental shield also makes us more willing to put ourselves out there and less afraid of failure or rejection. Knowing that the world can't easily penetrate your inner firewall means that you don't need to live your life in fear of attracting criticism or denigration. Your mental armor will absorb the impact of negative words or actions and protect you. For any person who wants to take you down a peg, you can deny them the power to do so. With a mental shield, you'll be able to become bolder, braver, and more daring in the life you live.

Another benefit of a shield is that it's there when you need it, but it doesn't have to be a constant force in your world. After all, we can't shut ourselves off from others completely. That's an incredibly lonely and isolated way to exist. Mental armor is meant to be used when you need it.

Hormetic Effect

The word *hormesis* comes from the Greek word *hórmfisis*, which means rapid motion or eagerness. In medical terms, hormesis refers to the body's strengthening response to the administration of low doses of stress. This is how vaccines work—a low-dose virus is introduced into your body, which causes your immune system to produce antibodies to fight it. This defense mechanism is how you become immune to certain diseases. It's the same reason calluses form on the palms of your hands after being exposed to repeated stressors such as swinging an ax, doing pull-ups, or hoisting a shovel. It's also how muscles grow. Lifting weights causes microtears in your muscle fibers, such that when your muscles repair themselves, they grow back bigger and stronger to better handle the same load next time. So, if you want your muscles to keep growing, you have to keep adding greater amounts of stress onto them either through lifting heavier weight or completing more repetitions with the same weight.

The Hormetic Effect, however, isn't just about physical adaptation; it's about adapting mentally as well. Our Secret Service training was designed around this concept. Over the course of months, our instructors incrementally exposed us to greater and greater amounts of stress to the point where we could function highly, both mentally and physically, while under extreme cognitive loads. We needed to learn how to run AND shoot AND maneuver our way out of a burning building AND keep our protectee safe—all at the same time. That way, for example, when our presidential motorcade was assaulted by multiple adversaries from multiple directions, we were able to logically think, swiftly move, and effectively fight our way to safety without losing the life of our protectee. It's one thing to try to save yourself when you're under attack—it's a whole other thing when you have to save two lives, one of which just happens to belong to the president of the United States.

The first time we ran this scenario, it's fair to say I slightly panicked. I may have run in the wrong direction, and it's possible I became so tunnel-visioned that I couldn't locate where the threat was even coming from. Tunnel vision can make you so hyperfocused on one particular threat that you're unable to see what else is happening around you, which makes it extremely dangerous. But the more we practiced, the more I learned to manage my mental faculties; the repeated bouts of stress were building up my tolerance to chaos. By the end, I was in a state of flow—that mindset where you're fully present and immersed in what you're doing, yet acutely aware of the world around you. In all honesty, though, in situations like these, I was at my cognitive limit. Had you asked me to recite the alphabet backward while engaging in a heated gunfight, I wouldn't be able to do it. I might not be able to do it from *A* to *Z*, either. I might be able to do only a portion of it. Or perhaps pause intermittently while my brain pivoted between lining up my next shot placement and visualizing what comes after *Q*.

The intentional addition of microstressors in our personal lives can help strengthen our minds as well. Ironically, today we seem to be constantly pushed toward seeking a life that is stress-free. But what these *purveyors of placidity* don't realize—or choose not to tell us—is that we need a certain amount of stress to make us stronger. Think of your mind like a muscle of adaptability. If you train it, it will get stronger. If you let it lie on the couch in sweatpants while stuffing your face with nacho chips and binge-watching Netflix . . . not so much.

So how do you use the concept of hormesis to fortify your mental armor? That depends on what it is you want to be less afraid of. If, for example, you fear public speaking, then consider signing up for an acting class. Stressful? Uncomfortable? Absolutely! But that's the point. By making yourself stand up in front of strangers, you're training yourself to deal with the discomfort (and stress) of performing without any extreme consequences. Once you get past the initial embarrassment—and having gone to acting school, I can assure you that you will—you'll be less shy and more confident the next time you get up onstage. Worst-case scenario, you feel foolish in front of people you don't really know, which is a great way to practice adaptability. By contrast, you don't want the first time you speak publicly to be when you have the most to lose—like when you're giving an important presentation at work or speaking in front of a large audience. The point is to gradually expose yourself to small doses of public speaking so that you can get to a place of doing it without having a full-out anxiety attack or letting your F3 run the show. Over time, you will get better and better, and your mental armor stronger and stronger.

Or perhaps you fear bombing an important job interview. If so, what's stopping you from applying to several postings for jobs you don't want and using these interviews as "rehearsals"? It may seem like a lot of work, but here's the thing—becoming bulletproof is work (in fact, it's some of the most meaningful and lifesaving work you will ever do). I can't begin to tell you how many interviews I've bombed over the years, but I go out as often as I can—even to this day. I put myself in front of people deliberately to get better at presenting my ideas and fine-tuning my social skills—all vital to fulfilling my goals. Becoming good at something involves practice, practice, and more practice. By the time it comes to interviewing for the job you really want, you'll be far more capable and far less likely to make a mistake based on nervousness or self-doubt.

Regardless of what you fear, stress about, or hope to improve upon, you can always find a way to conquer it, so long as you gradually work your way toward that goal. You can do so by implementing the following steps.

STEP 1: EXPOSE

Identify stressors that you can introduce into your life to help you strengthen your mental armor. Don't jump off the deep end here. Remember, you should start small, but these should be uncomfortable. They might make you feel awkward or even afraid, and that's okay so long as you don't overdo it.

STEP 2: EXPERIENCE

Observe and take note of your F3 response. Study yourself under the condition of heightened stress to learn all that you can about your natural reaction to the stimulus. Did you freeze up? Did you feel the sudden urge to quit or run away? Did you experience rejection or failure? Good! Believe it or not, all of these experiences help fortify your mental armor so take them in.

STEP 3: ADJUST

After analyzing your responses, identify areas where you want to make adjustments. What can you do differently to help you achieve the desired result? Perhaps you want to spend more time on your preparation and planning. Or hold out thirty seconds longer before quitting or walking away. Or manage your breathing by taking long, deep breaths, which provide more oxygen to your brain to help you think and stay calm. Every little adjustment you make will add up to big improvements over time.

STEP 4: OVERCOME

After you identify what worked and what didn't, choose one area to really focus on and correct. Don't overwhelm yourself by trying to fix everything in one fell swoop. It's too much of a mental load. The idea is to keep the task both manageable and attainable. For example, if there are multiple areas you want to work on in public speaking (fidgeting less, slowing down your speech, maintaining better eye contact), work on one until you've mastered it before moving on to the next.

STEP 5: REPEAT

Repeat steps 1–4. Having strong mental armor requires repetition, so you must keep at it. It's not enough to just attain it; you must also maintain it. Think of it like trying to improve your bench press. In the beginning you may be able to handle only twenty-five pounds, but with enough patience and practice, you'll be able to work your way up to 150 pounds. Also, keep in mind that when you strengthen one area of your life it will spill over into strengthening others as well.

Kill Fear While It's Small

Everything in our lives has a *first*; our first day of school, our first car, our first love. These firsts are like seeds planted in our minds, ideas, and efforts that we begin to nurture in the hope that they'll grow toward a positive outcome. But there are also those things we don't want in our lives, like heartaches and setbacks, or the loss of our vitality. These are the seeds in our mental garden that can grow into uncontrollable weeds, sucking the life and energy away from the things we love most. Fear is one of those seeds. Oftentimes, we find ourselves afraid of something that feels overwhelming because we've allowed it to grow unchecked. We knew it was there, but we chose to ignore it rather than face it. It's those small fears that I want to discuss here, the ones that if we catch early enough, we can take action to keep them at bay.

Here's a personal example: I fear the cold. Okay, it's a little more than that—I hate it. And I hate it because I've been exposed to frigid temperatures countless times against my will.

As Secret Service agents, we were required to physically maintain a ring of security around a protectee at all times, regardless of whether they were outside at a rally or inside the White House. As a group, we stood watch—what we called *standing post*—through every weather condition for as long as the assignment required. Many a night, I stood outside in the freezing cold at 3 a.m., wondering if my hands and feet would ever warm up again.

During the 2005 presidential inauguration for George W. Bush, I was posted at the outside checkpoint where all public attendees entered. It was the middle of January in Washington, DC. It was freezing. It was windy. And it was brutal. Because I had to maintain the agency standard of looking professional, I came dressed in my typical black suit, my long black trench coat, and my nice pair of shiny dress shoes. No down-filled North Face jacket, no thick winter hat, no insulated boots were allowed. It was you and whatever you could fit underneath your Secret Service attire versus Mother Nature. And on that day, she came to play.

I began my shift at 5 a.m. and spent the next twelve hours on my feet. As I stood, I could feel the cold dampness of the cement creeping into the soles of my shoes. Subtly, I began shifting my weight back and forth, picking each foot off the ground looking for some reprieve, if for only an instant. The burn soon became unbearable. Medically speaking, it was the onset of frostbite. Hours later, when my relief agent arrived, giving me only a few minutes to take a break, I wobbled my way over to the nearest government building, found the restroom, and locked the door. Inside, I pulled out my buck knife, removed my shoes, and began cutting through the multiple layers of pantyhose and socks. Feverishly, I began rubbing my feet, which by then had turned a light shade of blue.

They were nowhere near normal when I started rewrapping them using medical tape from my bag and pieces of destroyed socks; I still had several more hours left of standing in the bone-chilling cold.

When I got home that night, I walked right into the shower. As the steam rose slowly around me, I shook uncontrollably. Admittedly, that was the first and last time I cried from the pain of being so cold. It's also the time when the seed of fearing the cold was planted.

Unfortunately, assignments like this weren't uncommon in the Service. I've stood in knee-high snow at 6,200 feet of elevation in Jackson Hole, Wyoming, protecting the residence of Vice President Dick Cheney; outside the Oval Office in the middle of a snowstorm while President Barack Obama worked into the evening; and on the perimeter of a military base in Duluth, Minnesota, during a winter visit from President George W. Bush.

My lack of agency in those situations combined with some pretty negative experiences with the cold meant that, over the years, I grew to truly hate it. You will rarely find me with the AC on or the windows open at night, and I pretty much always have a jacket nearby, even if it's a warm day.

But because I know it's a fear of mine, I don't want it to control me, so I condition myself to face it. I take cold showers. I go for runs when it's raining or snowing. And last winter, in the middle of January, I headed to Long Island, New York, slipped on a 4mm wet suit, and surfed the Atlantic Ocean. None of it was fun, but all of it was empowering. I still hate the cold, but I refuse to let it dictate what I can and can't do.

In order to keep your own small fears from taking root, you must take notice when that first seed is planted. And then using the concept of the Hormetic Effect, begin exposing yourself to it in small doses. As you start to acclimate to your fears, you'll learn to become familiar with them, begin to understand them, and eventually be able to control them rather than the other way around.

I know a lot of people who fear being alone. Not because they're afraid something bad will happen to them, but rather the idea of loneliness, of not having companionship or someone to talk to. Although it's quite natural to want to surround ourselves with people who make us feel good—we are, after all, social creatures by design—your happiness and well-being shouldn't solely be dependent on the presence of others. When your daily life is determined by a fear of loneliness, you end up missing out on some of the great advantages of spending time by yourself. In fact, left to our own devices, we are actually more productive and creative when we're able to work independently (we'll discuss why in chapter 22).

If this happens to coincide with one of your own fears, you can begin to take control by finding ways of spending meaningful time alone. Consider taking yourself on a date to the movies or call up your favorite restaurant and reserve a table for one. The idea is to do things that will help you gradually realize you don't always need others around you to feel fulfilled. Think of your alone time as a personal adventure, but always pay attention if the fear of solitude begins creeping in. Notice it and gather intelligence on yourself. Observe yourself when you're under the influence of that fear, as well as when that fear is inactive. In time, and with practice, you'll begin to appreciate your solo excursions as much, if not more so, than your time with large groups of people.

Fear is like fire. If you extinguish it while it's small, it won't become an inferno.

Avoid the Hot Zones

Technically speaking, the president of the United States can travel to just about anywhere in the world he wants. With enough prior notice and enough agents, he can set foot onto some of the most inhospitable soil, speak to some of the unruliest crowds, and stay overnight in some of the most hostile countries. These dangerous situations are referred to as *hot zones*.

But even though he *can* do these things, that doesn't mean he *should*. As agents assigned to the president's detail, we took every precaution to ensure his safety. And that meant most of the time not putting him into a bad situation to begin with. If there was an area where his life was at risk, we avoided it. If there was an audience that might turn violent, we advised his staff to cancel his appearance. And if there was a road deemed too unsafe to travel, we found an alternative way to get him where he needed to go.

The point is that sometimes it's better to simply stay away from those environments that are potential hot zones for you. This includes people who could cause you some level of harm, whether done intentionally or not. And I don't just mean physical harm—I mean the kind that could undermine your sense of self-worth. One of the first strategies for building mental toughness is taking inventory of who you surround yourself with. Do you feel mocked or diminished by those in your social circles? Are the people closest to you good for your well-being? Are they supportive of your decisions, but stern and honest when they feel you're heading down the wrong path? How do you feel about yourself after spending time with certain people? Do you feel energized and good about yourself, or disheartened and depressed? It's vital for us to honestly assess every person in our circle and decide whether or not they're truly a friend or foe.

If you're not sure which relationships in your life should qualify as a hot zone, then ask yourself:

1. When I present my ideas or opinions, are they met with criticism or acceptance?
2. When I express my feelings, are they quickly dismissed or deeply considered?
3. Am I routinely the butt of the joke or am I in on the punch line?
4. Am I usually the last to know something or the first to be informed?
5. In my absence, do I go unnoticed or am I missed?
6. When I am there, do I feel like an intruder or part of the group?
7. When I leave an interaction with someone, do I feel worse or better about myself?

If you find yourself answering "Yes" to any of the negative phrases in these sentences, you should begin to think about your exit strategy.

Get Off the X

Oftentimes it's not possible to shield ourselves from the harshness of others, because sometimes the most negative people in our lives may be members of our family, the colleagues we sit next to at work, or the friends we've grown up with since grade school. But even though we can't fully disengage ourselves, we can find ways to lessen their impact on our mental well-being. If you find yourself, for example, in a toxic sibling relationship, a hostile work environment, or hanging out with a bunch of assholes who take pleasure in denigrating you, then you should start identifying ways to avoid them or minimize your interactions.

One of the realities of being a Special Agent was the understanding that carrying a gun meant you might one day have to use it. And if that day ever came, it was very possible that whomever you were shooting at would be shooting back at you. Which is why one of the first things they taught us in firearms training is that the worst thing you can do in a firefight is stand still. After spending countless hours at the Secret Service shooting range learning the fundamentals of marksmanship, our instructors began teaching us how to accurately hit our targets while on the move. Even when reloading our weapons, we kept moving until we positioned ourselves safely behind cover. We called this constant motion *getting off the X*. This training ensured that we never stood still long enough to give our adversaries an easy target.

The get off the X lesson carries over to all facets of our lives. When it comes to building up your mental fortitude, don't remain in the same place long enough to get hit, hurt, or insulted. And when I say "don't remain in the same place," I literally mean "don't remain in the same place." As in, physically get up and leave.

While on a protection assignment, if we ever got the inkling that shit was about to break sideways, whether in the audience the president was addressing or a volatile situation with protestors, we didn't stick around to find out. Why wait for things to go really wrong before deciding to pack up and go? We knew that if we hung around any longer than necessary, two things would inevitably happen: 1) it would encourage further and possibly bolder attacks, and 2) it would make our eventual departure even more dangerous or difficult.

Get off the X means keep moving for your survival and well-being. Get out of the area of danger. Adjust. Pivot. Because when you stay static—that is, when you remain in a bad situation—you *will* get hurt. And what many people don't realize is that removing yourself from a bad environment actually helps deescalate a situation before things get really bad. So the next time you get the feeling that the conversation or mood in the room is turning against you, I want you to think about immediately removing yourself from the scene.

There is no shame in leaving. In fact, leaving will save you the shame you'll probably end up feeling by staying put and taking it.

Which leads to my next point:

Have the Courage to Walk Away

There is this epic misperception that when you walk away from a fight, it's a sign of weakness or cowardice. Many of us are taught to believe that standing up for ourselves means doing so only with either strong words or clenched fists. And because no one wants to be considered a coward, we have become conditioned to instinctually strike back anytime we feel disrespected.

Society has ingrained in us the need to firmly stand our ground, or else we run the risk of being preyed upon. Although that's true to some extent, it doesn't necessarily mean that we have to fight back every time and in the most obvious of ways. Most people mistakenly believe that the proper reaction to being attacked is to directly and immediately confront their aggressor. In many instances, however, these transparent responses are the worst ways to defend your honor. The foundation of these responses really has more to do with protecting your pride than anything else. As a result, we end up wasting all our physical and emotional efforts engaging every fool that crosses our path.

Walking away isn't about weakness—it is about implanting strength and strategy to deal with conflict. The true essence of inner strength is seen in how you respond to conflict. It's about checking your superficial ego and being smarter than your adversary. And if, on occasion, you need to deal with an issue, it means being methodical in deciding the most appropriate time to engage so that the odds are in your favor and not in your opponent's.

Your goal should never be to fight every battle. Rather, to be selective and thoughtful about which battles to fight and why, and to avoid pointless confrontation whenever possible. It has nothing to do with being weak or afraid. It is about controlling your emotions, and being intelligent and calculated in how you handle certain individuals. If you confront every opponent with aggression, you become predictable. Your emotional reactions will become transparent, and ultimately you will be perceived as common as the fools you deal with. The key is to be able to determine when it makes sense to fight and when it makes sense to walk away.

Don't Catch the Ball

Throughout your life, you're going to cross paths with a lot of people eager to goad you into conflict or confrontation. There will be times when, despite your best efforts, you may find yourself getting baited into an argument, pulled into a game, or sucked into an agenda. And since we can't always avoid these *hot zones*, we need to have strategies in place to handle them. This section is about managing those specific situations; the daily annoyances and problems that arise at work, school, or with our family and friends.

Despite Newton's theory, not every action needs a reaction. Just because someone is demanding your attention doesn't mean you have to give it, especially if that engagement seems emotionally charged. When you decide not to dignify an irrational communication with a response, it's about preserving your personal dignity and mental clarity. Just because someone throws the ball doesn't mean you have to catch it.

Think of it this way: How would you feel if you sent someone an emotionally charged email but never received a response? You'd initially be confused. First, you'd double-check your Sent folder to make sure it went through. Then you'd start obsessing over the audible "ding" of your incoming messages, thinking it might be their response. Finally, you'd begin wondering if they even got your electronic tirade, somehow found a way to block your emails, or what else they might be doing that was more important than sending you a reply. In the end, you'd feel embarrassed, your pride deflated, and the fire you had to engage in keyboard karate would burn out. That's the power of not reacting.

When faced with a situation in which you're being provoked, take a moment to let your emotions pass, and then ask yourself, "Do I really need to respond?" Assess the situation from a logical vantage point—

rather than an emotional one—and base your decisions on what will ultimately benefit *you* in the long run.

This mental strategy, however, isn't solely for dealing with insults or slander. It's just as effective when trying to handle people who constantly want your time and attention. Sometimes you simply don't have it to give. Or giving it will distract you from things that are more important. When it comes to time allocation, it's good to separate the signals from the noise. If *everything* in your life is important, then *nothing* is.

Think about all the junk emails you receive. Every morning you may wake up to a barrage of unwanted and unsolicited messages in your inbox, eager for you to *buy*, *click*, *read*, or *respond*. Do you sit and methodically go through each one? Of course not! Otherwise, you'd be there all day getting nothing productive done in the process. Instead, you quickly identify them as spam, hit Delete, and move on. The daily interactions and intrusions you're exposed to are no different.

Of course, there will be certain times when you have to respond. When it directly relates to a relevant issue, then by all means reply, just do so from a place of logic. Focus on the issue at hand, be methodical in the words you choose, and condense your communication to the bare minimum, when appropriate. Politicians are brilliant at this. If they don't like a question or don't want to answer, they don't. Or if they do, they'll respond in a way that sidesteps the question. Over the many years of holding post in front of the dais, I've heard firsthand presidents and First Ladies asked the most ridiculous or inappropriate things. Do they respond? Nope! At least not in the way the questioner was hoping they would. This is the true essence of not catching the ball.

If you ever find yourself struggling to identify whether or not you need to respond, either in person, or via phone, text, or email, ask yourself these questions:

1. Is this a true emergency that requires my immediate attention?
2. Is this a relevant issue that I must respond to?
3. Is this something I can ignore?

4. Is my response going to invite unnecessary drama?
5. If I don't respond, will there be negative repercussions?
6. Are they trying to make their problem my problem?
7. Am I being baited into an argument?
8. Is this distracting me from more important tasks?

Sometimes the unnecessary stress in our life is our own doing, because we intentionally engage with the people or situations creating it. Although we often don't mean to, we find ourselves instinctually catching the ball out of habit or obligation or because of our history with that person (ex-spouse, childhood friend, overbearing parent). You may not be able to control what another person says or does, but you can always control your response, or lack thereof, to it.

If you don't like drama, then don't invite it in.

Playing the Long Game

A few years into my career as a Special Agent, I became a polygraph examiner for the Secret Service. I was often sent around the country to assist local law enforcement in active investigations. This meant talking to people who had done some really horrible things. Such as sexually abusing children.

When my colleagues heard about some of these interviews, they would often ask me, "How could you just sit there listening to him tell you what he had done to that poor child? Didn't you just want to punch him in the face?"

When I told them that no, I didn't want to punch him in the face, they were often indignant. And from their perspective, I get it. How could anyone not feel a sense of rage? It's a visceral reaction, and a totally understandable one. In fact, I'd argue that I understood it even more than they did, because no matter how good your poker face may be, every interrogator is still a human being. It is always heartbreaking to hear about a child being hurt, because out of all victims, they are the ones least capable of protecting themselves.

But here's the thing: As an interviewer, I wasn't there to pass judgment on the offender. My job wasn't to threaten or yell or tell my interviewee what I really thought of him. My job was to get the information I needed so no more harm could come to that child or any other; to ensure the guilty person would face consequences for their actions and that justice would be done. That was my end goal.

I can assure you that no one wanted to punch those suspects in the face more than me (Fight, as we all remember, is my go-to F3 response). But what would that have gotten me? A few seconds of satisfaction? That immediate tactic, what I refer to as *the short game*, would have worked in complete contradiction to my overall mission—*the long game*—which was to collect as much information as possible to send this predator to prison.

For the sake of argument and observation, though, let's map this out using what I call the *Gaming Framework*:

A: Short game tactic: Immediate response = punching him in the face:
Pros:
1. *I feel good about myself for roughly 60 seconds*

Cons:
1. *I lose the confession*
2. *I get arrested for assault*
3. *My law enforcement career is over*
4. *Suspect walks free*
5. *Suspect sues me and US government for violating his rights and wins*
6. *That vigilante feeling soon vanishes*
7. *Victim never receives justice*
8. *Other children become victims of the suspect*

Versus

B: Long game approach: Collecting information to send him to prison = not punching him in the face:

Pros:
1. *I get evidence and confession*
2. *I'm still employed*
3. *Victim is vindicated*
4. *I spend my night at home and not in a jail cell*
5. *I feel professionally competent*
6. *I get fulfillment knowing someone in prison will punch him in the face probably a lot harder than I could have*

Cons:
1. *I lose a minute of emotional satisfaction*

When putting forth any type of effort, the *long game* means achieving a specific goal—getting the highest grade, setting the best time, or losing a certain amount of weight. Simply put, it usually means winning. The *short game* is each independent decision made within the long game that affects whether you get closer to or farther from that goal, for example, how long you study before an exam, the marathon pace you set, whether you eat sandwiches or salad for dinner. If your short game is in harmony with your long game, you win. If it's not, you lose.

This applies to most everything we do in life when trying to achieve a particular objective—finishing school, saving more money, not arguing with an annoying in-law. Yet, there are times when somewhere along the way we lose focus on the long game and begin acting based on what we impulsively want in the short term. Part of having emotional intelligence is keeping your impulses in check and having the foresight to step back and evaluate your behavior. Are you heading in the right direction? Will this course of action bring you closer to your ultimate goal or farther from it?

With every endeavor I take on, I constantly ask myself if my immediate actions are in line with where I want to eventually end up. Although most of the time I can game out the strategies in my head, I still use the *Gaming Framework* if I feel like I'm too emotionally involved or unable to see the objective truth clearly. The next time you find yourself pursuing a goal but feeling like your compass is broken, pull out a sheet of paper and write down your long game. And then record what short-game strategies you need to use to get there. Don't worry if you don't exactly know what to do. The point is to rein in your impulse behavior and use your emotional intelligence to begin thinking about the goal logically. If the short-game tactics you're considering don't make the list, pivot and create new ones that do.

Chapter 4

Mental Resilience

You don't develop courage by being happy in your relationships every day.
You develop it by surviving difficult times and challenging adversity.
—Epicurus

Becoming Resilient

While it's crucial for us to take as many precautionary and proactive measures as possible to shield ourselves from the potential perils of the world, there will always be those threats capable of penetrating our defenses. No matter how great the plan, no matter how many layers we've meticulously wrapped around ourselves, nothing is 100 percent foolproof. There will always be that unexpected person or unimagined situation that will catch us with our guard down. This is where mental resilience comes into play. Research on resilience shows that it's not a genetic trait that some people luck into. Rather, it's a learned skill that can be built over time like an internal scaffold capable of bearing the weight of our emotional burdens.

Mental resilience is our ability to analyze, adjust, and psychologically rebound from adversity. It's seeing a problem for what it is—a problem—then swiftly and effectively working toward a solution. But to do so, you need a strong foundation of strategies.

This chapter is about giving you the tools to do just that; to enhance your resilience for when you find yourself contending with a mental crisis.

Mental resilience serves three purposes:

1. To keep you emotionally composed in a moment of crisis.
2. To help you effectively problem-solve using logic and reason.
3. To quickly recover from any mental hardship.

Live in Your Reality

Admiral Jim Stockdale was a navy pilot who, in 1965, was shot down during the Vietnam War. After parachuting into enemy territory, he was taken prisoner. Over the next seven and a half years, he was severely beaten and tortured by his captors, until he was released in 1973. During his time in captivity and despite his continued mistreatment by the North Vietnamese, Stockdale survived while he watched several other men die. During an interview with author Jim Collins, when Stockdale was asked his thoughts on who didn't make it out of the camps, he said it was the optimists—they died of broken hearts.[*]

Although having a level of optimism is important, facing the facts of your reality matters even more. If you're focused only on a positive outcome, you may find it impossible to cope should a less favorable one arise. When I was on the president's protection detail, I was optimistic that my security plan was strong enough to deter an assassination attempt, but I certainly wasn't arrogant or delusional enough to think it could never happen. I accepted the possibility, which in turn kept my mind sharp and open to finding solutions to unexpected problems or unforeseen threats. As an agent responsible for the lives of my protectees, my colleagues, the public, and myself, I knew it was better to wear clear glasses and see things as they truly were rather than rose-colored ones that gave me a skewed version of the truth.

Your ability to accept a situation—the real situation—will ultimately help you overcome it. This means that when unplanned shit happens, and it will, you must forgo the *I can't believe this is happening to me* attitude, and instead adopt the mindset of *This is happening to me. This is my reality. So now what?*

---

[*] https://www.jimcollins.com/media_topics/TheStockdaleParadox.html

Understanding the Real Problem

One of the complexities with trying to solve a problem is making sure it's the *right* problem to solve. Have you ever gone to a chiropractor with an ankle pain only to find out that your hips are out of alignment? Or suffered the onset of sudden headaches only to find out you need glasses? Sometimes we get so focused on what we think the underlying issue is that we fail to even consider it could be something else altogether.

When you find yourself unable to fix your dilemma, despite attacking it from multiple angles, it's usually time to reassess your perspective in order to determine whether you're focusing on the right problem.

At one of my speaking engagements on dealing with confrontation in the workplace, a young woman came to me afterward with an issue. She worked in the research and development division for a Fortune 500 company. "I work in this unit with a man who is very mean to me. He won't share any information with me and won't offer help or guidance when I need it, even if it's for something we should be working on collectively. He's just a mean guy. What can I do to get him to be nicer to me?"

I looked at her. "You think your issue is that he needs help being nicer?"

"Yes," she replied.

"How long have you been working at the company?"

"I'm new." I guessed that she was about twenty-five years old.

"And what about him?"

"Oh, he's been here for thirty years or so. He's older, maybe in his fifties."

"And you're both in the same unit. As peers?"

"Yes," she said.

"I don't think you're asking the right question here," I said. "Getting him to be nice to you is not the solution. You're making the assumption that he's just a mean guy and that his personality needs adjustment. But think about this: This is a man who has been at the company for thirty years and then you show up—a younger, newer version who is likely getting paid a lot less than he is. He sees you as his possible replacement. So he probably keeps you in the dark because he's afraid that if you learn what he knows, he will no longer be needed. Your problem isn't 'how do I make him a nice guy?'; what you need to figure out is how to alter his perception so that he stops seeing you as a threat."

I watched the realization of what I had said take hold. "Oh wow," she said, "I completely missed that."

Sometimes we become emotionally enmeshed in a problem or take such offense at someone's behavior that our perception of what's really going on becomes skewed. This young woman was so focused on her emotions and the belief that her coworker disliked her that she failed to see the situation from his perspective. She was making it all about her rather than stepping outside of the problem and looking for the true cause of his behavior, as well as a viable solution. In the end, I helped her find a way to make him feel more valued, less threatened, and how she in turn could reap the rewards of that shift in their team dynamic.

Sometimes, despite our best efforts to resolve an issue, we can get stuck. When that happens, try sharing your dilemma with a close friend or loved one. Even better, try talking to an acquaintance or someone that has distance from you and your issue—even someone you just met. Although it may seem odd to seek the advice of an outsider, sometimes a person who doesn't know you well may be able to give you a different and more honest perspective.

The Problem vs. Solution Mindset

Before we identify the most effective method for fixing a problem, we must first understand the mindset we're in when the problem occurs. When something happens that puts you at a disadvantage, do you have a hard time moving on? Say you're contributing to a team project at work and your coworker fails to put in her share of effort. Do you go home and spend the evening bitching to your spouse about your colleague who left you with the higher workload? Do you show up at the office the next day complaining to anyone who will listen about how unfair this is? Do you continue to spend the next several days focused solely on how you've been wronged? Although your anger is certainly justified under the circumstances, the real question is, How is this actually helping you complete the project?

Often, when things don't go as planned, we become more fixated on what went wrong than we are about solving the issue at hand. We get stuck in the *problem mindset*, looking for anything and anyone to blame. Focusing on all the reasons why something can't be done, rather than on how it can be done.

Research shows that as humans, we have a limited amount of mental bandwidth to utilize when it comes to problem-solving. Our *executive function* is the part of our brain that helps us creatively think outside the box, stay focused on a task, and deal with unanticipated challenges. When we tax that function with a series of seemingly insurmountable challenges, we actually impair our ability to handle impending problems. This is why, when forced to deal with unexpected issues, it's wiser to use your finite mental energy to have a *solution mindset*, wherein you focus on the solution rather than obsessing over the problem.

But how do we do that? How do we pull ourselves out of the mental loop where we ruminate over the issue? By following these steps:

STEP 1: SET AN EXPIRATION DATE

Sometimes before you can move toward the solution, you need time to process the situation and your emotions around it. The length of time can vary depending on the depth of your hardship. Give yourself enough time to gripe or grieve over what has happened to you—because if you move on too quickly, you may end up suppressing the issue rather than accepting it.

When I find myself grumbling to my husband about a frustrating situation, I set an expiration date. It can be anywhere from one hour to twenty-four hours to a week, depending on the emotional fallout. And then I make myself move on. You need an expiration date to mitigate the length of time you allow yourself to spend on an emotional hardship. It takes about twenty-eight days for a behavior to turn into a habit, so if you dwell in anger or misery or self-pity for too long, you'll end up making it much more difficult to extricate yourself from those emotions, and you don't want this to become the blueprint for how you deal with future conflicts. It's important to be able to adapt and overcome without burdening yourself with bitterness or unnecessary suffering. Even when you're wallowing, always keep one eye moving forward toward the solution.

So, when things don't go your way—you get a nasty email, or the negotiation you've been working on falls through, or your relationship takes a nosedive—give yourself time to process it. If that means crying your eyes out, throwing things against the wall, or eating a pint of ice cream while binging Netflix, do it. But do it only after you commit yourself to a designated amount of wallowing time.

STEP 2: ACCEPTANCE

Once you've moved through your emotional hurdles, accept where you are now. Don't try to start from where you *had been* or where you wish *to be*. Live in your new reality along with the mindset that this is *your* problem to solve. Remember, the mark of a resilient mind is one that can look frankly at the circumstances surrounding you. Don't expect someone else to intervene and fix it for you. This is not about accepting blame or taking responsibility for what went wrong when it's not your fault. This is about taking ownership of your problem so that you can also take ownership of the solution.

STEP 3: SHIFT TO THE SOLUTION MINDSET

Solutions require innovation. Creativity. Stepping outside your mental and emotional confines and looking at the situation from a bird's-eye view. Shift your mindset away from the problem and toward the solution. You may have already begun coming up with some possible improvements. It's time to start putting those plans into action. They may not magically fix things right away, and that's okay. The good news about following these steps is that your ability to rebound will only increase the more you implement this process into your life. If one kind of solution isn't fixing your problem, try something different. Be persistent and inventive. Don't give up.

Prototype thinking is a great way to pursue the *solution mindset*. In fact, I teach this method to my students at the City University of New York (CUNY), where I'm an adjunct professor of criminal justice and criminology. During one class assignment, I ask my students to come up with solutions for reducing the recidivism rates of juvenile offenders. I divide them into groups, hand out several yellow sticky pads to each group, and give them five minutes to write down any and every idea that comes to mind, no matter how foolish, how expensive, or how illegal. The point is not to *judge* ideas, but to *generate* them. At the end, my class often has more than a hundred ideas. Although some may be outside the realm of possibility, many have true potential that we can use to begin solving the initial dilemma.

Finding Meaning

For two years, I was a law enforcement analyst on HLN's *Dr. Drew On Call* show. Dr. Drew, whose full name is Drew Pinsky, is both a radio and television personality as well as a board-certified addiction medicine specialist, and a dear friend. One evening prior to going on air, Dr. Drew and I were discussing why some people are able to overcome trauma while others are not. He then asked me if I had struggled getting back to a normal life after my experience on 9/11.

I thought for a moment as to the truth of it all. "No," I said. "Although I was incredibly saddened by what happened, it didn't affect me that way."

I then told him how immediately after the attack, I went back to work and volunteered to help with the search and rescue efforts. I was assigned to the Secret Service command post at Ground Zero, where I worked twelve-hour shifts doing what I could to be part of the collective effort. I grieved at the tragedy of it all, but what I was doing felt important: I was helping others. Contributing. And offering support to those who had lost more than I had. Somehow, I was able to find light in all that darkness.

"That's why you didn't struggle," Dr. Drew said. "You found meaning in that tragedy."

Psychiatrist Viktor Emil Frankl came to this same realization nearly eighty years ago. In 1942, Frankl was imprisoned in Auschwitz, where he witnessed and was exposed to unimaginable suffering at the hands of the Nazis. After he was liberated and returned to Vienna, Frankl wrote a book called *Man's Search for Meaning*, where he described his observations that people are primarily driven to "find meaning in one's life."

This meaning, he said, is what enables people to overcome pain and suffering, to remain who they are in spite of enduring terrible hardships. After experiencing the camps, Frankl concluded that even under the most abhorrent and dehumanized situations, life has purpose—and in turn that suffering and loss can be purposeful. It is the sense we make from our pain that can be the difference between emotional collapse and having the will to get up and resume our lives. If we can't find meaning in a meaningless tragedy, there is nothing to get up for. Unbeknownst to me, my volunteer work after 9/11 had a positive impact on my physical health and emotional well-being. Research shows that when we offer to help others, our brains release oxytocin—the feel-good hormone—throughout our bodies. Volunteering has also been shown to reduce depression and increase our overall vitality.

When we can find meaning in our personal tragedies and use them as a way to enhance our lives, or the lives of others, we'll emerge stronger and more resilient. So if you ever find yourself in the middle of your own tragedy, the loss of a loved one, a diagnosis of ailing health, or the victim of a senseless crime, take inventory of what you can do to help yourself. And if there are others who have also been affected, do your best to help them, too. I know firsthand how it can be difficult to summon the strength needed to climb out of bed after a life-altering trauma, but it's vital that you stay active both mentally and physically.

Mental Attitude: Powerful vs. Powerless

Think about the differences in these two sentences:

Look what I became.
Look what became of me.

Despite the small word difference, what do these sentences say about the speaker's mental attitude? Although they're nearly identical statements, one is active and the other is passive. In the first sentence, the speaker has taken ownership over their life and became *something* by doing *something*. She owns the results, regardless of what those results are. Her approach and self-commitment have made her powerful, and that power came from within—hence a powerful mental attitude.

In the second sentence, however, the speaker allowed something to be done *to* him. He is a mere recipient, accepting whatever the world is dishing out at that particular moment. He doesn't own anything—instead, he is owned by his circumstances. He is coming from a place of no power—hence a powerless mental attitude.

When you have a *powerless attitude*, you're constantly blaming external forces for your difficulties. Simply put, nothing is your fault. Say you fail a school exam, and you decide to blame it on your professor's poor teaching methods. This means the only way you can pass your next exam is to have a different professor. If that doesn't happen, according to this logic, all future failed grades are the teacher's fault, not yours. Unfortunately, when you adopt this pattern of thinking, you put yourself at the mercy of others, relying on others to change or behave differently in order to fix your situation. As a result, you have no power over the outcome.

A *powerful attitude*, on the other hand, allows you to take ownership of your situation. You acknowledge and accept that you have played a role in some way, and by doing so, you have the ability to change its course. To turn the exam scenario around, you might say, "I know I failed my test, and maybe my professor does suck, but I can study harder, join a study group, work with a tutor, or talk to my teacher to see what more I can do." Now you have power; there are actions for you to take to alter or enhance your circumstances. You are at no one's mercy but your own.

In the Service, we were primed from the first day of training to take responsibility for everything we did. Accountability was paramount. No one wanted to hear excuses—they wanted to hear us take ownership of a problem and fix it. If you had a breach in security, physically lost sight of a protectee, or failed to report to your post on time, they didn't care about the *why* (the stairwell wasn't secured, my radio stopped working, my car didn't start). They wanted to know the *how*, as in *how* it happened and *how* you were going to make sure it didn't happen again.

I have always opted in life to risk making the wrong decision rather than taking someone else's advice and then blaming them if things went wrong. Because two things are bound to happen here: 1) you come to resent the person you listened to, and 2) you come to resent yourself for listening to them. There is nothing worse than looking at a parent or spouse or friend and thinking, *I'm in this shitty situation because I listened to you.*

So instead, my mindset has always been, "Okay, I did what I thought was best. Right or wrong. But if it doesn't work out, there is no one else to blame but me." Now, this doesn't mean I never take advice or heed the recommendations of my personal counsel. It just means that after identifying, discussing, and analyzing all my options, I take full ownership for the final decision made. Regardless of whether in the end I'm a hero or zero, I own the outcome by virtue of a powerful mental attitude.

Third-Person Solution

Let's face it—it can be extremely difficult for us to accurately identify and solve our own problems. Research shows that when trying to resolve personal issues, we're much more granular in our perspective and reserved in our options. We are, both literally and figuratively, too close to our problems to handle them objectively.

However, when trying to fix the dilemmas of someone else, like a friend or loved one, we're quite capable of viewing their difficulties from an overall more adventurous and less emotional perspective. We cut straight to what needs to be done with a swift and decisive course of action. How good are you at giving advice to your friends versus yourself? When someone tells you their problems, does the solution immediately pop into your head? Do the next words that come out of your mouth sound something like, "You know what you should do . . . ?"

Say, for instance, your friend tells you that her boyfriend cheated on her and asks for your advice. Without a second thought, you reply, "That's easy. Just leave him. Pack your shit and go." Boom! Done! But then your friend quickly counters back with all the reasons that she thinks she should stay: "But we were going to get married. He told me he loved me. He told me it was a terrible mistake. He told me he was drunk." On and on and on. And despite hearing all of this, you still keep thinking to yourself, *So what? He cheated. He'll cheat again. If you want to avoid getting hurt in the future, you need to leave him.*

Now, I'm not trying to oversimplify the "cheating" scenario here, as I know it's sometimes more complicated than "leave him." The point is that we're good at giving advice, but bad at taking it when the advisor is us. We become so paralyzed by our inability to take action or even make intelligent decisions that we don't effectively do anything.

One of the best strategies toward objectively fixing a problem is to use the *Third-Person Solution*. Take whatever dilemma you're facing and project it onto someone else. Perhaps a friend or a family member. Now, look at the issue as if they're coming to you with it. What would you tell them? What guidance would you give? If you can avoid making it about *you*, you can begin to see it as a more simplified and less muddied version of the problem, and then begin making clearer decisions.

Disrupter

Because of the emotional turmoil that usually accompanies a shitty situation, sometimes it takes having different approaches to help switch you from a powerless mind to a powerful one. When you find yourself so upset or pissed off that you can't think clearly, it's time to introduce a *Disrupter*.

A disrupter is something that mentally distracts you from the problem at hand. You can't solve anything when your head and heart are not clear or your F3 is running in high gear. You're also not likely to make intelligent decisions or interact well with others.

The point of a disrupter is to change your environment in order to interrupt your state of mind. It helps you create space between a stimulus and your response to it. Below are the three disrupters that I deploy every time I'm seeing red, white, and fuck you:

1. Place: Placing physical distance between you and your hardship is a great way to shift your emotional outlook. Perhaps you need to put some space between you and someone you're in conflict with, such as a loved one or a professional colleague. Or maybe it's a toxic household, or stressful work environment, that you need to step away from to clear your head and your heart. Distance limits our ability to act irrationally or impulsively, which can often worsen the situation. Sometimes a simple drive to the beach or the park can suffice. Other times it may require an impromptu vacation to get some perspective and objectivity.

2. Activity: Do something to physically alter your mental state. Maybe sign up for a sculpting or cooking class. Or head out dancing or bowling with your friends. Perhaps a tough workout in the park is a more doable option for you. Of course, you could also opt for the extraordinary, such as backpacking through Europe or hiking Mount Vesuvius. Whatever the physical activity, make sure it's challenging enough to draw your full attention. Doing something you don't want to do—like the laundry or cleaning the bathroom—is probably not the best activity for you in that moment. The point is to draw your attention away from your problem and onto something else that draws you into the present moment.

One of my favorite disrupters is Brazilian jiujitsu because it requires my full attention and physical effort. Often, by the time I'm done with class, any emotional turmoil I may have had has passed, allowing me to reevaluate my situation from a much clearer perspective.

3. Time: Using time as a disrupter is another way to pull yourself out of the mental mess swimming in your head. We tell kids, "When you're angry, count to ten." I say count to twenty-four hours. I actually have a twenty-four-hour rule that I follow when I receive an email, call, or text that I don't like. Because my default typically is to tell someone to go fuck themselves (hello, F3 response), I've learned that it's better if I step away, knowing that response won't help me in the long game, nor will it make me look good. When I use Time as my disrupter, I make sure not to focus on my dilemma for that designated period of time; otherwise, I know I'll quickly fall back into the cycle of ruminating on the issue. Usually after twenty-four hours, if I still want to respond, then I'm able to reapproach the situation without the unnecessary emotional nonsense that would have made its way in a day earlier.

Chapter 5

The Secret Service Mindset

Pay attention to your enemies, for they are the first to discover your mistakes.
—ANTISTHENES

Advance Team

Up to this point, we have focused primarily on strengthening your mindset. But protection is more than just harnessing mental grit; there's a physical element to it as well. It requires intentionally thinking about the things that can go wrong before they happen. No one wants to spend all day pondering worst-case scenarios, nor should you. You'd only end up hyper-fearful, which would defeat the point of reading this book. It's not about dwelling on the negative—it's about understanding the reality of our world so that we are less fearful of it. As described in chapter 4, resilience is about accepting things as they truly are. Unrealistic or overly optimistic fantasies help no one. You must live in the truth of things so that you can endure that reality with courage.

After spending the first eight years of my Secret Service career in the New York Field Office, I was assigned to the Presidential Protective Division in Washington, DC. In the Service, the majority of what we did was *proactive*. These were security measures we put into place *before* something happened. *Reactive* was what we would do in response to something happening. The Presidential Protective Division consists of two teams: The Advance team and the Shift team. Agents on the Advance team create the multiple layers of security that you don't typically see—all the precautions and preparations made ahead of time to ensure the president's safety.

The Shift team, on the other hand, is the innermost protective layer. They're designed to react defensively should a threat penetrate the Advance team's safeguards. As an agent assigned to PPD, I rotated between both teams.

The threat we were always on the lookout for had a name. We called him *the Jackal*. He was the unknown assassin with the potential to strike at any moment, the one we always kept in mind while formulating protection plans. "Think of the Jackal," our instructors would tell us during our months at the USSS Academy. "Could the Jackal penetrate this defense? How would you stop him?"

The best way to protect yourself and your family is to be proactive. While the Jackal is unlikely to be a big concern in your daily life, when it comes to personal safety, 90 percent of protection is prevention. Everywhere you go, you want to create your own advance plan. It takes only a few minutes, but the more you do it, the more efficient you will become, and eventually it will be second nature. Think about the places you go most often and start there, mapping out your ingress and egress points (more on that in a minute), working out how you'll get from A to B.

Oftentimes, people would rather put off thinking about a crisis until they're in the middle of it, forcing themselves into a reactive state of mind. When we're reactive, we are at our most vulnerable and least effective at problem-solving. Remember F3? Trying to figure what to do in an emergency with limited knowledge and practice puts you at a great disadvantage. And in a crisis situation, it can be extremely dangerous. Arming yourself with knowledge and tools will free you from unnecessary stressors and worries so that you can live fearlessly.

Turquoise

In 2009, I was the assistant detail leader for Barbara P. Bush, one of the twin daughters of President George W. Bush. This meant that as one of her primary protection agents, I went where she went and did what she did. Barbara was, simply put, a mover. And I loved it. Her code name was *Turquoise*, and we traveled throughout Africa for her humanitarian efforts and went to Texas and Maine to spend time with her family. And while other protectees went to bed early, we spent the evenings experiencing the New York City nightlife—of course I was always in work mode—but even so, it felt good to be out as well. Becoming a Special Agent at a relatively young age meant I missed out on a lot in my own personal life. While my friends were in the clubs dancing, I was in Egypt standing post for President Bush. When my family got together for holidays or celebrations, I was called in to do an interrogation. Even going on a date required I put in a request for leave with my supervisor at least three weeks in advance. In truth, my life was not my own. So being with Barbara was a chance to make up for some lost time. Hell, I even got to go to Coachella. (Though I'll admit that when Barbara first told me about it, my response was, "Great! What's a Coachella?")

When you're a Secret Service protectee, you're not only physically protected 24/7, but most of your daily logistics are handled as well. You don't have to drive, find parking, or fill the car up with gas, because, well . . . you don't drive—we drive you. You don't have to stand in line at the airport because we escort you through. You don't wait for an open table at a restaurant or even choose your own seat, because we've already handpicked it for you. You can go anywhere and do anything with little worry because we've taken the necessary safety precautions far in advance.

This type of personal attention tends to increase a protectee's confidence as to what they can do because they know someone else is there to worry about the minutiae of getting it done. Unfortunately, these perks can also come at a cost. When you become accustomed to relying on others to do things on your behalf, you tend to not learn how to do those things for yourself. Once that "protector" goes away, however, a sense of panic can quickly set in.

As George W. Bush's presidency was coming to an end, the Secret Service was winding down their protection of both Barbara and her twin sister, Jenna. Although all presidents and First Ladies are authorized by Congress to receive Secret Service protection for life, their protective detail ends for their children over sixteen years of age once their father leaves office. Prior to George W. Bush's eight-year term as the nation's forty-third president, he was also the governor of Texas for six years, which meant his wife and twin daughters were under the protective care of the Texas Rangers for all that time. This meant that for the first time in nearly fifteen years, Barbara would no longer have someone watching her every move.

Although I knew she was ready to be free from her constant security shadow, I also knew that a sense of fear and uncertainty would likely show up in our absence. Since Barbara was my protectee, she was my responsibility. I couldn't help but feel protective of her and her long-term well-being. So in the weeks before our protection was scheduled to end, I knew I had to do something—I couldn't just leave her defenseless. She needed the tools she never had the opportunity to learn. On my own time, I created a personal security plan for her. And in the time we had left, I taught her what I could.

What you're about to read is how I educated Barbara in the fundamentals of protection—with some extras thrown in for your benefit. Consider this your foundational protection plan for home, work, school, and travel.

Know Your Safe Houses

A safe house is any place you can go to be safe and secure. If you've ever played that game with your family or friends where you talk about where you'd go in the event of a zombie apocalypse, you've most likely already identified a safe house. Before I traveled anywhere with a protectee, I would find a place we could go in case of an emergency, or if we needed somewhere to lie low. Below is a list of places that you could use as a safe house in a pinch.

HOSPITALS: As Secret Service agents, we always knew where the nearest hospital was for every location we visited. But it wasn't enough just to find any hospital within our proximity, because not all hospitals are the same. Some are better equipped than others, have more resources, a different level of skill set and even competency. As an Advance agent, I always wanted to know where the nearest Trauma 1 hospital was—the place where the medical team is trained to handle gunshot wounds and other complex traumatic injuries. Being that I protected some of the most threatened people in the world, this was an important factor for me. When President Ronald Reagan was shot on March 30, 1981, during an attempted assassination, he was rushed to George Washington University Hospital—a Trauma 1.

Just knowing which hospital was rated highest or closest wasn't enough. I'd actually drive there, figure out how to get to the emergency room entrance, walk in, meet the staff, and get the layout of where everything was. It helped me save valuable time in case one of our protectees needed help ASAP. In the midst of an emergency is not the time when you should be working all this out.

We also never waited to be rescued, and neither should you. Don't wait for help to arrive. If you are able to, go find it! In mass emergency situations, such as an earthquake, hurricane, or terrorist attack, first responders may be overwhelmed with multiple calls for service, so it could take a long time for help to arrive. This is especially important when it comes to injury and trauma. Most people's immediate reaction is to call 911 and wait for an ambulance. Although this is prudent protocol in some situations—especially when the person can't be moved or there's no way to get them to the hospital—this waiting period begins to cut into what medical officials refer to as the *Golden Hour*, that small window of time in which prompt medical attention can be the difference between life and death. If you call an ambulance, you must wait for it to arrive (think traffic), wait for EMS officials to stabilize the person (think limited resources), and then wait for them to arrive back to the hospital (think traffic again). If it's an obvious emergency, and you have the means, take the injured person there yourself. Because as time passes, depending on the seriousness of the injury, the longer they go without medical care, the more dire their situation becomes.

POLICE DEPARTMENTS: Similar to the hospitals, I always identified the police departments closest to my protectee's location. I would reach out to those departments, drive by, walk in, and meet the officers face-to-face. This is critical, because in any emergency, the closest police department is a great place to go. They typically have a generator, which means power, and they have plenty of police, which means protection.

Anywhere I went on Advance and anywhere I go now as a civilian, I always know where the closest PD is located. I go in for a visit, introduce myself, and memorize how to get there without having to think about it. And while you're there, ask them about the crime in the area and any stats they can share or community meetings you can attend.

FIRE HOUSES: Fire houses are typically structurally sound, and like police departments usually have a backup generator as well. Plus, they are filled with firefighters who have emergency responder training.

You may be thinking this is all great for the president, but it's not for me. They're going to think I'm crazy if I go walking into the fire house to introduce myself. Not true. Knowing where the places of safety are in proximity to your home, your work, and when you travel is the smart thing to do. Police and firefighters are the men and women you want by your side in any emergency. They are there to help, so don't allow self-consciousness or insecurity to prevent you from taking important precautions for your safety. These informational visits could end up saving your life or the life of a loved one.

RELOCATION SITE: A relocation site is a place where you can meet up with loved ones should something happen. In the Service, if there was ever any type of emergency or natural disaster that meant we had to evacuate our offices or couldn't get to them, we had a designated area for us to relocate and regroup. Create one for your family and at work. Pick a site that is easily accessible, convenient for you and everyone who needs to reach you. It can simply be a few blocks away from your home at a neighbor's house, or a relative's home where you and your kids go all the time, or even a park or local coffee shop.

Know Your Routes

It's also imperative for you to know how to get to your safe houses by heart. In an emergency, cell phone services can go down and you shouldn't rely on technology to guide the way. You're better off relying on your own knowledge and experience. So take the time to visit each of these locations and commit their routes to memory, and know where your safe houses are in proximity to the places you frequent the most, such as home, work, and school. That way, if there is an emergency, you don't need to think—you can just go. If you go into an F3 response, it will be more difficult for you to plan, drive, and orient yourself. In the Service, we understood that we needed to account for that possibility, even though we were highly trained agents. We committed to memory the routes we drove, which made it possible for us to intuitively respond and save our cognitive functions to deal with the situation at hand.

During an emergency, you should not rely on Google Maps or Waze or any other navigation device. In fact, I was not allowed to use any of these as an agent—and I had to navigate all over the world. Aside from the difficulty of navigating to a location you haven't visited before in a state of high stress, depending on what the disaster or crisis might be, there may be no cell service to your phone or other device to help you get there. Cell phones are notoriously unreliable in natural disasters, simply because so many people are trying to use them at once. There could be no Internet, no cell communication. This actually happened on 9/11. The cell phone towers went completely offline—no one could make a call. And even if you do have some service, the time it takes you to find an address and search it out is vital time that you are wasting. Don't put yourself in that position. Plan and prepare your routes in advance, because when help can't come to you, you need to go to it.

Hard and Soft Targets

I recently went to the WWE's WrestleMania at MetLife Stadium. It was probably one of the coolest things I've done—I grew up watching wrestling and body-slamming my brother at every opportunity, so it was sort of a dream come true. That said, I am always hyper-aware when I go to large events like this because they can be enticing locations for an attack—what is called a *hard target*—which means that there is an inherent risk of vulnerability that comes with attending.

The three risk factors that determine this vulnerability are what I call the 3 P's:

1. **People.** Lots of them. At the WWE event there were more than 82,000 attendees.
2. **Place.** A large population of people densely packed into one location.

3. Press. Media. Attackers—especially terrorists—want exposure, so lots of cameras mean that an attack could be recorded and broadcast.

Whenever you see these three risk factors combined together, that means your situational awareness should be heightened.

Now, I'm not telling you to avoid places like this—obviously despite knowing this, I still went to WrestleMania—however, I remain cognizant of the fact that I am inherently more vulnerable under these conditions.

Other hard targets include places that are symbolic, like the Sears Tower, Yankee Stadium, or the Golden Gate Bridge. And although there is a higher risk, these places typically have additional security to account for it.

A *soft target* would be a school, restaurant, or movie theater. There is a lower risk here, as they don't usually make for particularly enticing targets. That said, we are lately seeing an increased number of attacks and shootings at these sorts of soft locations. While such places are less enticing to attackers, it also means that they typically have less security, which makes them easier targets.

Talk to Your Kids

It can be a struggle to talk to your children about safety and worst-case scenarios. But you do far greater harm by shielding them than by teaching them. You shouldn't rely solely on others—their teachers or their schools—to show them how to protect themselves. Educate yourself and give that knowledge to your children in a way that they can understand and use. Don't make them completely reliant on you either. You can't be with your children twenty-four hours a day, so give them the resources and tools they need to protect themselves when you aren't around.

Begin with teaching your children about your family's designated safe houses and relocation sites. Make sure they know how to get there. Walk the routes with them. Make sure they know your neighborhood and the lay of the land. Take them for a walk, disorient them, and then ask them to lead the way. Explain to them what each site is and the purpose it serves. Teach them how to get to these safe havens in case of an emergency, especially if they find themselves home alone or they ever get lost. If you feel that your children need extra precautions, teach them to think for themselves. Show them emergency exits and explain to them what they should do. Demonstrate for them what window is safest to climb out of or the best ingress and egress points (more on that soon). Then have them practice their escape routes more than once.

You should also have your kids memorize important telephone numbers—your cell or work line, a friend or relative who can look after them—so that they can call from anywhere if they need help. Make sure they actually know the numbers. Don't rely solely in saving it as a contact on a smart device.

Talk to their schools about lockdown drills. Educate yourself about the school's safety measures. Don't assume every school has one or knows what they are doing. I've had many schools reach out to me asking for help with this. Unfortunately, schools conduct drills where students mindlessly follow their teachers out a particular door or down a stairwell. Nothing about what they're doing or why they're doing it is explained. So what if something happens to a teacher? Now the students have to figure out where the exits are on their own. Help make them as self-sufficient as possible.

This is a tough one for a lot of parents, but it's important: talk to your children about what to do in an active shooter scenario. Some parents prefer to avoid this because they think it will scare their children. Here's the thing—discussing these scenarios will scare them only if you're scared. Be calm when you talk to your kids. If you're calm, they'll be calm. But if you're a hot mess, you'll just end up making them more afraid.

It's no different than a fire drill. Schools practice fire drills all the time. Fire can hurt you, just like a shooter. Yet fire drills are so common to us that we don't panic over them. In fact, they can seem mundane and boring. Approach lockdown drills in a similar fashion. Make sure your kids know what to do, and reinforce those protocols at home.

Finally, and importantly—teach your kids to fight back!

In the 2,574 abduction attempts reported to the National Center for Missing and Exploited Children (NCMEC) between 2000 and 2016, 70 percent of kids escaped by fighting back. Your kids have more power than either you or they think. Predators are on the lookout for easy prey, the ones who will be quiet and compliant. If you think your child can't ward off a potential predator by screaming their head off, think again. Don't be afraid to give them the tools and knowledge they need to defend themselves. Teach your children to yell, scream, kick, or bite to call attention to themselves in the loudest way they can. The bogeyman is the person they should fight rather than fear, so teach them to be unflinching.

Arrivals and Departures

We are often most vulnerable when we are in transit between locations. In the Service, we'd call those the *Arrival and Departure* movements of a protectee. That would be any movement from the White House to the motorcade or the motorcade to another location. It was within these few minutes where our protectee was most exposed. President Ronald Reagan, for example, was shot while walking to his armored limo after an event. Today the Service goes to great lengths to secure and even conceal those kinds of movements.

Similarly, when you are in motion, you are often at your most vulnerable. Take, for example, walking to your car—from the moment you step out of your home or leave the store to the moment you get into your vehicle, you are exposed. This is why remote parking lots and garages are high-risk places. Offenders are likely to frequent them looking for victims. This is particularly true near shopping areas and during the holiday shopping season, when thefts and assaults in parking lots are higher. Why? Because you've either got plenty of money on you or your hands are full with lots of newly bought merchandise.

When you walk out of the store, pause and look in the direction of your vehicle. Did anyone happen to follow you out? Notice who is around you as well as in proximity to your car. Scan the area. If it appears safe, then walk to your vehicle. If not, then go back inside the store or mall. You can wait till the area clears if someone is lurking nearby and you feel uncomfortable. You can also ask security, if that's an option (most malls have security), to walk you to your car.

Before heading to your vehicle, have your car keys in your hand. Try to always keep one hand free—meaning there should be nothing in it, apart from your keys. That free hand is for you to use should you need to respond to anything.

As you get closer, look to see if anyone is hiding near your vehicle. Also look at the cars parked next to you. Is anyone sitting in those cars with the motor running? If so, that may be a red flag.

Once you reach your car, get in and immediately lock the doors. Don't sit in your car with the doors unlocked while organizing your things or checking your phone. Get in. Secure yourself. Then do what you want.

If you have children, get them in as quickly as possible while maintaining awareness of your environment. Remain vigilant for people appearing in the background or moving around you. Attackers wait until you're distracted to act.

It's also a good idea to leave any dark, secluded areas quickly. It may be better to relocate to another area while you get yourself oriented, if need be. If it looks or feels wrong in any way, that probably means you shouldn't be there.

Away from Home

While on advances for presidents and First Ladies, I often traveled to foreign countries prior to their arrival to work out security for their visits. Traveling in another part of the world can be confusing, particularly when there are significant cultural or political differences, which means that more planning is needed. This is particularly true in countries with unstable governments, civil unrest, or high crime. Below is your advance checklist to use in preparation for visiting a foreign country.

1. Check for travel advisories. Before you make any international travel plans, do some homework on the country you plan to visit. I never board a plane without checking the State Department's travel advisories posted for countries all around the world.

2. Beware of road pirates. When traveling to remote locations or countries where there may be instability, stay off the roads at night. In some places it may be dangerous to drive after dark. When I traveled to Tanzania with Barbara P. Bush, the local authorities warned us not to drive anywhere at night due to road pirates, so we made sure to travel only during the daylight.

3. Know your US embassy or consulate. Before hopping on that plane, find out where the nearest US embassy or consulate is located for your intended destination. Should there be any type of emergency, that is where you would want to go. Also, with certain countries, it doesn't hurt to reach out and let them know you will be visiting in advance to help them keep tabs on you if need be. In fact the State Department has a website where you can enroll your overseas trip and get alerts.

4. Use reputable agencies. If you're going overseas to participate in any type of local tour or excursion group, such as a safari, for example, make sure you are working with a reputable agency. Sometimes employees can tip off locals, letting them know unsuspecting tourists are in town, so be cautious. If any person or situation feels untrustworthy, listen to your instincts and walk away.

5. Plan your routes. For road trips, do some prep work and know your travel routes before getting on the road, especially when going to new and unfamiliar places. Print them out or take screen shots and save them on your phone. This will protect you during those times you have poor coverage or lose service.

6. What's the 911. When overseas, make sure you know a country's version of 911. This way, if you are alone and need assistance, you know what to dial. And don't assume every place has a local emergency service. There are some locations where emergency services may not be available or able to get to you. In those cases, keep a backup safe house or two in mind.

7. Where's the hospital. Just like when you are at home—know where the nearest hospital or medical clinic is to you. Should there be any type of medical emergency, you'll want to know beforehand rather than waste valuable time trying to figure it out.

8. Know the culture and laws of your destination. When traveling internationally, be sure to brush up on the dos and don'ts of the social etiquette there to help you remain as safe and respectful as possible. When you're in another country, you have to abide by their laws—no matter where you come from.

9. Leave your valuables and expensive jewelry at home. Don't assume all hotels or room safes are created equally. Some hotels are more secure than others. And hotel employees can have access to room safes, so don't trust them implicitly.

10. Keep the cash low. Tourists are highly targeted by thieves and pickpockets, so don't carry lots of cash on your person. Keep just enough for when you may need it. Credit cards should be your go-to method of payment. This way, if they're stolen, you can put a hold on the card and won't lose all the money you would have been carrying otherwise.

11. Carry a mini first aid kit. Pack a mini first aid kit and add anything extra you may need, such as medications, sunscreen, and aspirin. Take it with you wherever you go. You never know when you may need it, especially in places where medical care may be hard to find.

12. Ditch the Wi-Fi. Don't use public Wi-Fi. It opens you up to hackers who are just waiting for someone like you to log on. Public Wi-Fi puts all your personal information at risk. Use only trustworthy networks with a passcode.

13. Take a travel buddy. My top safety tip—have a companion with you at all times. Whether you're going sightseeing, heading out to dinner, or walking back to your hotel room. I'm all about globetrotting around the world, but when you're alone, you're also at your most vulnerable.

Chapter 6

Be Your Own Shift Agent

He is a man of courage who does not run away, but remains
at his post and fights against the enemy.
—SOCRATES

Shift Team

In the previous chapter, we talked about the Advance team and their proactive mission of creating layers of security to deter potential threats. This chapter is where we discuss the final layer of security—the ultimate force: the Shift. This is the reactive element of the Secret Service, those agents who are there to respond quickly, swiftly, and violently to a threat. Just as the president of the United States needs Shift agents to protect him against volatile and unpredictable threats, you too need a Shift force in your own life.

When Hollywood makes a movie about a Secret Service agent, it's typically about a Shift agent. There's the 1993 Clint Eastwood suspense thriller, *In the Line of Fire*; Nicolas Cage's 1994 comedy, *Guarding Tess*; and the 2013 action adventure, *Olympus Has Fallen*, starring Gerard Butler—all of these films portrayed Shift agents saving the president's life—or driving a former First Lady around. In real life, these agents are the ones walking with the president onto and off *Air Force One*, riding shotgun with him in the limo, aka the *Beast*, and standing next to his stage during rallies. When I was on the president's shift, we worked around the clock, making sure that if a problem showed up, we were ready to handle it head-on. We trained in the tactics and techniques needed to deal with any threat quickly and effectively. That's the mentality I want you to have when obstacles arise in your life.

I recently took a flight from Los Angeles to New York City. My ticket hadn't been assigned a seat yet, so I approached the gate agent before boarding to see what my options were.

"I'm so sorry," the agent said, looking truly contrite. "There's a middle seat left toward the back of the plane, and one window seat next to the emergency exit available."

Did I hear him right? There were only two seats left and one of them was the exit seat next to the emergency door, which had a window and extra leg room? Obvious no-brainer. "Yes, thank you," I said. "I'll take the exit row, please."

As I turned and headed toward the waiting area, I paused. Walking back to the gate agent, still standing behind his desk, I said, "Excuse me again, but why did you feel the need to apologize for offering me a seat in the emergency aisle?"

"Well, some people don't want that seat," he explained.

"Why's that?"

"You know, in case something goes wrong. For some people, they don't want to be responsible during an emergency."

I thought about this for a second. I know in the event of an emergency landing, or in any emergency for that matter, I would 100 percent prefer to be the one in the position to save my own life versus allowing someone else, most likely a complete stranger, to save it for me.

"How many people refuse to take that seat?" I asked.

"Well, it's hard to say. . ." he said, a bit cagey before finally admitting, "but quite a few."

There are times in our lives where we are quick to surrender power to someone or something else, to avoid the burden of responsibility. But by physically and mentally preparing yourself for a potential crisis, there is no reason why you can't be the most equipped and capable person in an emergency. You shouldn't surrender your personal safety to strangers who may or may not be better qualified than you. With the situational and strategic awareness I'm going to teach you in this chapter, you can learn to effectively and prudently navigate through a crisis situation.

Situational Awareness

Assessing your environment when you go somewhere is key to protecting yourself. On the Shift team, we call this *situational awareness*. The intent is to recognize dangerous behavior and make ourselves fully present in our surroundings. In the real world, your situational awareness does not need to be quite as vigilant as that practiced by the Shift agents guarding the President of the United States, but you still need to be aware of where you are and what's going on around you. Because when you're aware, you can see a problem coming and have time to respond.

In everyday life, we can expand our understanding of situational awareness to involve some simple and swift measures to keep us safe. Whether I'm at a restaurant, a movie theater, or a concert, I spend the first five minutes assessing my environment and creating a situation report in my mind. It's a simple but potentially lifesaving process. Having a plan in place allows me to relax and enjoy where I am and who I'm with without worrying about what I'm going to do if things break bad. It means that I won't be caught off guard or surprised by something or someone that I didn't see coming. And often a predator will look elsewhere if they observe that you're aware and cognizant of what's happening around you. Predators look for easy prey, someone who is lost in their world or clueless about their surroundings. You can think about situational awareness like driving; you're not only looking forward—you're checking your side and rearview mirrors, glancing over your shoulder, remaining vigilant about your surroundings.

We can be so absorbed by our own thoughts, by communications with others or the stimuli perpetually demanding our attention that we end up oblivious to our environment. Most of us can walk down a city block or drive somewhere on complete autopilot without any presence of mind or having absorbed anything going around us. Our smartphones have also severely diminished our ability to be present, which is actually quite dangerous. They dull our senses and lessen the cognizance we need to be safe and smart.

Becoming bulletproof is becoming present. *Situational awareness* is more important to your personal protection than learning how to handle yourself in a fight. If you're aware of your surroundings, odds are you won't need to fight. On the other hand, you can learn all the fancy self-defense moves and techniques and strategies out there, but if you don't see the problem coming, none of that matters. You will be blindsided when things go wrong, which means you won't have the chance to thwart the threat or get to safety.

Cover and Concealment

One of the first things they teach recruits at law enforcement academies is how to effectively use *cover* and *concealment*. Cover is anything that can shield you against the piercing effects of a bullet, shrapnel from an explosion, or a sharp blade. It's something strong and durable, like a thick tree trunk, a heavy piece of furniture, or even that blue US Post Office mailbox you see on every corner.

If you've ever seen police officers position their vehicles during a traffic stop, they usually park with the nose of their car angled to the left. That way, if they get into a shootout with the driver, they have instant cover to get behind.

Cover doesn't have to completely hide you in order to work. A fire hydrant, for example, can be just as effective at protecting you, so long as you make yourself small enough to fit behind it. Good cover needs to do only two things: make you harder to hit, and be strong enough to stop whatever is trying to hit you.

Concealment, on the other hand, is what you look for when you can't find cover—either because there's none around or you don't have time to find any. In order for concealment to work (unlike cover), it needs to completely hide you. Think of the game hide-and-seek; the better you're able to hide, the less likely you are to be found. The same is true when the stakes are much higher. Concealment can be anything from a curtain to a blanket to a closet door. Although they can't stop a bullet, they can keep you out of an attacker's line of sight—and what an attacker can't see, they can't engage.

Of course, the best option is finding something that acts as both cover and concealment, like a fortified door or brick wall. But when it calls for immediate action, think cover first, then concealment.

Ingress and Egress

On any given day, most of us enter and exit the premises of our favorite businesses, stores, or cafés with little thought. We walk in through the front door of our local coffee shop, grab our morning espresso, and walk back out the same way. It's simple, it's automatic—and in the event of an active shooter or mass panic, this sort of autopilot orientation to the space could be tragic.

Nearly every restaurant, movie theater, and grocery store in the United States has two ways in and two ways out. In the Service, we call these *ingress* (in) and *egress* (out) points. Most of us are familiar with the main one—the front door—but we often fail to think about where the second one may be. Typically, they're found in the back storeroom, kitchen area, or loading dock—wherever a business gets their products in and their trash out without inconveniencing their customers. Whenever you arrive at any location, finding two ways out is the first thing you should do—and it's the simplest. Just put your head on a swivel and have your plan in place in case you need to make a hasty exit for any reason. And remember that not every secondary exit needs to be a door—it can be a window as well.

When I made security plans, this was a common concern of mine. Because I wasn't just worried about the safety of my protectee, but for all the people attending an event. Sometimes the number of attendees were in the hundreds or even thousands, and I knew the dangers of mass panic, so I worked closely with local authorities to create two contingency plans—one for my protectee and one for attendees. When you're looking for your two *egress* points, think like a Shift agent and take a moment to strategize about how you would get yourself out of a situation if things broke bad.

In a full-blown panic, most everyone will try to escape the same way—through the doors they came in. This herd mentality is what causes people to be severely injured or trampled to death. On February 17, 2003, twenty-one people died and more than fifty were injured when security guards at the E2 Club in Chicago used pepper spray to break up a fight. The smell of the fumes confused partygoers into thinking they had been gassed in a terrorist attack. As fear spread, the crowd of nearly 1,500 began pushing toward the only exit they knew—down a steep stairwell. Those who had been walking up the stairs were knocked back by the ensuing mass of bodies. Later testimony by the security team highlighted their efforts to save the fallen, but the sheer force of people made it impossible. This is why you need to take stock of egress points, and remain cognizant of this herd mentality. If hundreds of people are making their way toward one exit, have another one in mind. You want to go against traffic—not with it. Just because everyone is moving in one direction doesn't mean that they know what they're doing. Look for ways out that may not be obvious. You know how flight attendants like to remind you that the closest exit may be behind you? It's a useful reminder on the ground as well as in the air. It takes almost no time to find alternate ingress and egress points, and making a habit of this could one day save your life.

If it isn't possible for you to reach an exit in the midst of a volatile situation, here are a few other guidelines to help you stay safe.

1. Hard Rooms: These are mostly impermeable rooms where you can shelter out of sight. They are made of materials such as wood, steel, or tile that are more likely to stop a bullet. Bathrooms, pantries, or walk-in coolers make great hard rooms.

2. Stairwells: Walk your stairwells. They can be unpredictable in design, not go straight down to the ground floor, zigzag, or break off onto another floor, forcing you to regain entry elsewhere. If you work or live in a tall building, or if you're staying at a hotel, you need to know where the stairs empty out to. Also, doors may be locked or jammed. Familiarize yourself with the stairwells you might use in case of an emergency. The last thing you want is to be surprised by a locked door.

3. Rooftops: Don't automatically go to a rooftop unless you know that help can reach you there. We've all seen one too many movies that might make us think that a helicopter is going to magically appear and save us from danger. This doesn't typically happen. Also, you probably won't know in advance if the exit to a rooftop building is open or blocked. On 9/11, the doors to the roof of the World Trade Center were locked. People couldn't gain access to the roof, and even if they could, there's no telling if a helicopter would have been able to safely land and evacuate them. I'm not saying that rooftops aren't a viable option in a pinch, but they may not be the best option available to you. If you live or work in a high-rise building, take a walk to the roof and see if you can access it.

4. Elevator: We know there are certain risks associated with the use of elevators. They get stuck. They malfunction. They lose power or, worst-case scenario, drop. While we can't control every factor when it comes to elevator functionality, we can still use them sensibly. Pay attention to the occupancy weight of elevators. If it looks overcrowded to you, it's better to wait. Don't get into an overcrowded car just because you're in a hurry.

It's also a good idea to check the emergency phone to make sure it works, particularly for your apartment or work building. The first time you use an emergency phone shouldn't be during an emergency. Don't be embarrassed. Frankly, I do it all the time. When the operator asks how they can help, I reply, "Hi! There's nothing wrong. I was just checking."

Strategic Seating

1. Restaurants: Whenever my husband and I go out to a restaurant, we usually argue about who gets to sit with their back to the wall. Neither of us wants to sit with our six o'clock unprotected. That's also why we don't like to sit in the middle of a restaurant. Having your back exposed and being unable to see behind you is a vulnerability, whereas having your back to the wall means that you can see everything coming toward you. Maybe this makes us slightly more high-maintenance customers, but usually we will do a walk-through of the place, assess the seating options available, and tell the hostess where we want to sit. Doing so means that we can more comfortably enjoy our meal, which makes it worth it.

2. Movie Theaters and Concerts: I love going to the movies, but I'm wary of people in a crowded theater—and pretty much all movie theaters in New York City are crowded. When I choose a seat, I don't look for the seat with the best vantage point for the movie—which is typically mid-center of the theater, surrounded by tons of people. I also never sit in the middle row. Instead, I look for the seat that is closest to an exit—not the primary exit, because I know that's where everyone is going to run to in an emergency. I look for the exit closest to me and farthest from other people. I also pick an elevated seat because it gives me a better line of sight to see who enters the theater and what is going on.

You want to be able to get out quickly. If you are sitting dead smack in the middle of the theater, you will pretty much be at the mercy of everyone around you to get out of your way so that you can exit. This is where it becomes dangerous, because even if you keep it together in a crisis, it doesn't mean others will. How they react will directly impact you, so if they freak the fuck out, good luck.

Whenever you attend a crowded venue, look at how many people are between you and your exit. Because they are going to be a hurdle that you might literally have to overcome.

Making Your Plan

As soon as you arrive at any location, take the first five minutes to gain your situational awareness and put a quick plan in place.

1. Assess: Identify two egress points, preferably on opposite sides of a room. In a restaurant, this might be the main entrance and kitchen back door. If something happens, head to the kitchen, because a perpetrator is most likely to come in through the front. When outdoors, such as an amusement park or concert, locate the exits away from the main area and general population.

2. Evacuate: Map your exit route. How fast can you get there? What obstacles are in your way? How many people are between you and the way out? Remember that in a crisis situation people will panic, and their instinct will be to go out the same door they came in, which is usually the main entrance. If at all possible, you want to avoid this by heading to a different exit.

3. Harden Up: If you can't evacuate, it's time to find cover and harden up. Look for anything durable—wood, steel, tile—that could potentially shield you from an attacker. In a restaurant, it could be a table, counter, or refrigerator. In a theater, it could be under the seats, or behind a stage.

4. Cover and Conceal: Identify the places you can hide. Be creative; think like a child playing hide-and-seek. Curtains, posters, a large plant, these things can't stop a bullet, but they can keep an attacker from seeing you. An attacker is looking for moving bodies, easy targets. If there's no place to hide, be prepared to get low and get out of the shooter's line of sight.

5. Fight: As part of your five-minute assessment, look around and see what is nearby that you could use as a weapon if needed. Anything can be a weapon—silverware on a table, a hot cup of coffee, a chair, a pint glass of beer. Anything you can throw, smash, or stab with. I'll share more tools and strategies for how to fight in chapter 8.

Trust Your Instincts

Though this advice might sound less tactical and concrete than much of what we've discussed thus far, it is no less important, particularly where your personal safety is concerned. Our instincts exist to help shield us from harm. Even if we don't know why a certain person or situation gives us a bad feeling, we must listen to and trust our instincts.

While preparing to be interviewed on a popular morning show for a segment on self-defense, I was talking off camera with the anchor, who told me this story:

"You know," she said, "I was in a situation once where I was walking down the street and there was a man walking not too far behind me. I noticed him and something about it made me uncomfortable. I thought about crossing the street or running off, but I didn't. I told myself I was overreacting. And funny enough, I didn't want to offend him. After all, he hadn't said or done anything to me. He just happened to be walking in the same direction I was. So I ignored what I was feeling and kept on going.

"Well, it turns out, I should've listened to my gut," she continued. "Because he grabbed me and held me at gunpoint. He stole my wallet and jewelry. I was lucky he didn't do anything worse. I often think back to that day. And since then, I always, always trust my instincts when something feels off."

What happened to this anchor is unfortunately quite common. While working investigations for the Service, I came across countless stories of victims who had made similar choices. They failed to listen to what their intuition was telling them. In the anchor's situation, she chose to let herself feel uncomfortable rather than to offend a complete stranger. She tried to logically rationalize what she was feeling, even though she couldn't. As a result, she dismissed that vigilant inner voice telling her to be cautious, that something was wrong.

This is something that a lot of people do, and yet there is science to support the notion that people possess a sixth sense capable of detecting potential perils. In 2014, the Office of Naval Research embarked on a four-year, $3.85 million research program to explore how soldiers used intuition or "sensemaking" to avert disaster. This program came about from incidents reported in the Iraq War when soldiers preempted Improvised Explosive Devices (IEDs) by using their intuition or responded prudently to a novel situation without having consciously analyzed it. Based off this research, the Defense Department has designed training to help marines hone their precognition skills. Even if we don't fully understand why or how this intuitive sense emerges, it is widely accepted by the military and scientific community as indisputable fact.

Throughout my life and career in law enforcement, my instincts have saved me in more ways than one. They have protected me from bad things and people, and they have guided me toward the good. I know that my discernment is there to help me and keep me safe. When I go to the park for my typical late-night run and something about my environment feels off, I'll turn right back around and go straight home. Just because I've been well trained to physically defend myself doesn't mean that I'm invincible, and I have no interest in putting myself in a dicey situation. I trust the internal intelligence I've developed that tells me that the smartest thing I can do in a given moment is get the hell out of there.

The unconscious mind picks up on extraordinarily subtle warning signals before our conscious mind is finished assessing or making sense of them. Think back to a time in your life when you met someone and had a strong negative reaction to them. You felt from that first moment that something wasn't right. That person may not have said or done anything specific that you could point to, but for some inexplicable reason, you were unsettled by them. How many times have you dismissed this feeling, the same way the news anchor did? I'm guessing that in those times when you didn't listen to your intuition, you ended up regretting it. That's because the majority of the time your instincts are right, even when you logically can't explain why.

I'm a huge proponent of treating people with dignity and respect, but when it comes to your safety, don't be worried about whom you offend. Manners and politeness have zero to do with minimizing risk and vulnerability. Don't let being nice get in the way of being smart. Start paying attention to that *force* inside you. Allow your instincts to lead you in life. You can start small to begin honing this ability. Pay attention to your feelings and sentiments around people. Who are you drawn to? Who are you repelled by? What does your gut tell you to do? Whatever feelings you notice, good or bad, *believe yourself.* Embrace this special gift of your sixth sense and listen to what it is telling you.

Chapter 7

If You Must Fight, Then Fight

We are twice armed if we fight with faith.
—Plato

Embrace Confrontation

I went to Mexico as part of the Advance team for the G20 Summit. President Barack Obama would be attending along with other prominent heads of state. I was the site agent responsible for the security preparations and planning for the summit.

The majority of the president's time at the summit, which was being held at the Los Cabos Convention Center, was split between large group events and private one-on-one meetings with other world leaders.

During one such closed-door conversation, I was holding point outside the door to the room where President Obama and the president of China had just entered. Due to the sensitive nature of the topics being discussed, my State Department counterpart told me that only a handful of delegates, all of whom had already entered the room, were authorized to attend. No one else was allowed in. Any remaining members of the Chinese delegation or otherwise would have to wait outside.

While I was securing entry into the room, a man who looked to be part of the Chinese delegation approached me. With an air of arrogance, he gestured with his hand for me to step aside so that he could enter. Although I didn't speak his language and he apparently didn't speak mine, I held my hand up to politely indicate that he wasn't allowed in.

My respectful directive toward him, however, was immediately dismissed. From the instant scowl on his face and look of disgust, I could see that I had both insulted his ego and likely embarrassed him in front of his fellow delegates, who were standing close by. And so, in an effort to intimidate me with his physical size, he stepped in even closer, locked eyes with me, and aggressively gestured again for me to move.

My stance in front of that door, however, wasn't about him, nor was it personal. It was about the job I had to do and my reason for doing it. It was something I had grown accustomed to. Everyone wanted an audience with the president of the United States. Although the man was more than twice my size, he wasn't the first "big man" to challenge me, nor would he be the last. However, in a diplomatic effort to defuse the situation, I asked my State Department counterpart to check whether he'd been accidentally left off the access list. She checked again and said, "He's not on the list."

This third denial only infuriated the man even more. And that's when it dawned on me that a person in his position, whatever that was, probably doesn't get told "No" very often. In a matter of minutes, he had gotten the Heisman three times by two women, which seemed to be more than he could handle. And so, in his seeming infinite wisdom, he decided to take matters into his own hands, literally. He grabbed me by my suit collar and shoved me—rather hard, I might add—straight through the door and into the room behind me—where the two presidents were meeting.

Now at that very instant I could hear two distinct voices:

One was of the president of the United States, who was seated only several feet behind me, addressing the leader of this man's country. The other was an internal voice in my head that said, "Oh no, the fuck he didn't!"

So as soon as I got my feet back under me, I kindly returned the favor. I grabbed ahold of *his* suit collar and shoved him—rather hard, I might add—straight back into the crowd of Chinese delegates standing behind him.

As we fell into the crowd, I distinctly remember a look of shock cross his face—as though my response caused the synapses in his brain to misfire as he struggled to comprehend the fact that I had dared put hands on him. Quickly recovering, however, he lunged back at me. But this time he brought friends. He must have been someone important because every Chinese official jumped in along with him. As I was again forced backward, I felt one man put his hands around my neck to choke me while another slammed me into the wall.

Within a matter of seconds, my colleagues caught wind of the ruckus and swept in to join the melee. And so there we were, the US Secret Service kung fu fighting with our foreign equivalents while our nation's leaders were attempting to peacefully resolve foreign diplomatic issues. The irony . . .

Thankfully, the president's first assistant, Hunter, stepped out and swiftly closed the door before we caused any type of international incident.

As the fight ensued, the Estado Mayor Presidencial—Mexico's equivalent of our Secret Service and the host of the event—witnessed what had happened and quickly intervened. As they separated our two groups, they adamantly expressed their displeasure with the Chinese official and his delegation's behavior.

When it was all over, an interpreter from the Chinese delegation came over to reprimand me, saying that the man I had dared to put hands on was one of their country's high-ranking generals. I told him to go tell his general that picking fights with women was not very general-like.

Fight with Conviction

In my line of work, I often had to tell people what they could and could not do. And I had to convey my message clearly and without hesitation. But my success in standing my ground wasn't really about my physical strength. It was about my mental conviction. I believed in what I was doing and why I was doing it. I had a job to fulfill and lives to protect, so I had neither the time nor the luxury to debate my authority. I had to speak with confidence to make sure those who heard my message heard it clearly the first time. And when I did act, I had to do so in a way that assured I would not be mistaken for being weak or uncertain of my abilities.

I am not an advocate for violence. Using conflict and force are by no means the most effective or strategic ways to get others to comply (more on this in Part 3). I believe that while we're guests here on this planet, we should make every effort to work together, respect each other's opinions, and live and let live. And I routinely use the strategies in this book to avoid drama as best I can.

But, sometimes no matter how hard we may try, that shit just seems to find us. Take the general, for example. Right up to the point he put his hands on me, I hadn't intentionally provoked him in any way; I was polite, but assertive. I wasn't condescending in my speech or body language. I even double-checked to make sure his name wasn't on the list. I made every effort to avoid conflict—which, despite my efforts, was escalating with every passing moment. Me denying him access wasn't personal, it was my job. However, once he crossed that line and put hands on me, he violated the nature of our interaction as two diplomats each representing our respective countries. My response was not impulsive, but fully thought out. It was quick and it was fierce. It was not only about doing my job, but also defending myself against a bully—which, in attitude and behavior, he was.

The world is full of people who will try to dismiss you, intimidate you, and violate you. And there are those moments in our lives where we must speak up, push back, and fight. These moments, however, should be few and far between. Yes, it takes great courage to fight. But it takes greater courage to know when to walk away. That said, during those times in your life when you decide to stand your ground, do so with conviction. You cannot waver or hold back out of fear. You must fully commit to it, both mentally and physically. Because if you lack conviction, the belief in what you are doing and why you're doing it, you will lose before the first punch is ever thrown.

Don't fear the fight when the fight comes looking for you. In full disclosure, the general was a big guy. A really big guy. Had it been a one-on-one fight, there's a good chance he could have taken me. I realized that in those first few seconds it took me to size him up. I knew I was probably going to get my ass handed to me. And you know what—I was more than okay with that, because I was going to make him earn it. I fully intended to stand my ground no matter what. He may have walked over, but I was going to make sure he'd be limping back.

Be a Counter-Predator

My goal with this book is to help you create a bulletproof mindset.

But doing so requires a change in your mental makeup. I want you not to fear conflict or confrontation, but to embrace it when you need to. I want you not to take on the role of the victim when a predator enters your life, but rather to become a *counter-predator* willing to defend yourself against anyone who tries to overpower you. To help you become someone who walks through life with a quiet sense of calm and inner strength.

I've come to learn that bullies and predators are essentially the same thing. Now, I'm not talking *predators* in the animal kingdom sense. I'm talking about human predators who seek to exploit the vulnerabilities of others. Most of us think of bullies as the street thug on the corner or that knuckle-dragging mesomorph in high school who was bigger than everyone else. But bullies can also be a deceptive family member, a manipulative supervisor, or a malicious boyfriend or girlfriend.

But here's the secret: Predators primarily seek out those they perceive as weak. The ones they think will go down easy, who won't put up a fight. You know why? Because they don't want a fair fight. They want someone they can conquer. They are looking for an easy target. Don't give them one.

Unfortunately, that's why children are targeted so often; they are the most vulnerable and least able to defend themselves.

Most predators' modus operandi is to test you before deciding whether or not to attack. A school bully, for example, may deliberately bump into you just to see if you make eye contact with her or keep walking. A pickpocket will invade your personal space while standing in line to test how close they can get without you reacting. A jealous coworker may spread rumors about you to see whether you confront them.

There is, however, a misperception about predators. We assume they're strong and full of self-confidence. We conjure this grandiose, dominant persona who can crush us. We project all our fears onto them, allowing them to take the role of predator while we volunteer to take on the role of prey. But the reality is that they are often the ones full of self-doubt and fear, which is why they choose those they think are weaker than them. What I have learned in my years as a criminal investigator and in my studies of human behavior is that predators prey upon others to conceal and compensate for their own insecurities.

Whenever I arrested or interrogated someone who was considered a predator, almost without exception, they were usually the ones who cried, confessed, or squealed on their friends. They weren't tough. They were feeble and deeply insecure. And often they themselves had been the prey of someone else.

In his book *On Combat*, Dave Grossman, a retired lieutenant colonel from the United States Army, writes about the psychology of killing:

> *There was research conducted a few years ago with individuals convicted of violent crimes. These cons were in prison for serious, predatory acts of violence: assaults, murders and killing law enforcement officers. The vast majority said that they specifically targeted victims by body language: slumped walk, passive behavior and lack of awareness. They chose their victims like big cats do in Africa, when they select one out of the herd that is least able to protect itself. However, when there were cues given by potential victims that indicated they would not go down easily, the cons would walk away.*

Predators will assess everything about you, both verbally and nonverbally. If they perceive you as strong and aware of your surroundings, aka a *counter-predator*, they will move on to someone less likely to fight back. Therefore, when you're out in the world, present yourself with an air of vigilance and assurance. Walk with your shoulders back and head up. Don't be afraid to make eye contact with people. Show awareness. And if something doesn't feel right, don't neglect it.

You dictate what role you want to play in this world.

Victimology

In my criminology class, we discuss *victimology*. Victimology researchers study the correlation between crime and victims. They also look for similarities and patterns among crime victims to understand why certain people are targeted while others are not. Most people think criminals target their victims randomly—wrong place, wrong time type of thing. Although that's true in some circumstances—referred to as *opportunity theory*—there are, in fact, situations in which the victim increases their vulnerability.

Victimization comes with a cost—both to the victim and to society. There are the literal costs of conducting an investigation and going through the justice system. And then there are the health costs for psychological and medical treatment. This includes the trauma that many victims suffer, such as disability, loss of work, and long-term therapy. Because even after the crime is over, victims are still left to cope, which can make it difficult for them to resume their daily lives.

A victimologist named Kathryn McCollister estimated the average costs of crime:

One Murder: $8,982,907
One Rape: $240,776
One Robbery: $42,310
One Burglary: $6,462
One Piece of Stolen Property: $7,974

I share this information with you to educate you on the true cost of crime. Understanding victims and their relationship to crime is not about blaming the victim for what has happened to them. But it is important to see what patterns may exist.

Here are some factors to consider when it comes to understanding and anticipating when and how crime occurs.

1. Location: Urban metropolitan areas have a much higher crime rate than suburban or rural areas. There is a correlation between high crime and population density. In other words, more people equals more crime.

2. Gender: Women are more likely to be victims of sexual assault. The harsh reality is that every two minutes in America, a woman is sexually assaulted. Globally, one-third of women experience some form of assault in their lifetime. Studies also show that women are more fearful of men despite the fact that men are more likely to be victims of violent crimes, such as robbery or aggravated assault.

3. Time: Violent crimes and assaults are more likely to take place in open public areas between 6 p.m. and 6 a.m. Lesser crimes such as theft are more likely to happen during the daytime. Burglaries tend to occur from 10 a.m. to 2 p.m., when people are less likely to be home.

4. Age: Those likely to commit a crime are between the ages of 16–25, and those likely to be victims of a crime fall into the same exact age group. Teenage males are considered to be the most dangerous population. That's why we tend to see high victimization rates in schools, exacerbated by the fact that there is little supervision outside of the actual classroom. Teens and young adults are more likely to commit crime and be victims of it because they tend to go out during peak crime hours. The elderly are less likely to commit crime or be victims of crime; however, they are more vulnerable to fraud schemes.

5. Season: Crime rates also increase over the summer months. The warmer weather combined with the fact that school is out are likely determining factors.

6. Socioeconomic status: People who are poorer are more likely to be victims of both violent and property crime.

7. Race: More than any other group, African Americans are more likely to be victims of violent crime. The black homicide rate is more than six times that of whites.

8. Marital status: Believe it or not, if you're married, you are less likely to be a victim of crime, possibly because you are less likely to go out in the evening hours.

9. Behavior: Studies show that certain impulsivity traits can make someone more vulnerable. Those who are more impulsive, risk-takers, or lack emotional intelligence and self-discipline are more likely to be victims.

10. Lifestyle: The lifestyle you lead will make you more or less vulnerable.

High-risk lifestyles, such as consuming alcohol, drugs, going out at night, or engaging in crime yourself, all increase the likelihood of becoming a victim.

Learn How to Really Fight

Recently, I was invited to be on a popular daytime talk show to discuss women's self-defense. As I spoke with the producer on the phone, she was eager for me to demonstrate all the fancy self-defense moves she assumed I had learned as an agent. A mental image of Keanu Reeves from *The Matrix* flashed through my mind as she described to me what types of moves she wanted me to perform: "Something really visual that looks good on TV," she said. After listening patiently, I told the producer that she was right—those types of moves exist only on TV. I also explained that showing complex moves in three minutes wouldn't help their viewers; in fact, it could seriously hinder them. In an emergency situation when someone needs to defend themselves, people won't be able to recall self-defense moves that they've seen only once, particularly if there's any complicated choreography involved. I went on to tell the producer that we could demonstrate something practical, simple, and easy to remember, but it still probably wouldn't help viewers much.

Why? Because when you're assaulted, your fine motor skills go out the window, along with your ability to think. So unless you've committed that move you saw on TV to memory, and practiced it over and over again, you're never going to remember it.

Instead, I offered to show viewers a few moves designed to distract or injure an attacker long enough to give a person time to escape. A violent strike to the groin. A swift kick to the shin. A hard punch to the throat. Or jamming a finger in the eye. Swift, violent, and fierce— using elbows and knees when possible—as that's where we have the most power.

The point is not to teach people to engage in hand-to-hand combat with an attacker; it's to move and strike and run. It's about switching your mindset from those beautiful slow-motion *Matrix* moves to real survival.

Seven Minutes

One of the fight training scenarios we had to face in the NYPD Academy was being able to fight an opponent for seven minutes without stopping. In New York at the time, that was the longest it took a subway train to get from one station to the next. So, if by chance you got into a fight on that railcar while on patrol, help wouldn't arrive until seven minutes later. Seven minutes is a *long* time to fight—especially when you're getting hit back. Mixed-martial-arts matches do only five-minute rounds and boxing matches go for only three. Within the first few minutes, the amount of lactic acid buildup from working so hard will make you feel like your muscles are on fire. You'll be completely out of breath, and your energy zapped. If you want a taste of what it feels like, set your timer for seven minutes and punch the air as hard as you can without stopping. And move around. No standing still. It's exhausting. Seven minutes is nothing when you're reading a book or watching television. It's an eternity when you are fighting for your life.

The most important piece of advice I can give you is to sign up for a martial arts or boxing class—a place where you can not only hit someone, but where someone can hit you back. There's a huge difference between shadowboxing and boxing for real. Yes, you want to learn how to defend yourself—but you also want to know how you will react in an attack scenario. You want to know what you're capable of and, more important, what your limitations are.

The first time you experience an attack should never be in a real fight. Give yourself the gift of knowledge and self-awareness, of knowing what your mind and body will do when someone comes at you. This experience is as important as the specific moves that a self-defense instructor could teach you. Once you know what it feels like to be attacked and experience the initial shock of a truly heightened F3, you'll become better at managing your response.

Knowledge is power, and the better you know yourself, the stronger you'll be should you ever need to defend yourself in real life.

Reality Check

My husband and I have similar training experiences and backgrounds. We frequently work out together and go running through the streets of New York City. Although he's six foot one and about two hundred pounds of muscle, in my mind, my skills are on par with his.

One day, during our jiujitsu class, I asked him to be my partner. Even though he's more experienced than me in this particular sparring style, I still had a ton of confidence in my own strength and skill. I thought it would be fun to put ourselves to the test. He simply smiled at my request and said, "Sure."

Now, my husband knows when it comes to training, he's not allowed to take it easy on me. Although I don't expect him to throw me across the room every chance he gets, I do expect him to make me earn my win. As we started our live standing drills, I was immediately caught off guard by the strength of his grip on my gi and the ease with which he swung me around to set up a single-leg take-down. When it was my turn, the move on him was quite a bit harder, though not impossible. Within the first few minutes, I found myself breathing a lot heavier and sweating a lot more than he was. The disparity between our strengths, however, didn't completely dawn on me until our next round of training, which began on the ground. Part of the move we were learning meant he had to pin me down with the full weight of his body—which he did. I felt all the air leave my lungs. Both my arms and legs somehow managed to get trapped underneath him. I was unable to move. And I was exhausted. I remember thinking, *Holy shit, this motherfucker is strong* (which I mean in the most loving way possible).

Let me be clear. I knew he was strong, but the reality of it didn't hit me until we sparred. My F3 was in full effect and I felt genuine fear. Not in the sense that he would hurt me—although I may not have spoken to him the whole car ride home—but in the realization that, up to this point, I had drastically overestimated my ability to effectively fight against someone of his size combined with his training background. It's one thing to think you're strong, but it's a whole other thing to test it. Yes, power lives in the mind, but reality lives in the body.

Have you ever watched a TV show where someone was being chased or threatened with a weapon and you sat there eating popcorn and thought to yourself, *Man, if that guy tried that shit on me, I'd hit him so hard his future grandchildren would feel it!* If so, I suggest you put that theory to the test. You have to know what you're capable of. And what you are not. It can be scary. It astonished me to learn how powerful my husband was compared to my own strength. And being who I am, I was pissed. Being humbled isn't fun. When I eventually calmed down and we talked about it, he assured me that with more time and training I would be much harder to submit. He himself is quick to tap when grappling against higher-ranked belts, even though he might outweigh them. That's the beauty of an art like jiujitsu, which translates into the *soft art*. It lends itself to being highly effective for everyone of all shapes and sizes because it's about technique, not just power.

If you're truly committed to becoming bulletproof, then it's your responsibility to find out where your limitations are when it comes to physical combat. There are a number of amazing schools that teach different fighting styles, such as boxing, jiujitsu, and muay thai, among others. I'm not advocating one style over another. Just make sure the school you choose allows for sparring against other classmates. Once you find out where your weaknesses are, then you can begin figuring out how to improve and mark the growth you want to make. This practice of self-knowledge and self-improvement will strengthen not just your physical armor, but your mental armor, too.

Chapter 8

Bulletproof Your Life

If you do not expect the unexpected, you will not recognize it when it arrives.

—HERACLITUS

This chapter is designed to give you concrete and actionable steps to help better secure your life. Whether at home, online, or out in public, you'll have the strategies you need to keep your property, possessions, and information safe. Taking these steps will give you better peace of mind and help you on your path to becoming bulletproof.

BULLETPROOF YOUR HOME

1. Exterior lighting: A well-lit home is a safe home. Make sure the exterior of your home has plenty of lighting, particularly the front and side doors. Darkness provides concealment for intruders, giving them plenty of opportunity to pick or break the locks on your doors or windows. Lighting deters break-ins because it allows intruders to be seen by your neighbors and the public. Motion-sensor lights are also a great way to bulletproof your home.

2. Landscape: Well-placed bushes and trees are a strategic way to keep the outside world from peering in. But they can also provide concealment for potential intruders trying to break into your home. It's best to design your landscaping—especially around doors and windows—with this idea in mind. Keep those areas open and visible. If your home already has shrubbery around its entryways, do your best to keep it well groomed. The less unruly they are, the less of a hiding place they can offer.

3. Manicure your property: Keep the area around your home clean and clear of clutter. Having the grass cut, weeds pulled, and the trash picked up (newspapers, trash cans, yard waste) shows that the person who lives there cares and pays attention to what's going on around them. If you don't have a fence, you can plant trees or large bushes, or place large landscaping rocks around the perimeter, which sets a natural boundary to deter trespassers.

4. Keep windows and doors locked: The frequency of break-ins increases during the summer months as more people leave their windows and doors open. Whether you're leaving for the day or heading to bed for the night, remember to lock your windows and close your doors. Don't take a chance by putting only a screen between you and a potential intruder. Even during the colder months, especially around the holidays, it's best to not risk running an electrical cord through your window as a way to get electricity to your outside holiday decorations. When your window is ajar, it can easily be opened from the outside.

5. Close your curtains: Be mindful of who can see inside your home. If your windows are unobscured, you're essentially advertising to the world what you have "for the taking." Burglars aren't going to waste their time breaking into homes unless they know there's something valuable inside to steal, so it's best not to give them any help in deciding whether or not to choose yours. Keep your curtains and blinds closed when you're not at home and in the nighttime hours when it's easier to see inside.

6. Trash: Be mindful of what your trash says about your home. That large empty Apple computer box sitting next to your garbage bin could be all a burglar needs to see to make your home his next target. When throwing product packaging away, especially electronics, cut the boxes into small pieces and stuff them inside a black or brown trash bag—something passersby can't see through.

7. Know your neighbors: Not all neighbors are good neighbors. Be careful whom you invite into your home or what personal information you share with the people who live around you. If you live in an apartment complex, try to avoid giving your neighbors a free peek inside every time you open the door. Also, if you happen to keep a spare key hidden outside, make sure you're not being watched—there's no telling if your neighbors, their children, or their friends have been eyeing your comings and goings, just waiting for a chance to break in.

8. Guard dogs: Dogs are one of the best deterrents for intruders. In fact, one of the primary deciding factors when it comes to breaking into someone's home is whether or not they have a dog. Keep in mind, the type and size of dog matters—the bigger the dog, the better the security. Even if you don't have a dog, simply posting a "Beware of Guard Dog" sign on your front and back doors can offer enough of a psychological effect to make a potential intruder think twice.

BULLETPROOF YOUR DOOR

Above we talked about the importance of making sure the windows and doors of your home are not easily defeated—the more difficult you can make it to get in, the more secure you'll feel. The steps below are all about making those primary entry points—doors—nearly impenetrable. When police tactical teams make entry into a house, they usually smash open the front door by swinging a *ram*—a large heavy circular piece of steel with handles—or they'll hit it with a sledgehammer. On occasion, however, if the door they're trying to breach is so well fortified, even the best law enforcement tools can't get past it. Our objective in this section is to make your doors as strong as possible, starting with the importance of the door frame.

1. King studs: Doors are typically set into a wooden frame. This is what the hinges hang on to and the locking mechanisms fit into. Adjacent to the frame are king studs. These are typically two pieces of wood running along the left and right sides of the door frame, from floor to ceiling, that offer extra support. King studs are what make exterior doors more secure. If you've ever seen someone kick down a door and the frame went down with it, that's because the frame wasn't properly secured into the king studs. It's important to understand the different parts of your door frame in order to know how better to secure it.

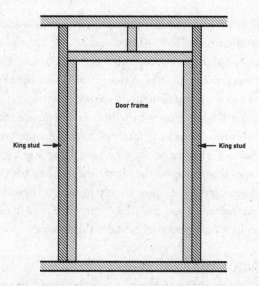

2. Dead bolt: The dead bolt lock of your exterior doors should go into the door frame as far as possible. At a minimum, it should be an inch long when extended so that the bolt passes through the doorjamb and into the door frame. The deeper it penetrates the door frame, the harder the door is to kick open. Also, make sure your strike plate is secured to the door frame with 3" screws (they typically come with 1" screws, so you may need to upgrade). The strike plate is the metal plate that's screwed into the door frame and has a hole in it where the dead bolt goes through. When someone successfully kicks open a door, it's usually because they're kicking the strike plate off the frame, not because the dead bolt failed. By opting for much longer screws, they'll go past the jamb and into the frame.

3. Secondary dead bolt: Although burglars try to avoid breaking through doors with dead bolts, there's no guarantee it won't happen. Therefore, in order to make your door even more impenetrable, you can add a floor dead bolt. A floor dead bolt is mounted vertically to the bottom of your door, which allows the bolt—when extended—to lock into the floor studs. This makes it even harder to force the door open because the door is now secured in two different places, its side and bottom. There's no key to activate it, which means it can be locked only from the inside.

Important note: Always make sure when adding additional locks that they're accessible for children to reach in case of an emergency.

4. Door strength: There is no point in trying to strengthen your door frame and add extra locks if the door itself is weak. Exterior doors should be made of solid core material, such as oak or metal; something that's not easy to punch a hole through. If you're not sure whether your door is solid or hollow, knock on it. If it echoes, that means it's hollow and should be replaced. Also, if your door is designed with custom glass or decorative paneling, make certain the frames around these sections don't have exposed screws, making it easy for someone with a screwdriver to disassemble them. It's also a good idea to avoid having an exterior door made of glass. Although it may be aesthetically pleasing, they're a lot easier to break through.

5. Door enforcer: If you're unable to make the aforementioned adjustments—either because you can't afford the installation or you don't own your home and aren't allowed to make changes to the physical structure of your doors—a door jammer is a great alternative. A door jammer is an adjustable metal pole with a rubber stopper on one end and a U-shaped clamp on the other. After securing the U-shaped clamp under the door's interior doorknob, you set the length of the pole so that the rubber end snugly pushes against the floor. This allows you to reinforce the door from the inside, but it can be used only when you're home.

6. Exterior wall: The exterior wall surrounding your door should be made with a resilient material. Often you'll find homes with strong front doors that appear impassable, yet they will be surrounded by glass or a weak wall made out of plaster. In this case, an intruder doesn't need to break down your door. They can just break the surrounding glass or wall to enter. There is no point in having a strong door if it is not reinforced by a strong wall.

BULLETPROOF YOUR WINDOWS

1. Glass: Understanding the kind of glass you have in your home windows is important. Regular glass is glass that has not been strengthened with any type of temperature or chemical. Of all the glasses we'll discuss here, regular glass is the easiest to break, especially at its center. And when broken, it typically shatters into large, sharp pieces.

Tempered glass is glass treated with intense heat followed by intense cold to enhance its strength and durability. This makes it harder to break than regular glass, although it is weakest at its corners. Unlike regular glass, when tempered glass is broken, it shatters into much smaller pieces.

Laminated glass, also known as safety glass, is tempered glass bonded together with a clear film to keep it intact when broken. This is the type of glass found in car windshields that, when damaged, cracks into a spider web pattern. Laminated glass requires more strength to break than both regular and tempered glass.

Plexiglas, which is actually a plastic, is also a good safety option, as it's more shatter-resistant. You'll usually see this type of glass around a hockey rink. But because it is not as good at insulating the home from outside temperatures, it's generally not used in home windows.

Of all the glass types, laminated glass is the best option to choose when enhancing the strength and security of your home's exterior windows and skylights.

2. Basement windows: Don't assume basement windows are too small for someone to break into. According to the NYPD, they are the most popular way for intruders to get inside your home, so treat them as you would every other window—free of clutter, unobstructed by landscaping, and well lit. Also make sure they're well covered from the inside, using vertical blinds or curtains, so would-be burglars can't see through them.

Most basement window locks are relatively weak, so consider upgrading them using dead bolts or window stoppers. You can also add an interior horizontal bar in the middle of the window, which secures to each side of the window frame. This not only helps to keep the window from being opened all the way but also prevents someone from squeezing past the window opening should they manage to break the glass.

BULLETPROOF YOUR SECURITY SYSTEM
Home security is much more affordable today and much less complicated than in the past. Because it's such a competitive market, most se-

curity companies are happy to come and install everything for you at a reasonable rate. But if you're unable to afford a security system or aren't able to install one in your home, consider adding a few fake cameras around the perimeter to act as deterrents.

1. Motion-triggered cameras: Cameras are a great way to deter break-ins. If a potential intruder sees a camera, they know there's a higher chance of being caught, making it less likely they'll attempt breaking in. Some cameras even have the capability of focusing in on specific features, such as a person's face at your front door or the license plate of a car in your driveway. This can be helpful information to share with law enforcement, should you need to.

2. Recording capabilities: Purchase cameras that have recording capabilities and store the footage for at least several days. This feature allows you to go back in time to see what occurred should there be a delay before discovering a problem, like a break-in or theft.

3. Cell phone accessibility: Some security systems now allow you to access them via an app on your cell phone, which can be set to alert you if someone enters your property or rings your doorbell. This feature both increases your home awareness while away and allows you to directly communicate with the "visitor."

BULLETPROOF YOUR EMPTY NEST

When you're planning to be away from home for any extended period of time, it's wise to take certain precautionary steps to ensure that once you've returned, you're not faced with the aftermath of a burglary or vandalism. The best way to do that is to make it look as though you never left.

1. Stop your mail: An overstuffed mailbox is a dead giveaway you're not home, so consider putting a stop on your mail via the US Postal Service. There's a simple online form you can fill out indicating the dates you'll be away. Or if you have a family member, friend, or neighbor you trust, have them grab your mail in your absence. And while they're at it, ask them to pick up any packages, newspapers, or circulars that have made their way onto your front steps or lawn.

2. Trash: Consider emptying your trash a few days before leaving town.

That way, you don't need to set out your full trash cans before trash day or your empty cans don't sit unattended for days afterward.

3. Social media: Everyone loves to let everyone else know they're on vacation. But if you're posting "wish you were here" photos in real time, you're also letting everyone know you're away. Although it's fun to gloat, don't do it at the expense of inviting unwanted guests. Post your vacation pictures *after* you have returned home.

4. Taxi/Uber/Lyft pickup: Although having a car service pick you up at home is super convenient, it's also an easy way to let everyone know—including your driver—that you're leaving, especially with several suitcases in tow. When hailing a car for a ride to the airport, consider using a pickup location not directly in front of your home, like a few doors down or on the corner. At the same time, be mindful of your conversations in the car or what you tell your driver. They don't need to know you're going to Disney World for seven days.

BULLETPROOF YOUR GO-BAG

A go-bag is a multi-purpose bag that's packed and ready to go with everything you and your family need to survive and thrive for a few days. People often don't think about putting one together until it's too late or when their F3 is activated in a crisis, which makes it harder to think and plan clearly. To help you get started, here is a list you can use and then customize to meet your individual needs:

1. Cash: In emergency situations, cash is king, especially if there is a power outage rendering your credit card and debit cards useless. Although money may be tight, try putting away what you think you'll need for a few days.

2. Credit card: Set aside at least one credit card with a zero balance to be used solely for an emergency. This way you have plenty of credit available to use.

Recommended Supplies:
- Flashlight with extra batteries
- Passports or a photocopy
- Change of clothing

- Non-perishable food, such as canned food, power bars, and nuts
- Bottled water and canteens to fill with water
- First aid kit
- Utility knife
- Cell phone charger
- Matches/lighter
- Extra clothes (warm for colder climates)

For those things you may not be able to leave stored in your go-bag, such as medication, consider writing them down and pinning the list to the outside of your bag. This way, in an emergency, you don't have to rely on your memory. Just grab the list, locate the items, and go.

BULLETPROOF YOUR WALLET

Don't be the person who carries their entire life inside their purse, back-pack, or wallet. By minimizing the amount of items you keep on you—credit cards, insurance cards, debit cards, work IDs—you'll make life a lot simpler should your wallet get stolen. The fewer number of stolen cards means the less time spent on the phone with your credit card companies freezing your accounts. As a rule of thumb, consider carrying no more than two credit cards—a primary and a backup. And try not to carry more cash than needed. If you don't plan on making any big purchases that day, consider leaving a majority of your cash at home. Keep it simple. Carry only what you're comfortable losing or having stolen. For purses, consider placing a light scarf on top of your contents to make it more difficult for someone to slip their hand inside to steal your wallet.

BULLETPROOF YOUR SOCIAL MEDIA

Avoid posting patterns: Be mindful of what you post and when. Letting your "friends" know every move you make may be setting you up for future problems. If you're always posting your 5 p.m. Taco Tuesday dinner spot, for example, you're alerting people to your weekly location, giving them an opportunity to take advantage of your empty home.

Avoid posting your home: For the same reason that people keep their curtains drawn at night, be mindful about posting photos showing the inside of your home. And while you're at it, avoid posting exterior photos that identify your address or the street you live on. Nowadays, it's too easy to use the Internet to find out where someone lives. The same goes for your vehicle. Try not to advertise the make and model of your car, and never allow your license plates to be shown in photos.

Avoid posting your real date of birth: Don't share your real date of birth with anyone on social media. It is a personal identifier and many financial institutions will use it to verify your identity. I know we all love it when our "friends" wish us a happy birthday, but it makes us more vulnerable to identity theft. And you don't always know who your real "friends" are. Social media accounts get hacked into and hijacked all the time, so be cautious about what you reveal.

Avoid posting about your children: Finally, for parents, stop advertising where your kids go to school or the local teams they play on. Child predators can use this information to track down children and use it as a means of showing that they know you. "I'm your mom's coworker, Todd. We work at the bank together. She told me to come pick you up and take you to soccer practice today. You play for the Golden Bears, right?" All of this is easily obtained from your social media accounts when you post pictures of where you work, who your colleagues are, where your kids go to school, and the sports they play. Child predators study social media accounts and collect small bits of information to create profiles for potential victims, so be careful not to leave any of this information exposed.

BULLETPROOF YOUR SECURITY QUESTIONS

Most of us worry about our accounts being hacked, so we create extremely complex and personalized passwords. But how many of us think about the answers we give to the security questions should we happen to forget our passwords? I'm sure your ex-spouse, your coworkers, or anyone looking through your social media posts know the name of your first pet, the town you grew up in, or your high school mascot. Using real answers to security questions is an easy way for both strangers and our "friends" to gain access to our accounts. Consider choosing answers that aren't easy to guess or verify to ensure you are the only person who has this information.

Part 2

READING PEOPLE

Chapter 9

Becoming a Human Lie Detector

All men, well interrogated, answer well.
—Plato

Golden Boy

The young man appeared golden on paper—the perfect candidate for the USSS: Ivy League college, ex–baseball player, confident, smart. If you were casting a role in a Hollywood movie for a Special Agent, you would have chosen this guy to play the part. He looked like a hero. But this hero had two prior inconclusive polygraph tests, and the recruiters wanted him badly. I was in the field office in New York City when I got the call.

"We need you to do his third poly. Get him through."

Two days later, I flew west to do the interview. Most people have the misconception that the polygraph machine is the complete test—that you hook a person up to some sensors, measure their pulse and blood pressure, and one way or another you'll get the truth out of them. The reality is that the real test is the interviewer. In other words, I was the polygraph.

To be in the Secret Service, you have to pass a polygraph exam. This consists of hours of conversation where the examiner (me) elicits information by asking the candidate questions about their life. The actual test—with the machine and the wires—is just to verify that the interviewee isn't hiding anything.

The fact that this applicant had two inconclusive tests meant that he was hiding something. It was my job to pull that out of him. If it was no big deal, he would tell me, and then I would be able to verify that he had answered everything truthfully and would pass the test. Often, with applicants, it's usually something minor that they're afraid to share, thinking it will automatically disqualify them. The truth is no one is perfect and people make mistakes. The Secret Service just needs to know that you're honest about your past, and that hopefully none of your mistakes are felonies. For example, stealing change from your mom's purse when you were fourteen does not preclude you from being a Special Agent. Stealing from your last employer might. So the question "Have you ever stolen anything?" is meant to cover your whole life.

That day in the interview room, the man was polite and respectful with a firm handshake. He didn't look overly nervous.

I can't share the specific questions the Secret Service asks potential candidates, but I can tell you that this is the time when people show who they are and tell me everything they've done—good and bad. Mostly bad.

For this particular candidate, the conversation started innocently enough.

"Have you ever hurt anybody?"

"No," he answered. "I mean, in baseball, yeah, I hit a line drive into a guy's leg once."

He moved in his chair. Not a lot. Just a shift. Leaned back. I mentally took note.

"Anyone else?"

"No."

"Did you ever hurt anyone away from the field?"

"I upset somebody once."

"Tell me about that."

"It was in college. Just a girl I was seeing. I went out with her and she said I made her feel bad after our date."

"Feel bad?" I repeated.

"She said I hurt her. I mean, I didn't. But she said I did."

I silently waited for him to continue.

"It was after we had sex. She said she didn't want to. I don't know."

"When you were having sex, did you hold her down?"

"Well, I held her wrists."

"Okay. Do you think you held them tight?"

"Well, yeah, kind of." He paused. "After we had sex she cried. Told me she was upset. And then she left."

I took him through some more questions, and at the end of the conversation, I didn't need to give him a third polygraph. This guy wasn't going to be an agent.

I walked into the boss's office where he was waiting, eagerly anticipating what he thought would be good news.

"Well?" he asked, excitedly.

"He's not your guy," I said.

"What?" He looked confused. A little annoyed, even.

"Your golden boy," I said. "He's a rapist."

Polygraph Training

To become a polygraph examiner with the USSS, candidates must successfully complete a highly challenging twelve-week training course at the National Center for Credibility Assessment (NCCA).

When I attended NCCA in 2004, it was known as the Department of Defense Polygraph Institute (DoDPI) and it was by far the hardest, most mentally challenging training academy I'd ever attended. To this day, it remains at the top of my "Well, that sucked" list. DoDPI was the who's who of federal agencies when it came to polygraph training. All federal agencies, including the CIA, National Security Agency (NSA), FBI, USSS, Drug Enforcement Administration, and Army Criminal Investigation Division, sent their selected candidates to DoDPI with the *hope* of getting back a certified examiner at the end of the three-month course. I emphasize the word *hope* because not all agencies did. It was so intense that some students simply couldn't keep up with the amount of studying needed to pass the barrage of tests being thrown our way each week. The school consisted of graduate-level courses on topics such as psychology and physiology, both of which play an important role in polygraph examinations. Not only did I have to become an expert in the mental and physical traits of people, I also had to do a deep dive into the laws governing polygraphs, research methods, ethics, and especially interviewing and interrogation strategies. By the end, I had earned nearly half the credits needed toward my master's degree in forensic psychology.

Despite polygraph examiners being highly sought-after positions, the vast majority of Special Agents don't put their names forward for consideration. We were a small agency, and despite our name, there were no secrets. If someone decided to pursue one of the coveted polygraph examiner positions and failed, everyone would know. For a lot of people, this was reason enough not to try.

I ended up at DoDPI at the encouragement of a senior examiner who was leaving the team to join the PPD. Initially, I declined the position when he recommended it to me, mostly because I didn't think I would be particularly good at it. A polygraph examiner's job is to get confessions, solve cases that other agents couldn't, get new leads, gather intelligence. There are a lot of expectations and responsibilities that come with being a polygrapher. And while my "fuck off" face was as good as anyone's, I didn't think I'd be able to intimidate people into confessing their crimes. But my colleague had a different perspective.

"People will be more likely to talk to you," he said. "If you aren't trying to intimidate them, they'll let their guard down. They'll be more open with you. I'm telling you—you'll be really good at this."

Despite the fact that I have master's degrees in journalism and forensic psychology, academics never came easy for me. At DoDPI, I quickly discovered that the way I learn seemed to be different from most of my classmates. Where they could read and retain information in one sitting and still magically have time to grab a beer with friends, I had to spend hours locked in my room, going through the same material over and over again. Even under normal circumstances (which the institute certainly wasn't), I'm not one of those people who can effortlessly retain facts and theories and recall them instantaneously days or weeks later.

My brain simply works differently, which meant that I needed to learn differently. My evenings quickly became a constant stream of study intensives. I'd stay up most of the night rewriting my notes from the day's lectures and even copying my textbooks by hand, word for word, in order to cram the concepts into my long-term memory. Night after night I passed on social gatherings at the local pub with my fellow classmates (including the prized buffalo wings I always craved), choosing instead to study until three or four in the morning, writing out all the information I needed to know on thick stacks of binder paper. And I wouldn't just copy my notes and textbooks once. I would do it twice. That's right—I'd literally copy my textbooks in longhand twice. If that sounds crazy, there's actually science that supports this method of memory retention. Research shows that the mental encoding process of writing out our notes during a lecture increases both retention and learning.

If that sounds extreme, well, it was. Most graduate students have an entire semester to learn the curriculum of psychology and physiology courses. We had one week. One week to read and retain an entire textbook cover to cover, prepare for a midterm and a final, and then move on to the next subject. And after every exam our grades were posted in the hallway for all to see. For all these reasons, DoDPI caused more stress and sleepless nights than I care to remember.

When I graduated from DoDPI as a polygraph examiner for the US Secret Service, I was one of only about thirty in the agency. And being assigned to the New York Field Office meant I handled the polygraph exams for the northeastern part of the United States.

Whether or not you have a strong stance on the validity of polygraph—some claim polygraphs are 80–90 percent effective, while others argue they're no better than the flip of a coin—I can tell you from my personal experience that they are extremely useful inside the interrogation room. Why, you might ask? Because people lie. Agencies like the CIA, FBI, and USSS use polygraph examinations as part of their pre-employment hiring phase to determine whether an applicant is trustworthy. Research shows that between 28 percent and 75 percent of job applicants will tell some type of lie during their job interview. During my years as an examiner, I learned how to look for those subtle clues of deception, identify misplaced nervousness, and key in on paralinguistic pattern changes that allowed me to politely call bullshit even before I hooked them up to the polygraph.

How Polygraph Works

The polygraph instrument—more commonly known as the lie detector—is a machine used to monitor and record changes in a person's body. When most people think of a polygraph machine, they think of a big box with a bunch of wires and several ink pens scrolling up and down a rolling sheet of paper, much like what Robert De Niro used on Ben Stiller in the 2000 movie *Meet the Parents*. But in 1992, that big box was replaced with a laptop computer. Now the modern-day polygraph machine and all its components fit discreetly inside a backpack.

Although polygraph components track an examinee's physical changes—sweating, blood pressure, and breathing—those changes occur because of what's happening inside their head. In other words, how they're reacting psychologically to something is what matters. Remember in chapter 1 when we talked about F3? That's exactly what's going on here. When a person gets stressed, their body goes through a bunch of physical changes that occur all at once; these are typically reactions they have no control over, and which the polygraph can easily pick up on.

Let me give you an example of how F3 relates to polygraph. This is the same example I gave to nearly all my examinees: Imagine yourself driving down the highway. It's a beautiful day. The sun is shining, the radio is on, sunroof's open. You're feeling pretty good . . . and going just a bit over the speed limit . . . by about 15 mph. As you crest the hill of a road you've traveled down a hundred times before, you see him. A state trooper. Sitting on the inside shoulder running radar.

Now, after saying "Oh shit!" what's the next thing that happens? Your foot immediately comes off the gas pedal; both hands go back onto the steering wheel. You'll likely even turn off the radio and close the sunroof.

As those things happen externally, internally your heart rate just increased, your body—usually your hands—begin sweating, and your breathing becomes noticeably shallower. In a matter of milliseconds, you went from feeling great to feeling anxious, simply based on seeing a "threat" parked on the side of the road.

As you pass the trooper, you obsessively begin checking your rearview mirror hoping he doesn't pull out . . . *shit, he's pulling out*.

Now with the threat driving directly behind you, your heart rate further skyrockets, your sweaty palms just got sweatier, your breathing feels more labored, and your stomach turns in knots.

And then he turns on his lights. *Damn.*

As you begin pulling onto the shoulder, your mind racing as fast as your heart, he suddenly whips around you and speeds off.

Relief.

You drive on for a while, still frazzled, but knowing the threat has passed. You begin to relax. Your heart rate decreases, your hands stop sweating, and your breathing eventually returns to normal. You may still drive in silence for several more minutes with the sunroof closed and both hands on the wheel, but internally you go back to the same person you were five minutes ago.

That's F3. In that moment, you couldn't Fight or Flee, although unfortunately some people try. And you couldn't completely Freeze, although most people become less able to process multiple stimuli, which is why they'll close the window (wind becomes a distraction) and turn off the radio (unable to concentrate with music on). The reason you experienced this is the perceived threat of getting pulled over and the consequences that come with it: Getting a ticket. Paying a fine. Penalty points added to your license. Your insurance premium going up.

Using that analogy, we can apply F3 to polygraph. There are lots of reasons why we might lie, but regardless of the "why," when we tell a lie, we know we're lying. And more important, we know the consequences of being caught in that lie—loss of a relationship, loss of respect, loss of an opportunity. So when we lie, our bodies physically respond to the psychological stress of telling that lie. During the polygraph exam, you're asked a number of questions to test the body's stress response. For example, if somebody's lied on their application about graduating from college, during the polygraph they are likely to have a strong stress response to questions associated to their education.

When we lie, we give off energy or what I call *red flags* of behavior. Although in some cases those red flags may be subtle, we all wave them in some form or fashion. If we didn't, the US government wouldn't spend millions of dollars every year training their agents to catch them. I also want to mention that I use the words *interview* and *interrogation* interchangeably throughout this section, because regardless of whether I was interviewing a terrorist or a candidate for the USSS, my approach and process remained the same. Polygraph isn't about intimidating people into talking to you. It isn't about ridiculing or insulting them. Everything I've learned in my career has taught me that treating people like they're garbage means that most of the information they offer will be garbage, too. Others might shut down or get combative, all of which works against your primary goal of uncovering the truth of what they know or what they've done.

Evil Doesn't Have a Face

There is one pivotal truth that not only became a pillar of my polygraph and law enforcement career, but remains an important part of my worldview even now—there are no absolute good guys or bad guys. I've interviewed hundreds of people, some of whom have done some truly terrible things. But I have never sat across from someone and felt that I was looking into the face of evil. I'm not saying it doesn't exist—but it's rare. In most cases, people are much more complicated than that, and if you want to read people and understand them, you need to leave that way of thinking behind you. Everyone has good in them, and everyone has bad. Most of us try to make sure the good outweighs the bad—which is why, when we do something wrong, we feel guilty about it. Some people feel this more acutely, some people less. But this is the constant balancing act we practice. In moments of stress, when we're weak, when we're insolent, when we're angry or not thinking clearly, sometimes there can be a shift when the scales tip and the bad dominates the good. Nobody is immune from this. Most people are good people, and sometimes good people do bad things, or stupid things, or both.

We like to put people into categories. Categories are simple and safe—black or white, virtuous or villainous. They save us the effort of looking beyond our own biases and become genuinely curious about someone else. But categories can sabotage our efforts to understand people, by reducing them to two-dimensional stereotypes. While it's easy to assume that the person who dings your car and drives off is an awful person, the truth is there's probably a lot more to it. Similarly, if someone you love or admire is accused of doing something hurtful, you might jump to their defense. "Oh, they didn't mean it," you might say. "They just made a mistake." Some would prefer to be willfully blind to the fact that a good or kind person did a bad thing if it allows them to sustain an uncomplicated way of viewing the world. We would rather judge people by who we believe them to be rather than by their actions. Conversely, we like to imagine that one bad action can determine a person's overall character or humanity. It doesn't.

Reading people means looking beyond categories and stereotypes. It means seeing people in all of their complexity and contradiction. Learning this skill is what made me a good interviewer. When I sat across from someone, I didn't reduce them to the sum of their wrongdoing. Instead, I tried to figure out what had gone wrong in their life that led them to this moment, in which they found themselves in the extreme situation of being interrogated by a federal agent. I gradually realized that the most effective way of understanding someone was to empathize with them, to learn not only *what* they had done but *why* they had done it.

As my interview style became more sophisticated and complex, so did the people I interrogated. It was no longer just some street criminal sitting across from me—it was John, a banker, who had four children and was struggling to pay his bills and couldn't imagine another way to handle the pressure he felt. It was Sarah, who struggled with an addiction. It was James, who had lost his father at a young age and been taken in by a gang that felt like family.

It was so many names and so many faces and so many stories, and so much more than what appeared on the outside. Some of the most dangerous criminals looked like someone you might see at a community potluck or on a yacht or anywhere but in handcuffs.

How to Become a Human Lie Detector

We all genuinely want to know how to make sense of the people we come into contact with, whether it's a love interest, a friend, a boss, or someone we've just met. We want to know if they have a hidden agenda. If they like us. If we can trust them. And so we try to read their facial expressions, their body language, and decode their quirks and habits of speech as we wonder, *Should I trust this person with my child? With my house? With my career? With my friendship?* Many of us have had the experience at some point in our lives when we felt betrayed by someone. Do you have one of those friends who constantly end up in relationships with the wrong people? Or a family member who is always picking the wrong business partners? Raise your hand if you've ever lost sleep trying to figure out what another person was thinking or feeling. At the core of many of the questions we ask ourselves about other people are two important ones: Does this person have my best interests at heart? Am I safe with them?

The answers to these questions are right there in front of you, if you know how to look for them.

This section will teach you the art and science of reading people. I'm going to show you how to spot certain behaviors and ask the right questions that will help you become a human lie detector. You'll learn to read body language and verbal cues to understand what people are really saying when they're talking to you. The best techniques of the interrogation room are equally powerful in our everyday lives. As a civilian now, I use them all the time. Whether I'm interviewing someone for a media story, deciding to work with a specific producer, having a difficult conversation with a family member, or corralling the energy of my students, communication skills are always at play. I've even used these skills to get a cheating confession out of a boyfriend—ahem, who became an ex-boyfriend shortly thereafter.

And since everything that you learn about how to read people and elicit information could also be used by the person who wants to read you, I'll teach you how to assess yourself for what you might be revealing to others. The next chapters will hone your discernment toward people and help you make better choices in your life about whom to trust and whom to avoid. The best part? You get to learn all this and skip the twelve grueling weeks at DoDPI. Ready? Let's begin.

Chapter 10

Everybody Lies

Learn to be silent. Let your quiet mind listen and absorb.
—PYTHAGORAS

Red Flags

When a seven-month-old baby girl with severe blunt-force trauma to her skull was brought to the hospital, a local police department called to request a polygraph. The injury was not the result of an accident, and the police had two main suspects—the babysitter and the father.

I interviewed and polygraphed the babysitter while another Service examiner did the same with the father. Both passed their exams. That's when my sights turned to the mother. Although the detectives advised that she was not a suspect, I wanted to polygraph everyone who had been in daily contact with the infant.

On the morning of the exam, the mother arrived at the police station, accompanied by a lawyer. Although it was her constitutional right to do so, this seemed odd because up until this point she had been voluntarily speaking to the authorities without one. And her husband had taken his polygraph without any legal representation. By all accounts, the mother was a victim by proxy. Her seven-month-old baby girl had suffered a massive head injury, which had yet to be explained. Prior to being asked to take a polygraph examination, the mother had been extremely cooperative. In fact, she was the one who had identified the babysitter as a suspect. But now she sat silently in the company of her legal counsel as she waited for her exam to begin.

First red flag.

Upon introducing myself, I advised the lawyer to wait in the lobby, as the polygraph exam would need to be conducted in private. The mother and I then walked into the interview room, where we took our seats across from one another.

From the moment the interview started, the mother was extremely antagonistic. She feigned disinterest when I spoke about the case and seemed annoyed at the fact that she too had been asked to take a polygraph. And on more than one occasion, she made it a point to tell me that she was in a hurry, requesting that I "make it quick."

"I have things to do," she told me. "It's hot in here. How long is this going to take?"

A typical polygraph exam can last a few hours, sometimes longer depending on the circumstances. And in cases such as this one, where the parent of an abused child is being interviewed, the exam can often take several hours or more because of the emotional anguish. Yet, this mother apparently had more important things to do with her time than to help me find out who had hurt her baby.

Second red flag.

As the interview continued, I asked the mother a series of questions about factual matters pertaining to the case. Describe how your daughter was found? Tell me who you might suspect? Explain to me what you think happened? But each time she was given an open-ended question (more on this in chapter 19), she gave only brief responses. Again, this was extremely odd behavior. A mother whose child has been physically harmed will try to offer as much information as she can to help find her child's abuser. She'll make wild guesses, offer hunches, and speculate on theories, anything to help the investigator put the pieces together. Yet this mother did none of these things. Truthful people will typically give very detailed statements, while deceptive people will offer vague ones. Liars say less because it's hard to create a story and then remember everything that was said.

Third red flag.

Prior to the actual administration of the polygraph, I could see the mother was anxious and wanted to leave. She was seated in the fleeing position with her body leaning toward the door (more on this in chapter 11). Right before the test, she stopped me and said that she now felt bad for the babysitter and wanted to leave it alone. She no longer wanted to press charges against the nanny and ruin her chances of working as a caregiver somewhere else. According to the mother, the babysitter was, after all, still young and had simply made a mistake. This was an extremely unusual statement to make under these circumstances. A mother whose child had been severely beaten would want whoever was responsible to be punished in some way. A truthful person's view of punishment will often fit the crime. A deceptive person's view of punishment will often favor extreme leniency.

Fourth red flag.

The mother of the seven-month-old baby girl took her polygraph. And failed.

I looked at her and told her that she had failed her exam. Upon hearing those words, it was as if a switch flipped inside her. She locked eyes with me, leaned in and, with a defiant grin on her face, said, "I think we're done here." At that moment, she knew that I knew the truth.

Sadly, I had known the truth even before I administered the polygraph. Everything about the mother's behavior indicated guilt. Her voice and speech, the way she sat in the room pretending this was no big deal—her feigned disinterest and cold demeanor toward me given that I was there to help—all of it was deeply incriminating. But there was nothing I could do. She could not be charged based on my assessments alone. I needed facts. I needed proof. I needed . . . a confession.

But because she was not in custody and had come to the interview voluntarily, I couldn't force her to stay. Although I wanted to lock the door and interrogate her, I wasn't allowed to do so. The law was the law.

And so she left. Without any formal charges, she freely returned home to continue to care for her abused seven-month-old girl and three other children.

As for me, I immediately went to the investigators who had up until this point focused solely on the dad and babysitter. "You've been looking at the wrong people," I told them. "It's the mother. She did it. Start digging."

Why People Lie

First, let me just say that everybody lies. Everybody. Some studies show that the average person lies between one to two times per day. Other studies claim people lie up to ten times over the course of a single conversation.

We often have very good reasons for lying. We lie to be kind. We lie out of embarrassment or fear. We lie out of self-interest. We lie to deceive and conceal sensitive information. And sometimes we lie just because we want to. Although lies can certainly be told for personal gain, the majority seem to arise for psychological reasons related to saving face. Lies also allow us to be accommodating and make things easier or more pleasant for others, to protect others' feelings, or keep something private. Have you ever had those moments where you feel like you've shared too much information, and then afterward wished you hadn't? It's because you feel exposed and vulnerable.

"How are you?"

"I'm fine. How are you?"

Meanwhile, you just had a huge fight with your partner and are not fine. It's natural to be reserved and to try to share only what we want others to see.

Professor Paul Ekman, long considered to be the world's leading expert in emotion recognition and whose work was the basis for the television show *Lie to Me*, conducted a study of 509 people to determine who among the group was best at spotting liars. This study included police officers, federal agents, judges, psychiatrists, robbery investigators, and college students, as well as professional polygraphers for the CIA, FBI, and NSA. Ekman's findings revealed that people considered experts in lie detection actually performed about as well, or in some cases slightly worse, than the average person—perhaps because experts in deception tend to assume people are being deceptive. The only group that scored consistently higher when it came to identifying liars and reading nonverbal cues were Secret Service agents. This skill set is likely due to our rigorous training as well as our heightened state of awareness and observation when it comes to looking out for potential threats in large crowds. We are constantly scanning and assessing human behavior.

The study also seemed to suggest that people had a more difficult time spotting lies made by those closest to them than the lies of total strangers. This may have something to do with the fact that we tend to judge people based on how they make us feel. Our emotions can become so clouded by the people who are always around us that we lose the ability to see them clearly or judge their actions for what they truly are. A husband might see his wife as merely having a bad temper rather than see a spouse who is emotionally and verbally abusive. We make excuses or dismiss the actions of those closest to us. "That's just how my wife is." "She has a lot on her mind." Only in retrospect, after we realize that a partner is abusive, do we start looking at all the evidence with clear eyes. To see a lie, we need to take ourselves and our emotions out of the equation.

All that said, you don't need a PhD in criminology or be a polygraph examiner to know when people are lying. You just need to trust your instincts and learn some of the important techniques I describe in the following chapters. Whether you have concerns about a cheating partner, a dishonest business associate, or your child's after-school activities, you can learn to find the indicators in their behavior that will help you assess their truthfulness.

How We Lie

People lie in three primary ways.

1. They tell a complete lie. In other words, they design a false statement that deliberately contradicts the truth.
2. They tell a lie mixed with the truth. Rather than coming up with an entirely false statement, they distort the lie by littering it with aspects of the truth.

3. They lie by omission. Lying by omission is the primary way most people lie because we feel like we aren't really lying. We all know lying is wrong—well, at least most of us do—and believe that we shouldn't do it. So, to alleviate our guilt, we just leave certain parts of the story out of our narrative and justify it by thinking, *Well, I'm not really lying, I'm just leaving that part out.* But leaving something out can drastically alter and even mislead the listener's understanding.

At the end of the day, a lie is a lie is a lie, regardless of which method a person uses. Remember, everyone lies, and we lie quite often. So, given that, here's your first piece of advice:

Don't Take It Personally

Once you begin to realize how often people lie, you will learn to take their lies less personally. Believe it or not, this is an important element in reading people. When someone lies to us, we tend to see it as a personal attack or manipulation. *How dare you lie to me. You must think I'm stupid.* Our ego feels injured when we learn that we've been lied to. The trouble is that when our egos get involved, it can often muddy our capacity to read people and understand their true motives. Egos color our ability to see the truth, and I've learned that in order to read people effectively, you need to be able to see them objectively rather than solely through the lens of judgment or emotional escalation. Reading people is about detaching yourself from the outcome and seeing past yourself in order to understand why that person is lying.

Gathering Intelligence

The goal of reading people is to collect information that allows you to make an assessment. As an agent, people would lie to me all the time. It was just a given. Even today—in business, in Hollywood, with the students I teach—I still get lied to. But mostly it doesn't faze me because I know that it's just part of human nature.

Instead of allowing my emotions to interfere with my ability to assess someone objectively, I try to learn all I can about the person in front of me—who they are, what they care about, the choices they make, and the motivations that determine those choices. The more I know, the better armed I will be, and the better I'll be able to respond to what I discover. Another advantage is that it helps prevent me from making the wrong assumptions. It's easy to assume the worst of someone if we're viewing them only through our personal biases, but by doing so we're more likely to miss something fundamental to who they are.

Gathering intelligence allows me to know whom I'm speaking to and how I should speak to them in order to communicate well. Whenever I begin a new semester of teaching, one of the first things I do is ask all of my students to write me an essay about themselves, why they're taking my course, and what they hope to get out of it. The information I collect from them always plays a big role in how I teach the class in order to connect with the different needs and interests of my students.

So what do you want to know? Whether an investor has honest intentions? If your business partner is stealing money? If your boss is looking out for your best interest or his own? If your spouse is cheating on you? Did your kids really do their homework? Whatever it is—you need to gather intelligence. And the best way to do this is to learn how to watch and listen.

Be an Active Listener

There is a misconception that I often come across when I teach interrogation and interviewing strategies. People believe that if they speak the most, they can control the conversation. *Wrong.* The exact opposite is true. The more you talk, the less control you actually have. When you're reading people, silence is your friend. Listening is your friend. I cannot express how important it is to be an active listener when people are speaking to you. Active listening is about using all of your senses to "hear" what the person is saying. Open your eyes and listen. Take people in. Watch them. Feel the energy or vibe they give off.

When you start to home in on the nuances of their verbal communication, you'll begin to understand their meaning and motives at a much deeper level.

Remember, if your goal is to accurately read someone, then it's not about you talking; it's about allowing the other person to talk and share information with you. When you are on the receiving end of a conversation, the more you receive, the better informed you will be.

Fortunately, most people love to talk about themselves.

So let them. Don't let your ego tell you that you need to take up space in the conversation. Also, don't interrupt people while they're speaking. Not only is it rude and disrespectful, but it can derail their train of thought and throw them off the topic you're trying to gather information about. Even a long, rambling explanation will give you a ton of useful information, so let people tell their story from start to finish and then later come back with any follow-up questions you may have. Even if what they're saying seems unimportant to you, it may be of great significance to them. So rather than cut them off midsentence or ask them to get back on topic, instead ask yourself: "Why are they telling me this story in this way? Why is this important to them? Are they being vague or overly detailed about certain parts of their story? Does anything in their narrative seem to be missing? Are they engaged in the conversation or do they seem detached?"

It's worth noting that a dishonest person's speech may sound rehearsed, as though they have been practicing their answers, while a truthful person's responses will be spontaneous. As we saw with the mother at the beginning of this chapter, deceptive responses also tend to be vague and brief. The speaker will try to minimize their dialogue to avoid getting caught in a lie while a truthful person will offer more details. So pay close attention to not only what they say, but also to what they don't say.

Active listening means being present. Get rid of any distractions and give your undivided attention to the person sitting in front of you. Make them know they matter and that you're willing to give them all the time they need to talk.

If this isn't quite what you imagined a seasoned interrogator might recommend, you've probably been watching too much TV. Movies and shows like to paint a dramatic portrait of the angry interrogator pounding the table and the terrified suspect cowering in his chair, but nine times out of ten, that kind of strategy will fail and fail hard. The truth is that active listening doesn't make for good TV, but it is the most useful technique I use. If you're committed to really trying to read someone, this is the best tool at your disposal.

Use it.

Chapter 11

Reading People

Eyes are more accurate witnesses than ears.
—Heraclitus

Body Language

Body language is an important part of every conversation—far more so than you might realize. When we communicate with someone in person—as opposed to over the phone, email, or text—we have much more information at our disposal to help us understand what that person is really saying or thinking. The gestures and poses people make with their body, whether intentional or not, inform our understanding of what they may be thinking but not saying. One of the ways I read people is by assessing whether their words and bodies are in harmony. When there is conflict or contradiction between someone's physical mannerisms and the story they're telling, even if that conflict is incredibly subtle, that's when I know to pay closer attention.

Understanding body language can provide additional insights at work, in relationships, and can be extremely helpful to parents with children of any age. In fact, a 1994 study by Dr. Judee Burgoon showed that approximately 65 percent of what we communicate is nonverbal—meaning there is a wealth of information people are unknowingly revealing about themselves at any given moment. We've already established that when a Fight, Flight, or Freeze response kicks into gear, most people have difficulty controlling how they react. When faced with the prospect of being caught in a lie, even though a physical threat may not be looming, many people will still experience some activation of their F3 response. Their jaw might clench. They may fidget with their hands. Their eyes might widen. They may cover their mouth when they speak. Or try to mask their awkwardness by smiling. This is because they fear the consequences of being caught, which could lead to them losing their job, family, social status, money, dignity, or in some cases even their freedom.

Don't Put People in a Box

You already know that learning to read people means being willing to see them in all of their complexity. When it comes to body language, the same is true—because the fact is that no two people are exactly alike in their habits or behaviors. Some people might look away when they're lying to you; others might look directly at you. Some people might scratch their heads. Others might clasp their hands. Every *body* expresses stress differently. Before you can begin to read someone's body language, it helps to become attuned to their habits by paying special attention to how they behave under nonheightened circumstances. We call this getting a baseline (more on that soon).

It would be great if there were universal indicators when it came to identifying dishonesty in a person. Certain experts and popular techniques claim that they have identified specific habits to determine a person's honesty based on their neurological and behavioral patterns. They'll tell you that a certain kind of person will engage in specific behaviors under a stressful scenario, but these designations fail to take into account the diversity of how people operate and behave, and therefore they won't help you uncover the truth. We are all products of a huge variety of things: our genetic makeup, biology, life experiences, the neighborhoods we grew up in, the kind of parenting we received, our socioeconomic status, education, and much more. Each of these elements interacts with all the others to determine our perception of the world and our response to it. They also shape our behavior to external stimuli. That's why these catchall methods and one-size-fits-all formulas don't work, because people are simply too unique to adhere to any one approach or methodology. Frankly, anyone who tries to convince you otherwise is trying to sell you something.

All this means is that you have to be super-observant. What we're going to be looking for are clusters of behavior—identifying a person's tell signs. These are the habits and physical traits that deviate from how a person normally behaves in a neutral setting. Because the fact is that most people are bad liars. Lying requires an impressive feat of multitasking—from tracking your story to delivering it in a compelling and convincing way to controlling your physical signals without letting your F3 response take over. At some point in the process, a liar is likely to slip up. Fortunately, most people have no idea what their tells are, but the more you learn to read people, the more obvious those signs will become. In this chapter, I'm going to show you how to turn your powers of observation into a personal superpower.

Find the Baseline

So we've established that people will vary in their mannerisms and behaviors during stressful circumstances or conversations. In order to determine what a person's stress tells might be, you first need to observe them when they're calm and collected. You need to figure out who this person is when they're on cruise control.

When I talk with people, I pay attention to how they sit or stand, their posture, the words they use, the way they speak. When people answer basic or benign questions about themselves, they don't typically feel worried. This is why I often begin by asking neutral questions that help put people at ease. I might mention something about the restaurant we're in, or compliment their shoes or ask about their kids. This helps me see how a person interacts in a casual context, and that information in turn helps me build a foundational understanding of that person.

This is why casual conversation is important. Before you bring up a heavy topic that may destabilize someone, ask them about their favorite show. Bring up the weather. How their day has been going.

Begin with safe topics to help them relax and then pay close attention. Observe how the person is holding themselves when they're discussing something easy and straightforward. Do they sit up straight, cross their legs, scratch their head? What do they do with their eyes, their mouths, their hands? Track and remember each of their mannerisms before you delve into the more difficult topics, and then look for what changes.

Clusters of Behavior

The important thing is not just to notice one habit, but to look for clusters of behavior. The more you notice, the easier it will be for you to pick up on red flags. When you start to see those red flags, you should become curious.

Imagine a woman talking to her boyfriend over their morning coffee. Things are relaxed and normal until she asks him what he did last night. Now he fidgets and covers his mouth before he answers. *Why did he do that?* she wonders as she observes him. It's a good question. Once you begin to notice shifts or changes in that behavior, you can probably assume that a person is being affected by some sort of stimulus. Perhaps he is worried about something. Perhaps he feels nervous or threatened. Perhaps he's about to tell her a lie.

At the same time, these red flags might not signify a lie at all. There are countless reasons why someone might react to a question they're asked. Maybe her questions simply coincided with his movements. You don't want to assume guilt based on a single moment's incongruence.

When I was interviewing people for positions within the USSS, I would often ask them whether they had ever been arrested. I remember one particular candidate who answered "No," and immediately looked at the floor. It was the first time he had done that during our conversation. Which prompted me to probe further.

"So you've never been arrested?" I asked again.

"Well, I haven't," he told me. "But my father has."

"Okay," I said. "Tell me about that."

When it comes to the truth, there's usually much more than meets the eye. While a red flag is important to notice and pay attention to, it may not indicate guilt or dishonesty. It may simply mean that the truth is more complex than a *yes* or *no* answer can convey.

Reading body language is about becoming an investigator of behavior. The body doesn't lie. In fact, regardless of a person's agenda, the body wants to tell the truth. Sometimes, no matter how much a person tries to remain composed and controlled, the body will signal when it's lying. Professional interrogators call this *bleeding information*, because information will leak from the body almost like an open wound. The following section will teach you about some of the most common places where information tends to bleed through.

Facial Expressions

A person's face can reveal a huge amount of information. This is especially true for folks who don't know how to control their facial expressions. You know those people, the ones who can't help but reveal everything they're thinking and feeling. This might be bad for their personal discretion, but it's good for you. Yet even for those people who have more controlled expressions, there's often a lot of information staring you in the face, so to speak. According to Paul Ekman, people often inadvertently display their true emotions through a series of micro-expressions, subtle facial signals lasting less than .5 seconds, which often occur without them even knowing.

Eye Contact

One of the first things to determine when you want to read someone is their normal level of eye contact. Some people (wrongly) assume that extended eye contact conveys honesty, whereas avoiding eye contact is a sign of deception. We expect people to look us in the eye the entire time they're speaking to us. But in fact, people tend to make eye contact only 60 percent of the time. For some people it may be more, and for others less—the research varies. However, it is absolutely normal for people to break eye contact with you when they are speaking. The important thing is to establish the normal level of eye contact that specific person maintains, and then notice how and if that changes.

If I want to get a good baseline on someone, I'll ask a question that requires them to recall something. Then I'll pay attention to see if their eyes shift during their recall process. For example, if someone looks up and to the left every time I ask them to remember something, then I have assessed a pattern. But some people may not shift their eyes at all. Again, each person is uniquely different.

Looking up and to the left

On the other hand, some people may look down when accessing their feelings or emotions. Kids, in particular, seem to perform this behavior, especially when they feel ashamed or know they've done something wrong. There is a popular video of a mother asking her child whether he had eaten a jar of sprinkles. The child, with a face covered in sprinkles, is adamant that he did not eat them. "Did you eat those sprinkles?" the mother asks. "You know it's not nice to tell stories and to lie, right?"

"Nope," he insists. But when he says this, he looks away from her. Each time the mother repeats the question, he looks away.

"John, look at Mommy," she tells him, and he does. "You're not supposed to lie. Tell me—did you eat those sprinkles?"

"No," he says, looking away again, his shoulders slumping forward, shifting side to side on his feet. "I did not eat those sprinkles."

"John," she says. "You have sprinkles on your face."

"Um, no, no," John tells her. "I did not eat sprinkles." And then he begins taking small backward steps toward the kitchen doorway.

A lot of parents believe that if their child is looking them in the eyes, they won't be able to lie.

"John, look at Mommy."

"You're not supposed to lie."

Two things are happening here:

1. Mommy is teaching John to look her in the eye when he lies, which will help him become a better liar over time.
2. She is correcting his obvious tell sign—looking away when he lies—which will make it harder for her to know when he is lying in the future. She's essentially sabotaging her own efforts to accurately read her son.

This holds true for adults as well, which is why it's so important not to ask people to change their behavior when you're trying to discern the truth.

"Look me in the eyes and tell me the truth."

"Turn around and say that to my face."

Any of these sound familiar? If what you're really after is the truth, the key is to notice the behavior, but not change it. If you're trying to extract information, why would you want to alter someone's tell? Plus, it's a pretty major misconception that people can't lie when they're looking directly at you. Personally, I can look you in the eyes all day long and lie, if I need to. So let people be. When you're reading people, don't try to change how they're acting, even if you don't like it. By interrupting someone's pattern of behavior, you're simply teaching them to become a better liar by concealing their tells and making it more difficult for you to assess them accurately.

I once interrogated a man who was being investigated for having taken part in a fraudulent ATM scheme. As a way to make more money, a legitimate ATM company designed their ATMs to capture the banking information off the debit cards customers were using in their machines, which they later sold to credit card counterfeiters. When I asked the man I was interrogating basic questions about who he was and his background, he sat slumped forward in his chair and kept his eyes on the floor while he answered. Although it may have seemed odd, I didn't try to adjust or correct his behavior. I didn't say to him, "Why are you looking at the floor?" I left him alone and proceeded with our interview. It wasn't until I turned to questions about the ATM scheme that he shot straight up in his chair and looked me in the eyes. There was a clear shift in his behavior—a huge red flag. His baseline was looking down at the floor, and his F3 was looking at me in the eyes. And by allowing him to be and not correcting his behavior, I was able to get a better read on him during the interview. Eventually he confessed to engineering the software used to skim the ATM users' card information.

Other Common Eye Expressions

OH GOD:

Some people may look up when exasperated. I call this the *Oh God, help me* look. Their eyes will roll straight up to the sky as if looking for divine intervention. People may do this when you pursue a topic they don't want to discuss, particularly when they hit a point of hopelessness or exasperation.

Oh God, help me!

DEER IN HEADLIGHTS:

This is that thousand-yard stare you get when someone's F3 kicks in. More specifically, it's the Freeze response staring you in the face. This can happen as a result of a perceived threat or the fear of being caught in a lie. In a moment of Freeze, a person's faculties will briefly abandon them as the fear takes over.

Deer in headlights

SHOCK:

Typically we see only the whites of someone's eyes to the left and right of the iris (the colored part of the eye). When someone's F3 kicks in, however, you might see the whites of their eyes above or below the iris as well. There is a Japanese term for this, *san pak ku*, which means "three whites." It is brief and can last for just a second but can be a good indicator that a person is under stress.

San pa ku

The Mouth

The mouth is an interesting place when it comes to reading people. As the origin of our speech, this is where we hold much of our tension. When we tell a lie, it is the delivery mechanism we use to convey our words. And so it is only fitting that it can give us away the most, regardless of the words we use.

When we are angry or stressed, we may see a clenching of one's jaw or the grinding of teeth. When we're nervous or afraid, we may see the biting down of lips, tightening of the mouth, or twisting the lips to one side. Dry mouth is also a common symptom of nervousness, which can be tipped off by exaggerated swallowing.

Another big tell is frequent sighs or yawns. Although the science as to why is not yet fully understood, it appears that we tend to yawn more when under heightened states of stress. This is partially due to the fact that stress causes our body to heat up and so, when our brains feel our internal temperature rise, yawning helps cool things off.

Smile

Don't take a smile at face value. After all, some people can smile to your face and stab you in the back. When someone smiles genuinely, the smile will affect their entire face. The edges of the mouth will almost reach the edges of a person's eyes. When it's real, conveying an authentic feeling of pleasure or humor or warmth, a smile will transform someone's face completely. There is actually a name for this expression—it is referred to as the *Duchenne smile*.

Genuine smile   Fake smile

Guillaume Duchenne was a French neurologist in the mid-nineteenth century who identified what happens to facial muscles when we smile. The zygomatic major muscles in the lower portion of the face raise the corners of the mouth and the orbicularis oculi muscles raise the cheeks. (This repetitive movement is what causes crow's feet around the eyes.) Research also shows that a genuine smile typically lasts between 0.5 and 4 seconds.

Fake smiles, on the other hand, typically last for a much shorter span—a quick flash and then it's gone. Or much longer, as in those cases when the smile seems to be plastered onto the person's face. It's also easy to distinguish a fake smile from a real one in that fake smiles often affect only the bottom half of the face, leaving the eyes and cheeks relatively neutral.

Laughter

Have you ever had an argument with someone or asked them a serious question and they laughed? You might be quick to get offended and snap back with "Don't laugh at me" or "This is no laughing matter." When you do this, however, you're letting your ego do the talking, which as you now know is not what you want when you're trying to read people. In many of these instances, they're not really laughing at you—it's their F3 response kicking in, looking to release the tension they're feeling. In fact, they may not even realize they're doing it.

When someone smiled or laughed during an interview, no matter how serious the topic, I did nothing more than make a mental note of it. Although it seemed inappropriate, I knew it was a kind of release valve for the tension they were feeling rather than a response to something they found humorous. If I had interrupted that moment by pointing out their odd behavior, I wouldn't have been able to later use it to identify another leak the next time it happened.

Again, you don't want to point out this behavior because once someone becomes aware of it, they will try to correct it, and that in turn makes it more difficult for you to assess them. It will also put the other person on the defensive or cause them to stop talking altogether. Remember—the goal is to keep people talking, not shut them down.

Head Movements

A person's nonverbal behavior should align with their verbal behavior. This is especially true when it comes to head movements while answering questions. If someone answers a question you ask by saying "No" and then—almost without meaning to—nodding their head up and down as a nonverbal sign of saying "Yes," take note of it. The same holds true for a "Yes" verbal answer, but a nonverbal "No" head shake. Those sorts of inconsistencies matter when you're trying to decipher what a person says versus what they actually mean.

UPPER BODY
HANDS
Because most people use their hands as illustrators (more on this below), you'll occasionally see someone "put them away"—such as inside their pockets, under their legs when sitting, or tucked away in their lap. People will typically do this when they want to be less forthcoming, less talkative, or less open. When I see someone hiding their hands, I often question if they're hiding something deeper.

FIDGETING
People are prone to fidgeting when nervous. They may start playing with pens or other objects in front of them, rubbing their hands together, scratching themselves, cracking their knuckles, or biting their fingernails. All of this could be a symptom of an activated F3 response. If a person engages in any of these behaviors that show up right around the time the conversation gets difficult, it may be an indication that they're pretty anxious or trying to withhold something from you.

GROOMING
Beyond fidgeting, you may see people grooming themselves when their F3 kicks in. For women, hair twirling is a way of channeling nervous energy. For men, they may start pulling on their mustache or their beard. In the interrogation room, we often watched in amusement as people would start picking imaginary lint off their clothes right around the time they had to answer a tough question, while others would obsessively start to smooth out wrinkles in their clothing. Although fidgeting is not a sure sign of deception, when you notice this happening, see if it corresponds with any particular part of the dialogue that might be worth noting.

ILLUSTRATORS

People who frequently gesture with their hands when they're talking are called *Illustrators*. I'm one of them. Like most Greeks, when I speak, my hands are everywhere—flying up and down, right and left (except for when I'm interviewing someone, of course, but that's for another chapter). Typically, when someone tells a story—especially an event they're recalling—they may tell it with illustrators or gestures because they are reliving the event as they tell it, which is an indication of truthfulness. On the other hand, if they are stoic and rigid in their movements or don't gesture at all, that could indicate a manufactured or rehearsed narrative—a possible sign of deception.

POSTURE

A person's posture is a strong indicator of both their physical energy and mental composure. When speaking with someone, look at how they're sitting or standing. Are they upright, slouching, or leaning to one side? A person who carries themselves upright can convey confidence, arrogance, or defiance, while a person who slouches may convey weakness, fear, or guilt. Also, assess whether they appear rigid or relaxed. A person may freeze when stressed, nervous, or lying, whereas a person with a more relaxed posture may indicate a more relaxed mind.

Confident/upright posture   Insecure/slouching posture

Body orientation can also tell you what someone is feeling. A person who is interested in you or what you have to say will often lean in with their body frontally aligned to yours. If they're leaning away or turned to one side, it's a signal that they're less interested in you or the topic at hand. And if by chance you see them subtly leaning toward the door—the fleeing position—they are no longer invested in what you're saying. The same holds true when someone starts moving toward the exit while you're still talking. Rather than trying to finish your thought, it's best to save your words for another time when they're mentally present.

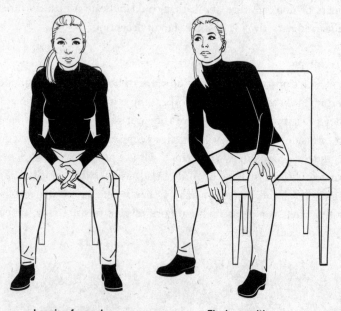

Leaning forward   **Fleeing position**

SUPPORTIVE AND DEFENSIVE GESTURES

Sometimes you'll see people lean forward with their elbows on the table and their chin resting in their hands. This is what's called a *supportive gesture*—meaning a gesture in which someone feels the need to physically support themselves. Maybe they're tired or feeling lonely or vulnerable. Gestures like this are meant to provide self-comfort. If someone needs to comfort themselves repeatedly throughout a conversation, you should begin to wonder why.

Supportive gesture   Defensive position

It is also natural for people who feel uncomfortable, defensive, or threatened to cross their arms in front of their chest. This is considered a *defensive posture*. If you think about it, when you cross your arms, you're effectively creating your own shield and protecting the most vulnerable part of your body—your vital organs. This could be an indication there's something that person is trying to protect or defend.

LOWER BODY

SETTING UP THE ROOM

Before I interview someone, I always spend a few minutes reorganizing the furniture in the room, if possible. I do this to ensure there's nothing blocking me from seeing the entire body of the person I'm talking to. My objective is to have them sit in a chair with nothing between us. That means no desks or tables, because the upper half of a person can tell one story, while the lower half can say something completely different.

During one polygraph I conducted for a prospective new hire for the Secret Service, I remember the applicant looked great on paper. Her background was flawless. As we sat and talked, she had perfect composure and all the right answers. Everything about the interview was going smoothly—until we got to the drug question.

"Have you ever experimented with drugs?" I asked her.

Up until this point, she had been calm and collected, sitting with her legs crossed. But as soon as we turned to the topic of drugs her crossed leg began to bounce up and down repeatedly. "No," she said.

For the entire interview prior to this moment, her legs had remained still, and now her foot was bobbing up and down, up and down.

First red flag.

Typically, when people refuse to admit to any drug experimentation, it's because they've either used so many different drugs or a particular drug so many times that by policy, they're unqualified to get the job. Most federal agencies have limits on illegal drug involvement. And so instead of admitting to some or all of their usage, applicants simply say nothing and roll the dice in hopes of not getting caught.

On her application, this candidate had listed "zero" drug use, and now she had just verbally committed to that answer as well. I silently took note of the change in her physical behavior and moved on to other topics. As I did, her bobbing leg fell still. I made a mental note of that, too.

Second red flag.

After we had covered the remaining questions on the exam, I returned to the topic of drug use. "I know we've already discussed this," I said. "But I wanted to revisit this question one more time to see if anything else came to mind."

When conducting pre-employment polygraphs for the Service, my job wasn't to browbeat or force information. Rather, it was to give the candidate the opportunity to amend their application or offer them an empathetic ear. And I gave her another opportunity to talk about her drug experimentation, if she so chose to do so. She declined. Instantly, her leg started bouncing again. So much, in fact, that in my mind she was no longer waving the red flag—she was kicking it.

Third red flag.

That's when I realized there was an issue—she likely wasn't being truthful about her drug use, which meant she was going to fail her polygraph. Although I was already fairly certain of the outcome, I attached the components to her anyway. I administered the polygraph and each time I asked her the drug question, she had a strong physiological response. She was lying and her body knew it. She failed.

The next time you're trying to read someone, keep an eye out for what their lower body is doing: legs bouncing, ankles rolling, feet tapping. And pay close attention to when they start and stop. Again, it doesn't mean they are lying, but it does mean there is likely something about that part of the conversation that's making them uncomfortable.

CROSSED LEGS

Like lower-body movements, lower-body positioning can be just as telling. Crossed legs, for example, can communicate everything from attraction and comfort to revulsion or the desire for more distance. The next time you see two people on a date, take notice of whether their legs are crossed, and if so, in which direction. If one of them crosses their legs toward the other, that can indicate the feeling of ease or even wanting to be closer. If crossed away, however, I'd bet money that date is not going particularly well.

Some people may also cross their legs as a way to create a barrier between them and someone else or they might lean away or clasp their shin in one hand to block off even more of their body.

SPACING

If you want to better understand the relational dynamics between people, look at how much space is between their bodies while interacting. Take an on-screen kissing scene between two actors. If their upper and lower bodies are fully engaged—meaning there's very little, if any, space between them—it's likely that they're both comfortable with the scene and each other. But if you see only their upper bodies pressed together while their feet are positioned much farther apart, perhaps they aren't fully comfortable, either with the scene itself or the person they're acting with.

The same holds true for hugging. Our hugs vary according to our level of comfort or intimacy with another person. Some hugs involve nothing more than a slight shoulder-to-shoulder touch accompanied with a single-arm wraparound and a light pat on the back—think of those once-a-year social gathering hugs where you haven't seen certain people in a while. As in, "I'm happy to see you . . . but from over there." Other hugs, however, are a full-on body hug—feet close together, hands wrapped around each other, a strong squeeze.

The next time someone hugs you pay attention to the details. Is it light and brief, or strong and drawn out? Does the person pull away quickly? Is it toe-to-toe or is there enough distance between your lower bodies to drive a truck through? Each of these factors can be indicative of the strength or weakness of the relationship.

Distant hug

My husband and I attended a wedding not long ago. Like me, the bride came from a Greek background, which meant that the reception was true to form a *Big Fat Greek Wedding*. It took place in a massive banquet hall with more than five hundred guests. Loud music poured through the speakers, energizing the room while we waited for the new couple to make their first appearance after the ceremony. At last, the emcee picked up the mic and loudly announced in a radio DJ voice, "Everybody! Please put your hands together to welcome the bride and groom!"

Everyone stood up and started clapping, hooting and howling, as the newlyweds walked in. The bride came in first wearing her beautiful white dress, one hand high in the air holding her bouquet, dancing and fist-pumping to the music. She entered with an overwhelming kind of energy. A bit over-the-top. Her other hand was down at her side, stretched out behind her, clasped in the hand of the groom. There was a small but awkward gap between their bodies.

First red flag.

He, a full arm's length behind her, walked in slowly—a bit rigid in his movements.

Second red flag.

He was smiling, but there was something off with his smile. It was frozen and plastered in place.

Third red flag.

I turned to my husband, who has the same training and experience when it comes to reading people, to see if he was seeing what I was. Before I could say a word, and without taking his eyes off the couple, he said, "Six months."

I looked back at the couple and felt a sense of sadness because I knew he was right.

Eight months later, they divorced.

For better or for worse, if you know how to pay attention to what people express through their movements and physical mannerisms, you will learn to see the truth beneath the surface.

Chapter 12

What Are They Really Saying?

*Most people, in fact, will not take the trouble in finding out the truth,
but are much more inclined to accept the first story they hear.*
—THUCYDIDES

How to Spot a Liar

I recently attended an interview training course at the Los Angeles
Police Department (LAPD). I was working on an investigative report-
ing story for my master's project for Columbia University, so I attended
not as a federal agent, but as a journalist. During one of the training
blocks, the instructors put on a scenario: They brought in two undercover LAPD detectives to tell two similar stories. These detectives were
masters when it came to deception; after all, their very lives depended
on not being caught in a lie.

The exercise was as follows: One at a time, and without the other
being in the room, each detective sat in front of the class and told a seven-
minute story about a trip he took to Egypt. The twist—one detective had
actually gone to Egypt and the other hadn't. Our task was to figure out
who was telling the truth and who was lying.

The first began with an elaborate recount of visiting family, seeing
the sights, and touring the pyramids, with a detailed description of everything that he saw. We all listened intently, but I didn't catch anything
that would have indicated he was lying.

Then the second detective came in and told his story. He too described in great detail his trip to Egypt, seeing many of the same sights, and his visit to the pyramids. Once again, everything he said fit. It seemed entirely plausible that he, too, was telling the truth—until he got to one little detail.

"So we walked into this tomb," he said, gesturing around as if he were back in the pyramid. "The doorway was here. And the column would be here."

In that moment I knew—he was the liar.

After the two LAPD detectives had told us their stories, one of the instructors asked everyone who they thought was the liar. At first no one said a thing. After a few moments passed, I raised my hand. "It was the second story," I said. "That was the lie."

"How did you know that?" the instructor asked me.

"It was the verb tense he used. Rather than saying 'the column *was* here' he said, 'the column *would be* here.'" He was imagining in real time where a column in an Egyptian pyramid might have been rather than recalling its location from memory. Though it was such a subtle shift that most people would never notice it, that simple verb tense slip-up is what gave him away.

Disclaimer

In this chapter, I'll describe and decipher some of the most common verbal red flags that come up in everyday conversations. It's important to remember that none of these are absolute indicators of deception. Not only are people uniquely different in how they respond to stress physically, but the same holds true for how they respond verbally. So it's best not to jump to conclusions based solely off one suspicious sentence or remark, but to take notice. That's why getting a baseline is so important—to establish a person's verbal patterns prior to engaging in any heightened conversation. Then when you see these phrases emerge from their normal way of speaking at a pivotal moment, it's time to pay closer attention. Some of these verbal tactics might be familiar to you already.

You're so dumb.

"That's a stupid question."
"I already told so-and-so about that."
"Do I have to answer that again?"
"You already asked me that."
"You already know the answer."

These are the sorts of things people say to try to shut down a line of inquiry. The person is hoping that by making you feel dumb or criticized for asking a question, you'll back off and let it go. Instead, you should recognize these avoidance tactics and press for answers.

You should know better.

"As I assume you already know . . ."
"You should already be aware . . ."
"You've already been told this, but . . ."

I recently received an email from a producer in which each of her first two paragraphs began with the phrase *"As I'm sure you are aware . . ."* The producer then went on to explain several things that I had zero prior knowledge about. Oftentimes, when people begin a conversation with statements such as these, it's an over-the-top effort to place the onus of having shared knowledge onto the recipient. Simply put, if you don't already know what I'm telling you, then you're either stupid or weren't paying attention. If anyone ever starts communicating with you using these phrases, and what they're telling you is not something you would have known prior, simply respond with "How would I have already known this?" That way, you put the burden of explaining their subtle jab back onto them.

You talkin' to me?

"Who, me?"
"Are you asking me?"

A person may also repeat the question back to you, such as:

"What did I do last night?"
"Did I miss the deadline?"

When someone answers a question with a question, it's typically a stalling tactic while they figure out how to respond. They're hoping that if they appear confused by the question or act like they didn't hear it, you'll ask it again or ask in a different way, giving them a few more precious seconds to think. The next time someone responds like this, ask yourself, "Did I stutter or mumble my words? Is there anyone else in the room whom I should be addressing?" If it feels like they are stalling and you know that you spoke clearly and concisely, then I suggest you respond with a simple "Yes" to indicate that was the question you asked. If their stress level wasn't already high, it will be once they see you patiently watching and waiting for their response.

I have better things to do.
"How long is this going to take?"
"I have more important things to do."
"I don't have time for this."
"Are we done yet?"

I'd hear this a lot from guilty suspects who wanted to make me feel like I was wasting their time. If you think back on the story in chapter 10 about the mom who abused her child, one of the things that tipped me off to her guilt was the fact that she acted as though she had better things to do than talk with me. Although not every situation will be as extreme as that one, it's important to realize that when someone uses *time wasting* as a tactic, it's usually an indicator that you've stumbled onto a topic they're uncomfortable with or don't want to discuss. When that happens, take your time, ask good questions, and don't let them make you feel rushed.

What's the Big Deal?
"Is this really that big a deal?"

"I didn't think it was that important."
"Let's not make a big thing out of this."
"You're making this into a bigger issue than it really is."

This is a tactic used by a person when they're trying to minimize the situation. They know it's a big deal—that's why they don't want to talk about whatever it is you're asking them. So, instead they'll make it seem as though you're the one blowing things out of proportion. The reality is, they just want you to move on to something else. Don't let them convince you that your questions aren't important. They are, so keep asking.

Refusing to Commit

"That's pretty much all I know."
"That's about it."
"I don't think there's anything else to say."
"Off the top of my head I can't think of anything else."
"Nothing else is coming to mind right now."
"I'm pretty sure I told you everything."

When someone uses this verbal tactic, they're trying to make it seem as though they've either told you everything or they can't think of anything else to say. But by saying things such as "pretty sure," "off the top of my head," and "that's about it," they're giving themselves an out in case more information comes up later. In that case, they can simply tell you, "Ah, yes, now I remember," or "I forgot about that until you brought it up." When someone answers your questions with such vagueness, probe further. Make them commit to their answers. If they won't, then you can bet there's more they're not telling you.

Lying by Omission

"I don't know."
"I can't recall."
"I forgot."
"I have no idea."

This is one of the most common things people say when they don't want to talk about something. Most often, it's stated as "I don't remember." My six-year-old niece has become an expert in using this tactic because she learned it was a great way to get people to leave her alone. It has become her go-to response to stop any line of questioning that she wants to avoid.

These responses are also used by someone willing to tell you part of the truth, but maybe not the whole truth. Their memory will suddenly grow foggy and imprecise. I sometimes refer to it as the "I think I have amnesia" tactic. Although hearing "I don't know" once in a while is common and appropriate, pay special attention to *when* it shows up. Ask yourself, "Do they really not know, or are they feigning uncertainty?" If their supposed amnesia begins clustering around a certain uncomfortable topic, consider it a red flag.

The Non-Answer

Q: "What time did you get home last night?"
A: "I usually get home around 6 p.m."

In the above scenario, does the person actually answer the question? People do this to avoid giving you the complete truth or having to tell you a blatant lie. They are answering your question without really answering it. They're telling you what they typically do. If you're not paying careful attention, you may miss it and accept what they say as an answer, but the example above is a clear evasion. The questioner doesn't ask what time do you *usually* get home. They ask specifically what time you got home last night. The appropriate response would be something like, "I got home at six."

Divine Intervention

"I swear to God."
"I swear on my children."
"I swear on my mother's grave."
"As God is my witness."

Here's the thing: The truth is simple. But when someone is trying to sell you a lie, they will work really hard to do it. They'll invoke deities and dead parents and any number of loved ones to try to exonerate themselves. A truthful person doesn't have to do this. They'll tell you the straightforward truth. So, when you hear these oversells, ask yourself, "Why is this person trying so hard to convince me?"

Catastrophic Event

"Professor, I'm sorry I didn't finish the assignment. My aunt died."
"My grandfather's house burnt down."
"My dog was hit by a car."

To avoid a deadline or shirk obligations, people may offer up some type of catastrophic event. This kind of excuse is also designed to make you feel bad enough to not ask follow-up probing questions. A relative dying is a common excuse—and it will usually be a distant relative because people don't want to use their immediate family members. It hits too close to home. Or being stuck at home deathly ill with the flu. I can't tell you how many of my students suddenly lose relatives, or suffer horrible illnesses right around the time of an exam or when a research paper is due. Of course, tragic things really do happen. But like all verbal cues, it's important to pay attention to how and when they happen.

Don't you know who I think I am?

"I'm a married man. I would never cheat!"
"I'm a doctor. I would never risk my profession."
"I'm a CEO. I don't need to steal."
"I'm a man of faith. I would never betray anyone."

These excuses may come up when people feel they should be given a pass because of their status. They may use their identity as a defense against being called out for any kind of wrongdoing. Let's take the first response, for example, *"I'm a married man. I would never cheat."* Just because someone is married doesn't mean they won't cheat. Some people are married and cheat all the time. One doesn't have anything to do with the other. When you hear someone invoke their status as a means of convincing you of something, ask yourself, "Why," and then ask them why that matters.

You're picking on me.

"You're just picking on me because you don't like me." (Kids love this one.)
"You're harassing me."
"You're doing this because of my race/gender/religion/sexual preference."

People may use this tactic as a way of frightening you off. Someone might say this when they're being disciplined or reprimanded in some way to avoid consequences or a difficult conversation. While I in no way want to discount the biases and prejudices that undoubtedly play a huge role in people's professional and personal lives, the fact is that people of all genders, races, and religions are equally likely to make mistakes *and* lie. Calling someone out for messing up is part of life, so be mindful when people use this as a manipulation tactic.

Emphatic Denial

"I absolutely did not stop for a drink on my way home!"
"Never! I would never do such a thing! How dare you even ask!"
"Absolutely not! I did not do that!"
"I categorically deny everything you just said."

Over-the-top denials are intended to be so emphatic and dramatic as to eliminate any trace of doubt from your mind. But remember, the truth is simple. When someone tells the truth, they tend to tell it directly and matter-of-factly.
Q: "Did you stop for a drink on the way home?"
A: "No, I didn't."
Truthful people know what they did and didn't do, so in their minds they don't need to work hard to convince you of the truth.

Integrity Qualifiers

"Honestly, I didn't see her there."
"In all truthfulness, I've never been to that place before."
"Well, to be perfectly honest with you . . ."

Unless someone's speech is normally dotted with these sorts of qualifiers, words like *honestly* and *truthfully* should be red flags. They're basically saying, "Don't believe anything I've said up to this point—now I'm telling you the truth." They're overcompensating in their response. Truthful statements don't need qualification.

Don't trust me.
"You're not going to believe this."
"This might sound crazy, but . . ."

This is another one of those unnecessary oversells, and this sort of statement should make you predisposed to doubt whatever the person is about to say next. If it happened, why wouldn't I believe it? Why assume I wouldn't? There's likely something off about a story preceded by this sort of framing, so hold on to some skepticism.

"Trust me. I know what I'm doing."

Whenever you hear someone say something like this, whether they're a financial planner, a car salesman, or a relative trying to fix a leaky sink, usually the last thing you should do is trust them. For example, when you ask your financial planner how he intends to invest your money and instead of explaining his investment strategy, he responds, "Trust me, I know what I'm doing"—take your money and run.

Oh, by the way . . .
"Oh, by the way, the deadline for that report is tomorrow."
"Oh, forgot to mention—I need to take a few days off next week."
"Oh, before you go, can I borrow your car?"

If you've been talking to someone for a while and they tack something on right before the conversation ends, you can assume that was the thing they actually were most interested in discussing with you. Some people use this tactic as a way of sneaking in a last-minute request or revealing an important piece of information when your guard is down. If a coworker or a friend has a habit of doing this, keep that guard up.

Third Person

"Joe Smith is an honest guy."
"Betty Jones would never do that."
"John Davis is not that guy anymore."

When people talk about themselves in the third person, it's called an *illeism*. In my experience, this typically signifies two things:

1. That person could be a narcissist. Narcissists tend to talk about themselves in grandiose, overdramatic ways, and referring to themselves in the third person definitely falls under that category of behavior.
2. That person is putting distance between themselves and their actions to avoid accountability. Think about the cheater who says, "John Davis is not that guy anymore. That guy had an affair, but that's not me." First of all, it is him. He didn't become a wholly different person—he just wants you to believe that. And second, he's trying to manipulate your understanding of the situation and his role in it. Don't fall for either of these.

The conclusion here is simple: if anyone talks about themselves in the third person, it's best to stay away from both them and their alter ego.

Verb Tenses

"So, I find this wallet and there's no money in it."
"This guy walks up and starts punching me."
"I'm walking to school and suddenly the wind blows all of my homework away."

True stories live in the past. What I mean by this is that when someone is recalling something that's already happened, they speak in the past tense. That is how recall works—we describe the sequence of events as they occurred in our memory.

When you're creating a lie, you're doing it in the present moment. If someone is telling a story and they switch from past to present tense, pay attention. *"I find,"* vs. *"I found," "walks up and starts punching"* vs. *"walked up and punched," "wind blows,"* vs. *"wind blew."* These descriptors become red flags when they're not in the past tense, usually because the person is making up details on the spot. This is a good time to ask some specific questions to determine if the person telling a story is actually recalling or creating an event.

Why "I" Matters

"Love you."
"Going to the store."
"Be home around eight."

People regularly use the word *I* when talking about themselves. It's a way of taking ownership of their actions. When a person avoids using *I*, they may be trying to distance themselves from whatever it is they're saying. Think about the difference between *"Love you"* vs. *"I love you."* The absence of *"I"* in the first instance diminishes the conviction of the statement. Of course, this is less true in texting these days, but in speech or even in long-form writing, the absence of *"I"* should be a red flag. In fact, *"I"* will occur about every sixteen words in writing, so keep an *eye* out for any conspicuous overuses or absences. Typically, anything more means the person may be narcissistic or depressed (self-consumed), while anything less means a lack of personal commitment.

No Answer Is an Answer

". . ."

If there is a delay or notable pause after you ask someone a direct question such as "Did you take the money out of my wallet?" it could be a major red flag. When an F3 response kicks in, people may Freeze and go silent. This means that the topic has affected them so greatly they may be unable to think, much less verbally respond. The truth is usually spontaneous, so if someone pauses, take note of that.

Chapter 13

How People Read You

*The way to gain a good reputation is to endeavor
to be what you desire to appear.*
—SOCRATES

First Impressions Don't Come Twice

"It's not what's on the outside that matters, but what's on the inside that counts." Although I agree that true power comes from within, our physical appearance is still the first thing people see when we show up. That being said, if you saw yourself walk into a room, what would you think? What do you imagine others think when they see you? In this chapter, we're going to talk about how to make yourself appear open, observant, and confident.

Every day, you control your image. This can be as simple as, did you brush your hair? Did you iron your shirt? Are your shoes shined and your teeth clean? Standing in front of the mirror, do you look put together and prepared or disheveled? Research shows it takes only seconds for people to form an opinion of your level of competence and composure. Are you someone they can trust or would rather avoid? Once first impressions are set, they're nearly impossible to change. If you take this into account, you can make life a lot easier by putting thought and time into projecting the image you want the world to see right from the start.

When I started appearing on TV, I was shocked by how much time and effort the hair and makeup people spent on my look. *My God, did I leave the house looking like a total mess?* I wondered. But then I realized that wasn't the issue. A few random hairs out of place might not be particularly conspicuous in daily life, but on TV it could make anyone look totally unkempt and unprepared. It wasn't about trying to make me look pretty; it was about making sure that viewers weren't distracted by my appearance so they could focus on what I was saying.

With that in mind, we should be thoughtful about our own appearance in the public eye. This doesn't mean spending an hour primping for a ten-minute drive to the local coffee bar—I certainly don't. But it does mean that when we know our appearance is about to become center stage—for instance, walking into a board meeting, a job interview, or giving a presentation—maybe it's not the best time to try a new fashion statement like a new makeup trend or ostentatious tie. Our outward appearance can be a huge attention grabber, and depending on the context, not always in a good way.

Because your clothing can have a powerful impact on how others perceive you, always consider your audience when you're picking out your wardrobe. If, for example, you're addressing a group of corporate executives, wearing a brightly colored outfit may make you look less professional, and in turn your input less impactful. Yet, if you're an elementary school teacher, wearing bright colors is probably an excellent choice because children love exuberant things. There are different versions of you for different situations and each might have a different look.

As Special Agents assigned to the PPD, we typically wore suits. But they couldn't be just any suits, they had to be dark gray, navy, or black, and our dress shirts were either white or light blue. There was nothing showy about our appearance, and that was the point. We were not there to draw attention to ourselves. Rather, we wanted to blend into the background, yet still make our presence known—or more important, *felt*. Our dark suits and muted colored shirts made us look professional, serious, and powerful. Throw in a pair of dark framed sunglasses and you have the signature Secret Service look. This look is not an accident.

It is specifically engineered to intimidate. The Service understands that our outward appearance has a direct psychological effect on the public. When used correctly, it becomes one more layer of security against a world full of potential threats. As agents, we were always playing a role. And we needed to communicate that role in the most effective way possible. I was taught to dress and groom myself such that, without saying a word, I could convey a strong message about who I was and who I wasn't. In that role, I was powerful and intimidating. I wasn't someone to be messed with.

Each presentation of *you* sends a different message. You can and should influence your appearance in order to mirror your message. When deciding on your look, ask yourself, "Who is my audience and what am I trying to convey?"

Master Your Poker Face

When trying to read people, you want them to speak uninhibitedly, so even if you don't like what they have to say, you don't want to openly judge them. When people feel judged, their walls go up. They begin to filter their words and behaviors, carefully choosing what they think they should and should not say to you. And in some instances, they may shut down completely. When this occurs, you lose the ability to read them accurately and collect the information you need.

One of the fundamental things I learned when talking to people is to maintain awareness of my facial expressions and body language. Because I know the person I'm communicating with is reading me as well, it takes conscious effort to maintain that self-awareness. They don't need to know what is going on in my mind. I need to know what's going on in theirs.

Having a good poker face is not just about sitting emotionless while the other person is talking to you. It's about masking your true feelings while collecting the details you need. So be attentive and nod politely as a way to encourage them to continue speaking. Make sure that you're actively listening the whole time and be aware of the signals your face and posture may be revealing. Don't roll your eyes, clench your jaw, or cross your arms in front of you. These subtle gestures can easily make people close themselves off. Instead, maintain a soft facial expression, hold a relaxed pose, and lean forward. Act like you really care about what they are saying and that you really want to be there, even if you don't. Make sure that you appear positive and interested, all the while revealing nothing and inviting everything.

It isn't just professional interviewers like myself who use this tactic; many power players use this technique as well. Take Anna Wintour, the highly revered editor in chief of *Vogue* magazine, who with one look can make or break a career. She goes to the extreme lengths of wearing sunglasses while seated in the front row of fashion shows. Wintour does this because she doesn't want people to know what she is looking at, let alone what her reaction is, to the clothes coming down the runway.

What Your Body Language Says About You
OPENNESS
Try to imagine your posture right now through the eyes of someone else. Do you appear open? Welcoming? Confident? What kind of shifts can you make in how you're positioned to better create that impression?

Start by making yourself physically open—arms and legs uncrossed, palms unhidden. Keep your hands out of your pockets or resting on a table if you're seated across from someone. Don't slouch—let your chest be open, your head level. If you appear inviting and relaxed, the other person may automatically pick up on that and will likely mirror you (more on this in chapter 21). Since you want to get a baseline with someone before you try to read them, being able to put people at ease is a great skill to learn.

EYE CONTACT
When you make eye contact, it increases that person's trust and confidence in you. It shows that you're engaged and interested in what they have to say, that they're worthy of your time and attention. You want the person you're reading to feel like they matter to you and maintaining easy eye contact with them is a great way to create this impression.

In a Cornell study, researchers looked at how characters on a cereal box influenced consumers' feelings about the brand. The study used two versions of the Trix Rabbit. One version had the rabbit looking down toward the cereal. The second version had the rabbit looking directly at the consumer. The study showed that consumers felt more trust and connection with the cereal box image of the rabbit looking directly at them, showing just how much value we place in eye contact.

FIDGETING

Just as fidgeting can signify anxiety or nervousness when you observe it in another person, the same is true of you. If you notice that you're going into a conversation full of nervous energy, try some breathing or meditative exercises to calm yourself first. You want to emanate ease and openness, so don't fidget or start picking lint off your clothing when you're having a conversation. Don't tug or twirl your hair—whether it's on your head or on your face. Don't play with pens or objects nearby. These behaviors not only demonstrate nervousness, they can be distracting or even annoying to the person you're speaking with.

BARRIERS

Whenever possible, remove any physical barriers that separate you from other people. Not only can tables or desks cut you off from seeing the lower half of someone you're trying to read, but these objects can create divisions between you and your audience as well. Every time I teach or am asked to speak to a large group, the first thing I do is get out from behind the podium because I know a podium creates a "me-versus-them" dynamic. I want my words to reach the people listening so they can feel connected to me, and that we are in this together.

For a lot of people, public speaking can be pretty stressful. They'll spend hours or even days trying to memorize countless facts and information in the hopes of appearing competent. But did you know that most people stop listening about three minutes into a presentation because their minds wander or they get bored. It's a challenge to hold people's attention for a long period of time. This is why connecting with your audience is just as important as knowing your facts.

Even in less public settings, people like to use barriers to hide their bodies. Some people will keep a purse on their lap, others a notebook or a resumé or a clipboard. All of these objects create distance and may even give off the impression that you're trying to hide something. Whether you're in a job interview or sales pitch or meeting someone for the first time, remember to keep your body open and unobstructed.

Think strategically about what you are trying to convey through your appearance, and how that can strongly influence the effectiveness of your communication.

Chapter 14

It's Not What You Say, But How You Say It

Be as you wish to be seen.
—Socrates

The Wrong Version of Myself

One of my first job interviews after leaving the Secret Service was at Fox News. At the time, I didn't know much about the network, or about how to pitch myself as a contributor. It was a bit naïve, but I trusted that my resumé and professional experience would speak for itself.

I had come from a paramilitary culture where you addressed a supervisor with near reverence. There was a chain of command, and over the years I had been groomed to respect that hierarchy and refrain from speaking freely. Most of my on-the-job speech consisted of "Yes, sir." "No, sir." "I will, sir." And just having come off the presidential detail, I had amplified that behavior even more. As an agent, I was meant to blend into the background. I spoke in hushed tones. Moved out of shots so I wouldn't be in any photos with the president. It was my job to protect and shield while trying to offer as much privacy as I could. My presence was meant to be felt, but not meant to be seen.

So when I met with Bill Shine, the senior executive at Fox News at the time, I still embodied this mindset. I listened. I was respectful and spoke in a cool, calm voice. I was composed and articulate as

I presented all of my accomplishments. My degrees. The languages I spoke. My expertise at being a trained interviewer. Surely that would be an attractive quality in a potential journalist?

But, it turns out the Secret Service persona doesn't really make for great television.

A week after my interview, my agent told me that Fox had passed on me. When I asked why, she told me that they didn't give a reason. I was perplexed. What had I done wrong?

I wanted to understand, and since I had already lost the job, I figured it couldn't get any worse. I decided to call and ask him directly.

"Hello, Mr. Shine—this is Evy Poumpouras. You interviewed me for a position with your network."

"Yes . . ." he said, clearly a little unsettled to be called out of the blue.

"Sir, my agent told me that you had passed on me."

"Yes. That is correct."

"May I ask why?"

He paused. "We just felt you might not be the right fit here."

"Mr. Shine, I appreciate your diplomatic answer, but it doesn't help me. I need to know what I may have done wrong. There is a reason you passed on me and I'd like to know why." There was silence on the other end, so I added, "It would help me so that when I go on future interviews, I can correct or adjust how I present myself. I'd really appreciate your feedback."

"Look," he said, "I'm sure you're as tough as they come. You were an agent and did all these extraordinary things. But you don't exude that. The way you present doesn't match up with what you are—and in TV, that matters. You seemed—demure. And . . . your voice—you need to work on that. It needs to be stronger. Deeper. You need to sound like you know what you are talking about. That's how to get people to listen in TV. People don't just listen to what you say—they listen to how you say it. Oh, and your speech."

"My speech?"

"Where are you from?" he asked.

"I'm from Queens."

"Yeah. You sound like it. But there is something else I'm also hearing."

"I'm Greek."

"You have to fix those two things. Your accent is too thick for TV. You need to learn to speak neutral American. This is how you can relate to people watching from different parts of the country."

"Okay," I said. "Thank you for your honesty."

"No problem," he replied.

I immediately hung up and dialed the number for William Esper Studios, where I had studied and graduated from acting school. I always had a passion for the arts. I minored in fine art in college and then enrolled in a two-year professional actor's program while I was an agent in New York City. Not only did it help hone my craft as an actor, but it made me a better undercover agent. Laith, a dear friend and actor who managed the studio, answered.

"Habibti!" he bellowed into the phone. *My dear.*

"Hi, Habibi," I replied. *My dear.* "Laith, I need your help."

"Anything," he said.

"I need to fix my voice. My accent, too."

"I hear you. I've been working for years to neutralize my accent. I got you, Habibti. I'll speak to one of the voice and speech instructors here to give you some lessons."

"Shukran, Laith." *Thank you.*

"Afuan, Habibti." *You're welcome.*

After I got off the phone, I did a Google search of the word *demure*. That word had stuck out conspicuously on my call with Bill Shine, but I had no idea what it meant. No one had ever called me that before.

This is what came up:

Demure *(adjective)*
(of a woman or her behavior) reserved, modest, and shy.
Synonyms: modest, unassuming, meek, mild, reserved, quiet, shy,
  bashful, diffident, reticent, timid, timorous, shrinking

What the fuck?!! That's not what I am. How dare he call me that?

And yet . . . my mind traveled back to my interview as I tried to look at myself through his eyes. I had been quiet. Overly respectful, still carrying myself as the subordinate I had been trained to be. As much as it bothered me, he had only told me the truth. His truth of what he saw and heard.

As it sank in, I realized I had made two vital mistakes:

1. I brought the wrong version of myself to this interview. Secret Service Evy was not what I should have presented.

2. My voice. Apart from maintaining a calm and quiet demeanor in the Service, I had never paid much attention to my voice or how I spoke. Not only had I never worked on building a more powerful voice, but in fact, I had tempered my speech. Because the truth is that the Secret Service draws mostly Type A personalities, and the vast majority are male. Add badges and guns to the mix and the level of ego and testosterone is on full throttle. And approximately only 2 percent of the agents on the president's detail at the time were women. It took a great deal of finesse to navigate that world, not to mention other law enforcement officials and members of the military. This was especially true during assignments where I was the one giving the orders. I didn't want to be perceived as bossy by my male colleagues (something that I had seen happen with my more forceful female peers), so I had created a habit of softening my voice so as not to offend those around me. Unfortunately, as a woman in this field, assertiveness and being a bitch seem to be one and the same. Though I had adapted my work persona for legitimate and strategic reasons, my interview at Fox News taught me that my so-called demure persona would no longer serve my new career in television. It wasn't a matter of changing who I was—it was a matter of amplifying my true voice.

Your True Voice

There is the voice we use. And then there is our true voice.

It is likely that the voice you're currently using is not your true voice. It is the voice that you have adopted over the course of your life. It contains all the markers of your confidence levels (or lack thereof), your insecurities, your fears, and your worries. It's probably molded by your race, culture, ethnicity, and gender. Girls, for example, tend to be socialized to have a softer, more timid voice. Boys, on the other hand, are told to speak up. Our voices are formed by our parents, the neighborhoods we grow up in, the schools we attend, whether we are nurtured or bullied by the people around us. Our voices can even be determined by socioeconomic factors or whatever current pressures may be weighing down on us.

The voice you're using belongs to all of the forces in the world that made you into what you are. And like any other part of you—your body, your mind, your soul—your voice is something that requires nurturing. But often it is the most neglected part of us. We put a far greater emphasis on what we say and what we look like. When we write speeches or presentations, we rehearse our sentences and memorize talking points. We pay attention to our clothes, to the image we present to the world. But we rarely pay attention to the vehicle we use to make ourselves heard. This is where the importance of our paralinguistics comes into play.

So what are paralinguistics? Essentially, it is the study of verbal communication beyond words. It's not so much about what we say, but how we say it. Paralinguistics include the accent and inflection we use, our pitch and tone, and not only the rate of our speech but the volume. Most of us haven't spent a great deal of time cultivating our voices, and so the habits we've formed in this domain are largely unconscious and automatic.

Studying your own paralinguistics is a remarkable opportunity for self-assessment. Once you begin to identify how your vocal habits reflect certain aspects of your life or life experiences, you can make conscious choices about which of those elements you want to keep and which you want to change—both internally and externally.

Have you ever listened to a recording of yourself and thought, *I don't really sound like that—do I?* If the voice that you hear doesn't feel like an authentic representation of what you imagine yourself to sound like, that means that the voice you're using is out of harmony with who you are. It's not your true voice. It might be the voice you were conditioned to use growing up, or the voice you learned to use to cope with a difficult situation in life like an abusive parent or an anxious sibling. Have you ever heard someone tell a difficult story from their childhood and suddenly their voice sounds higher and younger? This can happen with people who have experienced trauma at a young age. Those people are not in control of their paralinguistics, and so that younger wounded part of themselves comes through in moments of intense vulnerability. They're reliving that moment through the eyes (and voice) of their younger self.

We're also deeply influenced by the people around us. We pick up habits from others, in tone and pitch, inflection and pacing. When I spend time with my mom, I notice myself adopting certain parts of her speech patterns. It's entirely instinctive, and something that my husband always points out to me. But we all do this from time to time. If you have colleagues you want to impress, you may pick up some of their speech patterns. Or you might adopt the vocal mannerisms of your friends.

To begin gaining more awareness around your particular paralinguistics, the first thing to determine is where you habitually speak from. Some people who have a nasal quality to their voice tend to speak through their nose. Others who speak from their throat have a lower but more constrained sort of sound. People who talk from their chest tend to have a slightly higher, breathy tone of voice. And then there are those who speak from their belly, which gives them a deeper, louder, and more powerful resonance. After spending most of my life speaking from my throat, I trained myself to speak from my belly, which makes me feel more connected to my strength and power. As an exercise, try speaking through each of these distinct places—nose, throat, chest, belly—and listen for what sounds most like the voice you normally use. Then listen for which of those vocal tones feels best to you and then practice consciously speaking from there so you can project your most powerful voice.

How Others Hear You

University of Miami professor Casey Klofstad conducted a study of the 2012 election in which the vocal qualities of the candidates who ran and won were compared with those who lost. The study revealed that of the 435 candidates who ran, those with lower-pitch voices were more likely to win. And in another study, Klofstad found research subjects preferred a candidate with a lower-pitch voice. In particular, women with lower-pitch voices were seen as stronger and more confident, and therefore more electable.

Another multi-university study from 2002 looked into whether surgeons' tone of voice impacted the likelihood of their being sued for malpractice. The researchers listened to forty seconds of audio for each surgeon and found that those whose tone expressed dominance and apathy or lack of compassion were perceived as indifferent; as a result, they were more likely to be sued. Surgeons perceived to be warmer in tone and more professional in their communication were less likely to be sued.

Clearly, voice and speech play a major role in determining how we are perceived in the world, and can be equally powerful in influencing our success. Oftentimes we don't know what our paralinguistics are revealing about us or the impression our voices form in other people's minds. To begin gaining this awareness of yourself, let's break down some of the most common verbal habits that have the power to diminish or amplify your speech.

Pace: Fast vs. Slow

Fast: exudes nervousness

If you find that you tend to speak quickly, you likely sound like you are hurrying to get the words out. This creates the impression that you don't want to take up people's time because you think that what you have to say isn't that important. You are also more likely to stumble over your words and make mistakes. You may say things that you haven't clearly thought through and end up regretting later. Overall, speaking fast makes you appear overly nervous and less articulate.

Slow: exudes power

Now, I'm not necessarily talking about that slow, delayed sort of speech that you hear in the Deep South (no offense to my southern friends), but if you slow down your speech, you give yourself the time to think. Not only does this allow the listener to keep up and absorb the information you're offering, but it allows you to take the time you need to form your ideas and express them articulately.

Slow speech also sends the message that you and your ideas matter. It conveys confidence, that what you have to say is important and that you are worth taking up the listener's time. President Obama is a great example of this. As agents, whenever a protectee was moving from one place to another, we'd call it out over our radios to ensure everyone on the protective detail team knew. But with President Obama, it was almost a moot point because we could always hear him. When walking from the West Wing to the Residence, for example, his voice echoed through the corridors.

He also never rushed through any of his speeches, or any of his conversations. Do you think when President Barack Obama was speaking live on prime-time television he ever thought, *I better hurry up. I'm interrupting Grey's Anatomy?* No. He took his time, because he knew his words were both important and worth saying. And this mindset made him a remarkably powerful speaker. Yes, I understand that as the president of the United States his words mattered, but this isn't about *who* he was, but rather *how* he chose to speak. You don't have to be a world leader to speak with conviction.

Declarative Speech

The meaning and strength of a statement is determined not by its words, but by how it is spoken. When people are uncertain or insecure, their statements will often lift up at the end of a sentence, almost like they're asking a question rather than making a declarative statement. To take one of the most powerful and well-known declarative phrases of our time, hear this sentence in your mind as it was originally spoken: "I have a dream."

Now, imagine how the weight of that statement would change if it had been delivered differently: "I have a dream?"

Not quite so powerful.

This is the power of declarative speech. It means that you have something to declare to the world. Don't diminish your words by second-guessing them as they come out of your mouth. Give them the value and weight they deserve by saying them with strength and conviction. We can often be so afraid of saying something wrong or making a mistake that we shrink away from taking ownership of our thoughts and ideas.

I'm commonly approached by women who tell me about times when they've shared an idea in a meeting, only to have it swiftly seized upon by a male colleague in the room who then gets credit for it. This is far less likely to happen if you speak declaratively and passionately, if you claim ownership of your words while you're saying them.

Filler Words

Um. Like. So. Ya know. Sorta. Er.

These are filler words. We use them when we don't know what to say, so we throw them in the middle of our sentences to buy time. Sure, these are a great way to stall while your thoughts catch up to your mouth, but they also diminish what you're saying. Filler words will undermine the weight of nearly anything you say. Instead of relying on them to give you the time to formulate your thoughts, give yourself the time you need to articulate your idea thoughtfully and completely. If you want people to respect you, then give them a voice they can respect—and keep the *um*s and *like*s out of it. By the way, when you slow down your speech, you are less likely to use filler words.

Silence

Many of us are very uncomfortable with silence. Americans seem to be at the top of the list—we tend to view silence as something that must be eliminated rather than used, that all gaps in the conversation must be filled with words. And so we ramble on, saying things that have little to no relevance, repeating ourselves, bringing in more of those filler words.

But silence can be one of your best tools, if used properly. It does two things: First, it allows you to think before you speak, so that you can carefully pause and choose your words. This in turn makes your speech sound more deliberate and thoughtful. And second, it allows the listener to absorb what you are saying. They aren't being inundated by you and your random train of thoughts. You are giving them a meaningful, well-curated idea rather than spouting every thought passing through your mind. This means that your message will resonate better. When you say something and leave it there, the listener can take in the gravity of what you have said. But when you keep going, repeating yourself, or adding unnecessary details or comments, what you say loses its value.

Speak Up

If you're talking but no one can hear you, what's the point of having spoken at all? Speaking at a soft volume sends the message that you're insecure and uncomfortable, or that you're afraid of speaking your mind. But when you speak loudly and clearly, you send the message that you are worth listening to. Check in with yourself from time to time. Look for patterns—do you speak more softly with certain people? Are these people who have caused you harm, or do they intimidate you? Do you become quieter under certain situations? Often our inability to speak up can be tethered to emotional blockage, so if you find that this is persistently a challenge, it might be worth taking some time to reflect on the origin of your quiet voice and see if you can help yourself achieve some emotional resolution.

What Do You Really Sound Like?

Record yourself having a conversation. You could also do this while giving a speech or reading a news article or a passage from a book. Now listen to it. How do you sound? Is your voice too high? Too soft? Does everything you say end with an uptake? Do you speak with passion and authority? Do you sound confident or uncertain about what you're saying?

If your reaction is, *I hate the way I sound. I sound horrible. I can't listen to myself*—then it's time to rectify it.

If there is something in your speech that you don't like, take note of it and try it differently.

Identify those things that you wish to change. But do it one step at a time. For example, if you speak too fast, use lots of filler words, and have a high pitch, don't try to fix everything at once. Resolving to change your voice actually makes for a huge cognitive load because most of these behaviors are instinctive or unconscious. You've also been probably doing them for a really long time. Instead, start with one. For instance, try slowing down your speech and spend one month focusing solely on that adjustment. It takes about twenty-eight days to change a habit, and that's what we are trying to do here—change your paralinguistic habits. Once you've effectively changed one habit, then move to the next thing on your list.

Preparation Exudes Confidence

As an educator, I want my students to excel not only in their studies, but in life after college as well. So every semester, rather than assigning them a research paper, I assign them an oral presentation to give to the class.

I have on average thirty-five students and a three-hour class, so they each have five minutes to present their topic. The majority are uncomfortable and shy about speaking in front of their peers. But I know that helping them cultivate their speaking skills will pay dividends for them in the future. During the presentations, it also becomes quickly apparent which students come prepared and which do not. This is evident from the conviction in their voices when they present their ideas. When a student knows the information well, they are slower and more methodical in what they reveal. They come off as the authority on the topic they're presenting, and even if they're nervous their confidence still comes through.

Those students who have done a poor job researching their topic will hurry through their presentation. They'll speak so fast that they'll fumble over their words and use lots of filler language to fill the gaps from their lack of knowledge. Their sentences will sound like questions, and their poor preparation will be evident in the insecurity of their speech.

I'm usually able to verify this after each student's presentation during the Q&A. Those who spoke quickly will typically struggle because they don't know the topic well enough to answer spontaneous questions. Conversely, those who have mastered the information typically answer more thoroughly and confidently.

Less Is More

People often come to me with the dilemma of wanting to make their voices heard in meetings. They believe that if they go out of their way to say something in every meeting, their presence will be broadly recognized by their colleagues.

But here's the problem. People listen only when you have something notable to say. If you're just speaking because you feel that you're supposed to, then what's the point? It won't actually make your words matter more. If you don't contribute something relevant and valuable, it will be clear to others that you are speaking purely out of ego or insecurity. You are speaking for you—not the overall benefit of the discussion at hand.

Personally, I don't speak in half the meetings I attend. Mostly I listen. Sometimes I have nothing to say or nothing to contribute. Or someone else said what I was going to say. It happens. I don't leave mad or annoyed. Remember, you are there to learn and gather information. That's the most important thing. Because again, when you listen, you learn more. Then when you do decide to speak, you can do so more intelligently. Plus, the less you say, the more others will take notice and value your contribution when you do speak.

Chapter 15

Detecting Deception

The stars never lie, but the astrologers lie about the stars.
—HOMER

Lying Is Hard Work

The ability to detect lies and truthfulness has been a constant quest of mankind for nearly an eternity. In 500 BC, for example, priests in India required any subject who was accused of a crime to enter a dark tent where a donkey was tied up and pull its tail. According to the priests, if the donkey brayed when its tail was pulled, the subject was considered a liar. If, however, the donkey remained quiet, the suspect would be deemed truthful. Little did the suspects know that the donkey's tail had been covered in soot. If the subjects exited the tent with clean hands, the priests knew they had never touched the tail, thus finding them guilty.

Modern-day lie detection continues to remain a centerpiece in discovering guilt through various means, such as polygraph exams and assessing nonverbal behavior.

In recent years, through the continued work in the social, psychological, and neurological sciences, researchers have found something revolutionary—lies can be detected through the words people use. Up until now, this has rarely been talked about, much less published.

I'm not only going to talk about it here, but I'm going to explain to you exactly how it works, why it works, and how you can make this method of lie detection work for you.

By now, we've established the importance of allowing people to talk freely and uninhibitedly without any interruption. One of the main reasons we need to avoid disturbing someone mid-story is to ensure that we don't interfere with their cognitive ability to think clearly while speaking. Cognitive ability is something we all have, yet it is a finite resource. Think of a bathtub filling with water; you can add a lot of water into a tub, but if you put in too much, at some point it will start spilling out onto the floor. Our mind's ability to hold information is much the same way. Mental cognition is our capacity to take in and understand knowledge. We can simultaneously absorb and process a certain amount of information, but like the bathtub, there's a limit. Once we reach information overload, our ability to process multiple pieces of information at the same time while carrying out certain kinds of tasks simultaneously diminishes.

Here's an example: By the time we started first grade, most of us could recite the alphabet from beginning to end without much thought. With that in mind, I want you to take part in a little experiment that will give you a clearer understanding of what it feels like to reach cognitive overload.

Stand up and recite the alphabet out loud, starting with A and ending with Z.

Pretty easy, right? That's a simple cognitive task, something you know well and have likely done hundreds of times before. In your mind, it's relatively uncomplicated. On a cognitive difficulty scale of 1–10, with 10 being the hardest, for most people it's about a 1 or 2.

Now, I want you to do the same thing, but this time I want you to start walking while saying your ABC's out loud. A little harder? Maybe for some people. Have you ever heard the expression "He can't walk and chew gum at the same time"? Well, that's usually in reference to a clumsy person or someone who lacks good coordination. Their cognitive "bathtub" in that particular scenario is pretty shallow.

Okay, for those of you who found reciting the ABC's while walking easy, let's add another step. Walk, say your ABC's out loud, and clap the whole time. Harder? Yes, but not impossible. These three things—walking, clapping, and saying your ABC's aloud—are all skills you've been independently able to do since you were a child. So although you probably don't normally combine them in your day-to-day activities—unless, of course, you're a kindergarten teacher—it's not a far stretch to put them together and perform adequately. Cognitive difficulty scale? Maybe a 5.

Now, here's where the interesting part comes into play and how it connects to detecting lies: I want you to do this exercise one more time, but this time while walking and clapping, try saying your ABC's backward, starting with Z and ending with A . . . I'll wait.

Harder? Yes, a lot harder. Why? It's the exact same 26 letter sequence, just in reverse order. Cognitive difficulty scale: probably an 8–9. If you're like most people, you'll usually find yourself walking and clapping at a much slower pace, or stopping altogether as you try to remember what comes before X. Our lack of performance on what seems like it should be easy is based on one thing—we learned our ABC's only in one direction, starting with A. It's a linear memory. When asked to remember it another way, we can't. Or at least we can't at the same speed as we can reciting it forward. That's cognitive overload. Your brain was so overwhelmed with trying to think about and process something new that it lost its ability to simultaneously do other things. You simply didn't have the mental bandwidth to also walk and clap while saying the alphabet backward.

Now that you understand how cognitive overload works, we're going to use that understanding to decipher deception.

Lying Linear

When most people lie, they lie linear. They'll make up a story and then tell it in the order that it would really happen, such as, "First I did this, then I did this, then I did this," and so on—it's chronological. Because lying is cognitively hard, most liars will make their lies as simple as possible. They'll try not to add in too many details, in an effort to avoid having to recall so much information later. They'll also try to make sure they don't say things unnecessarily, meaning that their stories sound basic without a lot of actions, emotions, or complications that usually show up in truthful stories.

Take, for example, your teenage son who just came home from a Saturday night "sleepover" at his friend Billy's house. Being the inquisitive parent that you are, you ask him to join you at the kitchen table and tell you all about it. He begins, "So, after you dropped me off at five, me and Billy went for a swim in the neighbor's pool for about an hour. After that, we went back to Billy's house and ordered pizza because we were both starving. Billy challenged me to a game of darts, so we went downstairs and played for a while, until it got boring; then we switched to foosball. I was winning until Billy shot the foosball underneath the hot water heater and we couldn't find it. So we went back upstairs and decided we'd try and watch all the *Avengers* series—we rented them on Billy's mom's iTunes account. We made it halfway through *Iron Man 2* before Billy wanted ice cream. We walked to the custard shop on the corner by Billy's house, and ate it there so it wouldn't melt on our walk home. Once we got back, we started watching *Thor: Ragnarok* until we both fell asleep on the couch."

Now, you may be thinking, *No way, no teenager is going to give you that much information about their night.* And you would be right . . . but that was before you read this book. In Part 3, I'll teach you how to get more information out of some of the most closed-lipped stubborn people, including teenagers. But for now, let's just focus on the story in front of us. His story sounds legitimate, yes? Sure, but it could also be complete bullshit. With that in mind, here are a few things you can do to see if his "quiet night at Billy's house" starts to unravel.

Think for a moment about how you spent your day yesterday. I bet if I asked you to tell me what you did the hour before you went to sleep, you could do it. Maybe you meditated for twenty minutes, brushed and flossed your teeth, and then settled into bed for some light reading. Now, think about what you did for the hour before that. Maybe you had dinner or came home from the gym and showered. And the hour before that? The point is that even though you didn't plan to tell me about your day in reverse order, you can do it because it's a true memory. You didn't rehearse it; you just thought about what you did and the order in which you did it came naturally to mind.

When it comes to seeing if the storyteller can do the same thing, simply wait for them to finish their story without you interrupting and then ask them to tell you again what they did right before a specific part—similar to saying the ABC's backward.

Example:

Q: "What did you do again before you and Billy played darts?"

A: "Ordered pizza."

Q: "What movie did you and Billy watch right before you decided to go get ice cream?"

A: "*Iron Man 2.*"

If what he's telling you is true, then he will be able to answer without issue. But if not, you'll likely start seeing some fraying around the edges. He might begin to stutter and stammer while trying to recall what he told you and in what order. Pay attention as well to his nonverbal behavior. You may possibly start seeing some avoidance techniques, like turning away from you, breaking eye contact, fidgeting in his chair— subtle physical changes that weren't there before. If that's the case, maybe it's time you sent him into the tent to see if the donkey brays.

Spontaneous Corrections

Another great way to gauge whether someone is being truthful or not is to listen for any spontaneous corrections they make while telling you what happened. This often goes against conventional thinking—you might believe that if a person changes their story halfway through, they must be lying. Here's why that's not true. Research shows that when a person self-corrects in the middle of a story, it's more likely to be a sign of truthfulness because liars often think it's an indication that they're lying, and therefore they'll avoid making corrections. The key here is that the self-correction must be spontaneous—meaning they must do it on their own and not after you've asked them to clarify something. Using the same example as above: if midway through telling you about the games they played, your son says, "No, wait, we played foosball first then darts . . ." that's a spontaneous correction. What's especially interesting is that the order of the games they played doesn't impact the rest of the story, but in his mind, he's thinking back and remembering the order in which things happened. And so when that order gets out of whack, a truthful person wants to correct the detail, while a liar will not.

Remember what we said about cognitive overload. When people lie, they want to simplify their lie as much as possible so as not to overwhelm themselves with details. In this case, making an unprompted correction midway through the story is cognitively hard if you're also trying to remember all the other parts of the lie.

If the story is true, however, there's no cognitive overload, since there's nothing fake or made up. They're merely recalling true memories, which is significantly less taxing for their cognitive capacity. That's why spontaneous corrections are so important, because they actually indicate that a person is trying to remember things truthfully.

He Said What?

If quotations show up during a story, it's more likely that the story—or at least that part of the story—is true. In other words, if the speaker repeats something someone else said word for word, instead of just summarizing what they said, they're likely to be truthful. There is a difference between your teenage son saying Billy told a polar bear joke versus Billy ended the joke with, "Dad, I don't think I'm a real polar bear because I'm fucking freezing!" If the story is fabricated, adding quotations into it makes it more cognitively demanding, as now the liar has to remember the exact quote, if asked. If the story is true, however, adding in quotes further personalizes the story and solidifies the story line as something memorable that happened. It's important to know that the absence of quotes, however, doesn't mean the story is not true. It doesn't go in both directions.

Complications

Raise your hand if everything in your day went perfectly—meaning there was no traffic congestion on your commute, no annoying phone calls, no blue spinning wheel of death on your computer screen letting you know your document is still loading. Everything was essentially rainbows and unicorns. No one? I didn't think so. Mine, neither.

No matter who you are or how busy your day is or isn't, something invariably will go wrong. And that *something* doesn't have to be life changing—it can just be annoying. Do you remember the complication in your son's story? Billy losing the foosball underneath the hot water heater. Research shows that when complications are added into a story, they're more likely to be true. Again, liars are not going to intentionally burden themselves with trying to remember unnecessary details, such as things that went wrong with their day. So, the more complications a person includes in their story, the more likely they are to be truthful.

Ally or Accomplice?

Here's an interesting tactic if you suspect two people are involved in a lie: Interview them together. Most police detectives know that when you have two suspects involved in the same crime, you should interview them separately to see if their stories match up or if one of them will eventually break and begin telling on the other. This is definitely a great strategy, but if you're not in law enforcement, interviewing people separately isn't always an option. So, if you ever find yourself sitting with two people who you think may be lying to you, do this: Have them sit side by side so they're facing you. Then have one of them start telling you about whatever it is you're curious to know. In sticking with our teenage son and the Billy story, if you suspect that the story is partly or entirely made up, begin by asking them about the details of their evening.

After one of them begins, let him talk for about a sentence or two and then abruptly stop him (I know I said no interruptions, but this is the exception to the rule) and have the other person pick up where the first left off. If they're telling the truth, their back-and-forth should flow relatively smoothly since they both experienced the night in roughly the same way. They'll even correct each other, or possibly go off on a tangent, such as who was actually winning in foosball. But if they're lying to you, you'll quickly see that neither of them has any idea how the other person plans to lie. When it's their turn to talk, they'll try to add on to their partner's story, but stay as vague as possible so as to not make the story too complicated. In the context of cognitive overload, imagine trying to not only generate your own lie, which needs to sound believable, but doing it while trying to listen and remember what your accomplice is saying. The majority of people simply won't be able to pull it off.

Verifiable Information

If you're still not convinced after your son tells you everything about his evening at Billy's, there's something you can do: Verify the details. Most highly trained law enforcement agents know that the key to a good interview is not focusing on getting a confession, but getting enough details to either verify or disprove what the suspect said. That's why it's so important to ask good open-ended questions and allow the person to talk. In the case of your son's story, he gave up a lot of details that any astute parent could quickly verify:

1. The name of the neighbor with the pool he swam in and the time he swam there;
2. The pizza company he and Billy bought pizza from;
3. The electronic iTunes receipt showing the rented *Avengers* movies (ask Billy's mom);
4. The ice cream receipt or video footage of them at the store.

Sure, some of these you may think are impossible to verify, but if it's that important, it's worth asking, or at least telling your son that you're going to look into it. Even more important is that next time you'll know what types of questions to ask that will give you enough details to verify his whereabouts.

Part 3

INFLUENCE

Chapter 16

How to Influence

Character may almost be called the most effective means of persuasion.
—ARISTOTLE

The Truth About Influence

I distinctly recall the first time I was told how important my words could be. It was during a lecture in my Police Science class when I was a cadet at the NYPD. Sergeant Corrigan was teaching us about how to use our character and communication skills when dealing with people. I'll never forget what he said.

"Your words are your most powerful weapon. If you learn how to use your words deliberately and thoughtfully, you will be able to get people to give you what you want. When you communicate effectively with people, they will listen. When they listen, they will comply without the necessity of threat or the use of force. If you go your entire career without ever discharging your gun, then by my account you've had a great career."

In the years that followed, and especially as a federal agent tasked with arresting, interviewing, polygraphing, and protecting people, I came to realize that my words were indeed my most powerful weapon.

My friend Lee, a fellow interrogator, compared words to monetary currency, something he called *verbal economics*. Verbal economics is the understanding that, like money, our words have value, and the way in which we *spend* those words affects our investment in our desired outcome. Spent foolishly, our return on investment will lack both substance and worth. If it is spent wisely through strategic planning, we will reap the benefit of our efforts.

Unfortunately, rather than being calculated, we tend to use our words carelessly, without thought or any specific intent in mind, and often without awareness of their consequences. We speak just to speak, to satisfy our egos or emotional impulses. When we fail to offer anything of value to our listener, we risk losing their interest, or possibly being seen as having no currency at all.

To become a dealer of words, you must first understand that the words you choose are not about you. They're about the person who hears them. Instead of trying to force your listener to see the world through your eyes, try seeing it through theirs. Talk to people in a way that makes sense to them. A perfect example of this is watching adults interact with newborns. Without prompting, most will adopt a soft, high-pitched babble accompanied by an easy smile. Why? Because they know that's how babies communicate with the world.

When you're able to set aside your own viewpoints and focus solely on the result you want, you begin looking for ways to mentally maneuver people. Once inside a person's head, you can start influencing both the way they perceive you as well as how they communicate. Remember: Every word has a definition. Every definition has a meaning. And every meaning has an impact on your listener. As such, every word that leaves your lips should have a predetermined purpose—a strategy that collectively maneuvers the conversation in a particular direction. When you can master your words, you can master your future.

So, what do we really mean when we talk about *influence*? Influence is about using subtle strategies to affect someone's mindset or behavior to get what you want while staying true to who you are. At the same time, it's dependent on creating a genuine connection with another person. In order to mentally sway someone, they must first trust you. And trust comes through building rapport—a mutual investment of time, attention, and energy between two people.

What influence is not: Influence is not about bullying. It is not bulldozing people or forcing them to submit to your will. It is not about pretending to be someone or something you're not. It's not about manipulation and it's not about lying. A lot of people assume influence and psychological trickery are the same thing, but the truth is that you can't effectively influence someone if you're disingenuous. When people find out that you've lied or faked your interest in them (and they will), you'll lose all credibility. Your character will be questioned, your reputation tarnished, and you'll forever be approached with suspicion.

Influence, when executed well, is imperceptible to others. It can improve your relationships and create remarkable personal opportunities. Just bear in mind that if you want to master the subtle skills and strategies in this section, you must do so out of a sincere desire to understand others. When you come to recognize and appreciate another person, you add value to their lives, which in turn adds value to your own. This is the quintessential impact of influence.

Stop Trying to Change People

Before we continue, let's make one thing clear: When it comes to influence, there's a difference between trying to get a specific outcome from someone and trying to change them altogether. Influence is about shifting a person's specific mindset regarding a particular situation. Take, for example, trying to get your kids to do their homework—this is a short-term goal that, if strategized correctly, can be achieved relatively quickly. However, trying to get your kids to understand the value of a good education and how their academic performance will affect them into adulthood is a whole different ballgame. Here you're trying to change their inherent values, a long-term process that requires a great deal of time and effort.

When I interrogated a terrorist or sympathizer of terrorism against the United States, my focus wasn't on trying to alter their views about America or convince them that we were actually the "good guys." It was to get specific information from them, such as a plot, intelligence, or a contact. They could still hate America—and most of them did—but rather than waste time and energy trying to rewire their ideologies, I set my own aside and looked at the world from their perspective to get the desired outcome I wanted.

Influence isn't about permanently altering someone's character or long-established belief system. People change because they want to—not because you want them to. And if you truly want to effectively influence someone, you must first open yourself up to understanding their perspective.

Be Strategic

There's no better example of using another person's perspective to get what you want than the story of Hanns Joachim Scharff. Scharff was a German military officer who, during World War II, interrogated more than five hundred captured Allied fighter pilots. His techniques for getting Prisoners of War (POWs) to talk were so effective that they're now taught in the top interview training courses.

Scharff didn't use harsh interrogation methods, like the ones you hear about in the news or see on television. He was friendly, respectful, and soft-spoken. Instead of relying on pain or humiliation to force his prisoners to confess, he looked at their situation through their eyes, tried to understand their reasons for refusing to talk, and then found subtle ways to work around them. He didn't question his POWs inside interrogation rooms. Instead, he took them on long walks, or to the movies, or out for tea, all the while chatting about things that seemed unimportant. He never pushed for information; he simply talked and listened, helping his interviewees feel at ease. Gradually, his prisoners would speak freely about themselves, their comrades, and the war, all the while careful not to reveal more than they assumed Scharff already knew. Once the "interview" ended for the day, Scharff returned to his quarters, where he wrote down everything he had learned. He would then use that new information the next time he interviewed a new prisoner. The new POW, believing Scharff already knew the answers to the things he talked about, would also speak openly, often unknowingly adding a few more pieces of detail to the puzzle Scharff was quietly constructing.

Scharff used five interrelated tactics to accomplish this feat:

1. He adopted a friendly approach, by spending time with the POWs at cafés or strolls through the woods.
2. He never directly pressed them for information, but rather allowed their conversations to flow naturally.

3. He spoke with a confidence of "knowing it all," which lessened the prisoner's need to remain guarded.
4. He purposely misstated facts to see if the POW would correct him or add new details.
5. He never showed shock or surprise when new pieces of information made their way into the conversation—he always maintained an air of calmness and composure. Hence the poker face (more on this soon).

In the end, Scharff was able to compile a vast amount of intelligence about the Allied forces without his prisoners ever knowing what they had and hadn't told him. By adopting the perspective of his POWs and using that knowledge to influence them, he never had to lift a finger in anger to get them to talk. In fact, after the war, Scharff was invited to the United States to lecture at the War Department on his strategies. Eventually he was granted immigration status and moved to California, where he lived until his death in 1992 at the age of eighty-four. And his hobby after his interrogation career? A mosaic artist. He created elaborate pictures using thousands of little pieces of colored glass, stone, or tile, much like the pictures he constructed using the thousands of pieces of information he collected from his POWs. One of his most famous pieces hangs inside the Cinderella Castle at Walt Disney World.

Fast-forward to 2009, when the Obama administration created the High-Value Detainee Interrogation Group (HIG) as a result of the United States having used harsh interrogation tactics on terrorist suspects. Composed of high-level interrogators, behavioral analysts, and scientists, the HIG became responsible for overseeing the interrogations of high-value targets in US custody, as well as establishing a research program designed to identify the best methods, both ethically and effectively, for compelling suspects to talk.

Unlike traditional law enforcement interrogations tactics, HIG methodologies are based in science and come from decades of proven research drawn from professions where eliciting accurate and complete information is vital, in places such as interrogation rooms, intelligence briefings, sales and marketing seminars, and on psychologists' couches. Despite overwhelming requests, the HIG trains only an elite group of specialists within the law enforcement and intelligence communities.

The use of communication strategies that yield high volumes of reliable information without threat or coercion have become the cornerstone of a select few elite government agencies, including the Department of Homeland Security, the Department of Justice, and the Department of Defense. The interviewing approaches they are now beginning to use—what I call *soft communication skills*—are taken from the fields of social and behavioral sciences. These strategies, which we're about to take a deep dive into, aren't just for the interrogation room—they are for the boardroom, family room, or any other room where influence is needed. Whether we're talking with a coworker, chatting with our significant other, or interacting with someone we've just met, these methods work and work well. If you ever wanted to know how the world's top negotiators get people to talk, you're about to find out firsthand.

Chapter 17

Undivided Attention

All men by nature desire to know.
—ARISTOTLE

Make People Feel Special

Although I became a Special Agent toward the end of President William J. Clinton's administration, I spent years in close proximity to him. To date, he is one of the best communicators and influencers I have ever seen. People loved him and loved talking to him. He had a way of drawing anything out of anyone, of making them feel entirely worthy of his undivided attention. But it wasn't magic—it was skill. He'd walk into a room with hundreds of people, and when he spoke to someone, whether it was for a few seconds or several minutes, he made them feel like there was no one else there.

I was the agent responsible for securing site operations at one particularly important event for the Clinton Global Initiative. We had a banquet room filled with hundreds of people, all waiting for President Clinton's arrival. The problem was that he was running twenty minutes late. There was a cacophony of other agents yelling into my earpiece, demanding to know where he was. I was waiting anxiously outside on the curb for his arrival when at last his motorcade drove up. He got out—I let out a sigh of relief—and made his way toward the side entrance I had secured for him.

That's when the sigh of relief stopped mid-breath. There were people milling around on either side of the barricades we set up. I saw a group of onlookers not far from the entrance, and even though I already knew what was coming—he was President Clinton, after all— I remember thinking, *Oh no. Please don't go talk to them.* But his interest in other people was always more important to him than protocol or punctuality. Sure enough, he walked right over to the onlookers—and he didn't just go for a quick hello and a picture. He went over, shook everyone's hand, and had an actual conversation with each person in the group. He asked for their names, where they were from, and any follow-up questions that sparked his curiosity.

It wasn't just that President Clinton cared to talk to people—he cared to listen. He wanted to know what they had to say. It would be easy for someone in that position of fame and power to lose curiosity or interest in others, but he never did. People always describe him as charming and charismatic, and this is why—he makes people feel special.

Undivided Attention

At the start of any interview, negotiation, or business meeting I attend, one of the first things I do is turn off my phone. And not only do I turn it off, I make sure the person I'm meeting with sees me turn it off and place it inside my purse. One of the fastest ways to sabotage your rapport with someone is to keep your phone out. I've seen people go to great lengths to connect with others, and yet their phone will either be in their hand, splayed out on their desk or dinner table, signaling to everyone around them that there is something else of potentially greater importance waiting to take their attention away. This also sends the message that whoever you're with is less deserving of your time and that you're not fully present. Think of your phone as an uninvited guest to the table who's constantly whispering in your ear while you and your guest are talking—annoying, right? And turning it facedown is no different. If it's visible, it's a distraction.

We live in a time where our attention is continually being pulled in countless directions. When at work, we may think about our child struggling with her grades. When at home with our family, we're mentally back at the office, thinking about the to-do-list on our desk. While driving to the gym, we're emotionally caught up in world affairs and the barrage of political rhetoric. And when lying in bed at night trying to shut it all out, we stress about our health and the need to eat better. Rarely are we ever truly *present*.

Remember, this isn't just about showing respect—it's about influence. When people see you powering down your phone and stowing it away, this signals how much you value them and, in turn, demonstrates the importance of this interaction or the significance of your connection. More important, you'll be able to observe and read them better if you're giving them your full focus, which will allow you to pick up on behavioral cues that you might have otherwise missed.

Research shows that our brains actually don't multitask well. When we switch topics, even if only briefly, our brains have to expend effort to make the switch and will likely fail to retain information it was given in the process. That means if you're in the middle of a discussion and your eyes suddenly glance over to the text message that just buzzed in, you're likely going to miss the facial expression or body shift that could indicate the conversation is not going well.

Ironically, whenever I offer this "stow and go" advice, the response typically is "I can't be away from my phone. What if something important happens or someone is trying to reach me in an emergency?" Unless you're expecting an emergency call, such as news about a sick family member, then the statistical probability of your personal Armageddon occurring during the thirty minutes of being *unavailable*, is, well . . . statistically improbable. Never in my entire career as a Special Agent did I see any of the presidents—or First Ladies, for that matter—hold a phone in their hand or leave it out on a table while talking to someone. Whether they were negotiating with another world leader, chatting with the coffee shop barista, or asking the White House butler about his weekend, they understood the power of giving whoever they were talking to *all* of their attention.

Because I know how mentally distracting cell phones can be—whether it's mine or someone else's—every semester I spend about thirty minutes during the first-day class orientation on the subject of cell phones. I show my students proven studies about how they hinder academic performance and how social media use has been closely linked to depression. It might sound excessive, but it saves me both time and headaches come mid-semester because I'm not constantly telling people to put their phones away. Additionally, students are more likely to honor this request when I explain the rationale behind it. I tell them that although some professors may not care about cell phones in the classroom, I feel differently. I believe that I owe them an education and a nurturing space to learn, free of distractions from others. So my cell phone policy is not out of respect for me (although I certainly benefit from it), but out of respect for them and the sanctity of the classroom.

I also offer them the option to leave the classroom at any point to use their cell phones—no questions asked. This gives them autonomy over the situation, which is another influence strategy (more on that in chapter 21), because I am giving them a choice in the matter.

Remember People's Names

Dale Carnegie said, "A person's name is to that person, the sweetest, most important sound in any language." And he's right. Because our name is directly linked to our personal identity, we like hearing it. Researchers looked at how our brains react when we hear our own name, compared to hearing the name of someone else. When our name is called out, regions in our medial frontal cortex and superior temporal cortex—the areas responsible for how we judge ourselves and our personal qualities—are activated, which makes us feel good.

Among President Clinton's many talents was an uncanny ability to remember people's names. He would say the person's name repeatedly throughout their conversation, making them feel relevant.

"Bob, what part of Arkansas are you from?"

"Where did you go to school, Bob?"

"Bob, that's a great question. Let me tell you a bit more about that."

Imagine how special you would feel if the president of the United States—arguably the most important person in the world—spoke to you like a personal friend. That's the power of name recognition.

If you're like most people, though, you might be thinking, *I suck at remembering people's names*, and that's okay, because you can get better. And the primary way to start? Through incorporating small actions into your daily routine, which, over a period of time, will become a habit.

When you're interacting with new people, or meeting them for the first time, make it a point to address them by name.

"Hi, my name is Matthew."

"Matthew, it's a pleasure to meet you. My name is Evy."

Then repeat the person's name at least a couple of times in the conversation. This simple act of repeating a person's name out loud allows you to imprint it into your memory. It will also have the added benefit of making them feel more connected to you in the present.

"So, Matthew, where are you from?"

To put this to use, begin practicing the next time you can read someone's name tag: *"Hi, Annie, I'd like to order two green teas."* Or when speaking on the phone to a customer service representative who introduces themselves by their first name: *"Good morning, Mary, I would like to check on my account."* You may notice that, based on this simple act, the quality of service you receive will be higher than you expect.

Another way to remember names, especially if you're in a meeting, is to draw a makeshift diagram of the table you're at and write down the names in the places where each person is sitting. And if you're having trouble pronouncing a person's name, it's okay to repeat it back to them or ask them for help. I can't tell you how many times I've had to re-pronounce *Evy Poumpouras*, but I can tell you that I've appreciated the effort people invest in trying to get it right.

Chapter 18

Commanding Respect

Be modest in speech, but excel in action.
—Horace

Command Respect; Don't Demand It

After September 11, the technical security agents in the New York Field Office of the Secret Service decided that we needed to amp up our preparedness. They now wanted us to not only be able to effectively fight our way out of a gun battle without getting our protectee killed, but they wanted us to do it from inside a burning building. And since these scenarios could occur at any time, they placed us inside those fiery infernos without breathing gear or protective equipment. I couldn't see. I couldn't breathe. And it was so hot inside the building it felt like my skin was actually burning. Simulated bullets pummeled the walls as we fought our way out, basically blind, all the while vigilant about keeping our protectee safe.

Because this type of tactical training was new to many of us, we needed to become familiar with the personality of fire: How it moves and reacts under different situations, how it is influenced by water and oxygen, and the best way to defeat it—as well as knowing when you can't.

During one of these training courses, agents from my office teamed up with a local fire department in New York to learn the protocol of handling a fire hose. Due to the intensity of water pressure, handling a hose requires skill and strength, and at minimum is a two-person job. In the first exercise, I was chosen to take the front of the hose and two of my other colleagues were positioned behind me for support. I grabbed the hose and was shown how to angle the nozzle toward the ground.

The fire instructor turned to me and said, "Make sure you hold it exactly like this. And no matter what happens, don't drop the hose. Understand?"

I nodded.

When everyone was in place, the firefighters opened the doors and allowed oxygen into the burning house that had been set up for the exercise. The fire immediately roared to life and flames burst out, engulfing me in an intense wave of heat. Within seconds, an immense amount of water punched out through the end of the nozzle. I held my position and hugged the hose tightly into the center of my body. I made sure to angle it exactly as instructed, toward the ground at the base of the fire. As the pressure of the hose hit the fire, the flames curled up and over me in a vicious blast of heat and smoke.

It was both terrifying and surreal. Yet all I could think about was the instruction I had been given: *"Don't drop the hose."*

I bowed my head to shield my face, wondering if I still had my eyebrows, and held on tight to the fire hose. While fighting to contain the flames, I sensed some kind of commotion behind me, but kept my focus. After several minutes, the water from the hose stopped. The firefighters closed the doors to the burning house, and the scenario was over.

The fire official smiled. "I'm impressed," he said. "You held your position. Your two buddies behind you, however, didn't." Confused, I looked over my shoulder. The two male agents who had been chosen as my support team were no longer there. I had been left alone.

The official continued, "Just so you know, we purposely showed you the wrong way to hold the hose. The way in which it was angled, pointing toward the base of the fire, was incorrect. Instead of smothering the fire, the water from the hose pushed the fire up over your head and the flames came at you. But you stayed put. Nice job."

At the end of the training day, one of my colleagues who helped set up the training pulled me aside. "Hey," he said. "I just want you to know I'm proud of you."

"For what?" I asked.

"Because you didn't drop the hose," he said.

"I thought that was the whole point. I was told not to drop it. So why would I?"

"I shouldn't tell you this, but the guys deliberately chose you to hold the hose. They picked you because they assumed you wouldn't be able to do it. They wanted to set you up to prove a point. We've been doing fire training for three days now, and every time we do this specific exercise, we pick the strongest agents because you need a lot of power to handle the hose. And up until this point, every agent we've picked for this exercise has dropped the hose and left their position. They were certain that you would do the same. For what it's worth, I'm glad you put them in their place."

I suppose I should have felt better after being complimented by my colleague, but I didn't. These guys picked me because they assumed I was weak. They were certain that I would drop the hose and run as the others had done.

Despite being pissed, I never said anything to anyone about what my colleague had told me. I didn't take my anger to a supervisor, nor did I ever confront anyone about it. In the Service, you learned to fight your own battles; if you had an issue with another agent, you addressed it with them personally. But more important, I didn't have to bring it to anyone. My actions that day spoke louder than anything I could have said. Although I had been set up for failure, I held my own and let my actions speak for themselves.

"How do I make someone respect me?"

Whenever I'm asked this question, my response is always "You can't." Respect is not something that can be forced or demanded. It's a gift. If someone wants to give it to you, they will. And if they don't, they won't. That's it. Yes, your words are your most powerful weapon. But when it comes to commanding respect, sometimes it's best to hold your silence and simply show the world who you are through what you do.

At times, though, regardless of what we do, there will always be people who don't respect us. We can prove ourselves over and over again, and they'll never change their mind. Unfortunately, when we're unable to earn the respect we feel we rightfully deserve, we make it about us. We feel outraged or humiliated or confused about why our efforts are never enough. We try to come up with new ways to get people to respect us, oblivious to the fact that this person's lack of respect is entirely their own issue, something they've chosen to hold on to despite who you are or what you do. Maybe you remind them of someone they dislike or maybe they have a personal bias that happens to apply to you.

No matter the reason, it's important to remember one thing: The respect you seek must start with you. I was a female Special Agent for more than twelve years in a male-dominated profession. I wish I could say that during my career everything was fair, that I was always treated justly and as an equal, but that wouldn't be true. The path I walked was difficult at times and I faced many adversities along the way. But over the course of my career, I learned that I couldn't force others to respect me or see me as their equal. Once I came to accept that, I no longer allowed other people's opinion of me to determine my self-worth, my demeanor, or my performance. I achieved what I wanted to in the way that I wanted to do it, and then I let the results speak for themselves.

The measure of your success should not be respect. The measure of your success should be your resolve to carry out your particular purpose or mission in a way that brings you pride and satisfaction. At the end of the day, the person whose opinion matters the most is your own.

When you come to this realization, you free yourself from caring so much about what others think of you. You may want someone's respect, but you don't need it.

Give People Their Privacy

Have you ever had the experience of being denigrated in public? Maybe as a child your parents loudly scolded you in a packed restaurant for spilling your chocolate milk. Maybe a teacher called attention to your poor grade while passing back your test: "Good job, Ms. Poumpouras, you just failed your midterm." Or maybe your boss reprimanded you in a staff meeting for missing a deadline. In each scenario, my guess is that you not only felt humiliated and angry, but probably resented the person who publicly highlighted your flaws. The simple act of addressing people's shortcomings in private, rather than publicly, makes a world of difference in not only changing their behavior—studying harder, better time management, holding your sippy cup with two hands—but also getting them to comply with what you need.

Walking through the hallway of the New York Field Office one day after finishing an applicant polygraph, I heard a colleague call out to me.

"Hey, Genie, can you give us a hand?" he asked. "We're trying to get a confession out of this guy, and he's giving us nothing."

As I followed him into the small interview room, which had its door propped wide open, I saw the suspect handcuffed to the wall. There were three agents wearing full police tactical gear standing around him and a dozen or so agents congregating in the hallway. I took one look at the situation and pulled my colleague aside. "Of course, he's not talking to you," I said quietly. "There's at least fifteen people within earshot of his every word. Is he dangerous?"

"No, he isn't," the agent replied.

"Then I suggest uncuffing him from the wall, ask everyone to step outside, and you go sit with him in private and talk."

I understood what had happened. As agents, we became so accustomed to arresting and interviewing people that we at times forgot that anyone we took into custody instantly had their world turned upside down. Regardless of what they had done, they still deserved the respect of being treated with dignity—and part of that dignity is preserving their privacy. This is also a great influence strategy—providing someone with privacy will make them more likely to speak openly to you. Think about it: If someone were asking you to disclose deeply personal information, would you want to share it while sitting at a table in the middle of a busy restaurant within earshot of other diners or would you want to be in a secluded booth in the back corner? I would think the latter.

While offering the courtesy and respect of privacy is important, it's also worth noting that it will give you a tactical advantage. When you're trying to influence others, the more intimate you can make the setting, the more success you'll have. Even if the conversation doesn't feel particularly high stakes for you, it may be for them. People who feel exposed or unsafe are going to either edit what they're saying or shut down altogether. Conversely, people in private spaces will be more relaxed and open. Offering privacy is a meaningful gesture of respect, and since you're saving that person the effort of needing to save face in front of a bunch of strangers, the answers they give you are more likely to be expansive and truthful.

Preserving Dignity

After I left the Service and became an adjunct professor, I began to use the same privacy principles I had learned as an agent to handle disruptive students. In one class I had a student disclose to me that he had been arrested, so I knew he had a criminal past. This in itself didn't bother me, but the problem was that he was constantly interrupting the class, speaking to everyone in an abrasive manner, and making it almost impossible for me to teach. Despite being told by the dean's office to go in and discuss his behavior, he refused. It also became clear to me after a couple of conversations with him that there was possibly a mental health issue affecting his behavior, as well. On one particularly bad day, he became so disruptive that I knew there was no way I would be able to get through the whole class without some kind of intervention.

So, I called for a break and spoke to the student privately. "The dean would like to see you in his office. He would like to speak to you about your behavior in class."

"I'm not going anywhere," he told me, planting his feet and sitting staunchly in his seat.

At that point, I went into the hall and called public safety to alert them that a student in my class needed to be removed. They arrived a few minutes later, ready to come in and drag the student out, but I told them to wait outside.

"Don't worry," one of the officers said. "We can just go in there right now and take care of him. And then you can continue the rest of your class."

"No," I said. "If you drag him out in front of the whole class, you'll humiliate him. He's a volatile student and may react negatively—even violently—to save face." For the safety of the other students, and as a gesture of respect for the disruptive student, I knew that I needed to preserve his dignity, so I came up with a different plan. "This is what's going to happen," I said. "I'm going to let the class go early, and then you can come in and take him out once all the other students are gone. Do not approach him until everybody leaves. Try to talk to him before you physically remove him, okay?"

I released the class and the officers came in and spoke to the student calmly, as I requested. At that point, the student left willingly. The officers didn't need to handle him physically, and he didn't cause any sort of a commotion.

You should always have important or sensitive conversations with employees or colleagues in a way that preserves people's dignity. Whenever I have concerns about a student's performance, I always ask them to speak with me after class so that we can have that conversation in private. My primary objective as an educator is to support the success of my students, and I know that making them feel shamed or publicly humiliated will not help them in any way. This is the same for your employees, colleagues, and children. When you publicly reprimand others—even if you're in the right—people will often try to preserve their own dignity by responding defiantly or confrontationally. When you're trying to influence behavior, as I was with this student, it's important to take their dignity into account.

Chapter 19

The Right Questions

The right question is usually more important than the right answer.
—Plato

Ask the Right Questions

One of the most basic ways that people exchange ideas and information when communicating is by asking questions. The way questions are phrased will largely determine the sort of information you receive. Over the years, I quickly learned which words to use or avoid to prompt a truthful response, as well as how to draw out the information I needed without shutting a person down. Asking the right questions is a relatively simple technique and, paired with the strategies we've covered thus far—active listening and identifying red flags—this will pay dividends in influencing and persuading those around you.

Open-Ended Questions

As I mentioned in chapter 10, open-ended questions are important. They are invitations for someone to give you longer, personalized answers to an inquiry. For example: "Tell me about your meeting."

Closed-ended questions, by contrast, can usually be answered quickly and concisely with a "Yes" or "No" response—for example, "Did your meeting go well?"

The first question will prompt the person to go into more detail about what happened at the meeting. They might tell you what was discussed, whether they achieved a particular goal, or how they felt about how it went. To the second question, the person could simply respond, "Yes, it was fine." To them, that would be a complete and thorough response to your question, but you would gain almost no useful information about what the meeting was like.

Open-ended questions are useful for four main reasons:

1. You don't have to work as hard to get information. In most cases, the other person will offer it willingly.
2. By inviting someone to follow their own train of thought, open-ended questions allow you to see what is really happening within a person's mind.
3. Open-ended questions give you time to assess and observe someone while they speak, rather than putting the onus of the conversation back on you.
4. Open-ended questions invite someone to tell you a story, and storytelling can offer a wealth of information.

Whenever I finished administering a polygraph, I'd sometimes ask the person how they think they did. Invariably, the thing that each person was most uneasy or concerned about would be at the forefront of their mind. They would then elaborate on that topic, which in turn allowed me to follow up with deeper, more specific questions. Not only did this give me useful insight into each person, but it saved me the trouble of guessing what they were worried about.

More often than not, their concerns reflected their actual performance on those specific questions during the polygraph. By allowing them to tell me on their own and without my lead or influence to guide them, I was able to elicit the exact information that I needed. I also found that open-ended questions made it much easier to spot liars. Rather than answering with an easy "Yes" or "No," open-ended questions compel people to offer a more nuanced narrative. And as we know by now, narratives are difficult to fabricate on the spot, making it easier to see the red flags that could indicate dishonesty or omission. Remember, the more people say, the more they reveal, both verbally and nonverbally.

Open-ended questions can be hugely useful in professional settings as well. When I first went out to shop my proposal for this book, I wanted to avoid being the one to begin the conversation. I had no idea what the people in the room thought of me or my book concept, what they liked or disliked. So rather than trying to guess what they were thinking, my agent, Doug, and I prompted them to initiate the dialogue. After everyone made introductions, either Doug or I would begin by asking an open-ended question, such as "Tell me what you liked about the proposal?"

In every case, the editor would begin by telling us what really interested them in this book. They would tell us their favorite parts and what topics they were most excited about. Then they would typically invite another member or two of their team to share their thoughts as well. Fifteen minutes might go by without either Doug or I saying a single word.

This helped accomplish four things:

1. I didn't have to do any guesswork as to what they thought of my proposal. They would describe their favorite parts, what resonated with them, what was important to them, and their vision for the book. All of this information was valuable for me to know before I began to speak.

2. This allowed me to respond to their thoughts and vision, making it possible for me to enter the conversation in a meaningful way rather than blindly trying to figure out where to start my pitch. I didn't have to spend the meeting wondering which parts they did or didn't like. They told me on their own and the conversation flowed easily from there.

3. I was able to prime the conversation. Notice that we didn't say, "Tell us what you thought about the proposal." We asked them what they liked about the proposal. I wanted to begin the conversation on a positive note and prompt them to give me only positive feedback. Again, my goal was to sell the book concept. And I wanted to get each editor excited and primed so that we could discuss the book in the best mood possible, which is why I avoided the negatives. I knew constructive criticism would come eventually—but first, I needed to lock in a book deal (more on priming in chapter 21).

4. I could observe and absorb everyone while they spoke, as well as read the room, and decide on the best way to respond to their feedback.

(Sorry, Simon & Schuster. You know I love you guys.)

Be thoughtful about how you construct your questions—and equally thoughtful about how you begin a conversation. Give people flexibility in the way they speak. You want them to be comfortable, to speak openly and easily in whatever way their thoughts take them. Giving them this freedom gives you the luxury of seeing what's most pressing on their mind.

The best way to ask open-ended questions is by using the acronym TED. This stands for:

Tell: "Tell me how your day was."
"Tell me more of your thoughts on this partnership."
Explain: "Explain what happened."
"Explain to me what is important to you and your company."
Describe: "Describe your meeting with your boss."
"Describe your concerns with the situation."

TED is also a great tool because it allows you to phrase questions in a neutral way, without assuming how someone is going to answer. They don't lead a person in a particular direction with your own biases or expectations. Which leads us to the next section . . .

Avoid: Leading Questions

Leading questions do exactly what they say—they guide a person toward telling you what you assume to be true rather than what they know to be true. This might sound counterintuitive in the context of influence, but because the first step of influence is to actively listen and understand a person, you want to be careful not to coach them into telling you what they think you want to hear. A person may have extensive knowledge about things that you wouldn't know to ask, so if your questions focus only on your suppositions, you're likely to receive information limited to those topics. This will cause you to miss a fuller picture of the story.

If I were asking a witness for information about a suspect's vehicle that I think may have been used in a crime, I wouldn't ask a leading question like "Was the car a red or brown Chevy?" Even if I had prior knowledge of the car in question, I'd be careful to keep my questions open-ended. Here's why:

First, it would be leading the person to assume that the vehicle has to be a Chevy, when it may not have been. There is always a chance that my assumptions or prior knowledge could be incorrect.

Second, it would be leading the person to think that the vehicle could be only one of those two colors. Color can be subjective, and therefore someone's perception of red or brown might be different from mine. They might interpret those colors as maroon or beige.

A better question would be "Describe the vehicle you saw?" This allows a person to give information about the car without being unduly influenced in their answer. It also allows them to share details I may not have even thought to ask. Maybe the bumper or door had dents or scratches on it, or were painted a different color. Perhaps the windows were tinted. Maybe it wasn't a car at all, but an SUV or pickup truck. All of this would have been hugely useful to me in narrowing down the field of suspects.

Avoid: Compound Questions

When you ask multiple questions within the same question, it's called a *compound question*. These sorts of questions can be difficult for people to navigate or answer accurately. Here's an example:

"Did you enjoy reading this book, while finding it informative and useful?"

The problem here is there are three different questions being asked.

1. Did you enjoy reading the book?
2. Did you find it informative?
3. Did you find it useful?

Each question is asking something specific and distinct. So if a person answers "Yes," you'll have no way of knowing which question they're answering "Yes" to. One of the questions, two of them, all three? Because I decided to cram all my questions into one, I'm not allowing the person to think the question through or to answer expansively. If the listener is confused (and they probably will be), they may answer only part of the question, but not all. And if someone is trying to deceive you, this gives them an out to not answer you fully or to avoid part of the question without having to lie.

Avoid: Assumptive Questions

Assumptive questions are just what they sound like—they're designed around assumptions. Law enforcement detectives are notorious for asking these types of questions, either as a way to trick a person into confessing or hurrying along an interview. An example of this would be "When you went into the house, did you see the money?" Now, asking the question this way assumes the person being interviewed did go into the house. If the detectives already know this to be the case, then it's okay to ask. But if they're trying to get the person to admit to being inside the house, and he or she never went in, they just ended up ruining their credibility and any trust they may have built with the person.

Here's another example of how an assumptive question can cause problems in our everyday lives. Let's say you're trying to find out if your boyfriend ran into his ex-girlfriend again during lunch. If you assume that he, like most days, went to lunch with his two coworkers, you might ask, "When you were at lunch with Joe and Chris, did you see Jane?" By asking the question this way you assume three things:

1. That your boyfriend went to lunch.
2. That he went to lunch with Joe and Chris.
3. That he went to lunch with *only* Joe and Chris.

Now, in the event that you already know this to be the case—that your boyfriend did in fact go to lunch with Joe and Chris—there's nothing wrong with asking the question this way. If, however, you're asking the question because you're trying to find out more about his lunch, then it's better to simply say, "Tell me about your lunch today?"

That way, your boyfriend has to fill in the blanks with details and not just add on to what you already know—or think you know.

Or maybe your assumption is wrong; maybe your boyfriend didn't go to lunch with anyone, in which case your question is likely to elicit some type of unwelcome response, like a correction in your facts or even an accusation that you're being too nosy. Or maybe he did run into his ex-girlfriend, but not when Joe and Chris were around—so if he tells you "No," he won't feel that he's being dishonest. Either way, you're way off target, so keep it simple and open-ended.

When to Use Closed-Ended Questions

Though we've already established the importance of using open-ended questions as an information-gathering technique, there are a few specific instances when closed-ended questions can come in handy. Just to reiterate the difference, closed-ended questions are typically the kinds of questions that can be answered with just one word:

Q: "Did you go to lunch?"
A: "Yes"
Q: "Was the car red?"
A: "No"
Q: "Do you want to see a movie?"
A: "Maybe"

As we've already discussed, whenever you start any conversation, it's best to begin by asking open-ended questions. It's only later in the conversation when you want to know specific information that you should start asking close-ended questions. By asking too many closed-ended questions at the beginning, you'll wear yourself out by attempting to obtain individual facts rather than allowing the person to offer their information openly and freely. Or worse yet, you're giving them the opportunity to say as little as possible. Remember, when the aim is to gather information, the goal is to get the other person to do most of the talking.

Closed-ended questions are typically meant to be asked toward the end of a conversation. As a person is speaking, rather than interrupting or cutting them off, take good mental notes of anything they may have left out or details that you want to know more about. This allows you to spot any red flags and to follow up with more specific questions at the end. Doing this gives you three advantages:

1. You'll obtain as much information from the onset as possible.
2. You'll be able to think and process what is being shared.
3. You'll be able to read the person's body language and verbal cues while they're speaking.

If you want to enhance your communication skills and draw out all of the information you need in a given situation, learning how to approach a conversation strategically will be a big help in achieving the outcome you desire.

Chapter 20

The Principles of Rapport

You can discover more about a person in an hour
of play than in a year of conversation.
—PLATO

Rapport Is Everything

Have you ever started talking with someone you just met, or maybe it's someone you've known for a long time but haven't seen in a while, and the dialogue just flows from the start? No matter what direction the conversation seems to go in, you both keep chatting away, adding to each other's thoughts, sometimes even finishing each other's sentences. That's called *rapport*! And rapport is an incredibly useful ingredient when it comes to influence.

Rapport is that magical thing that happens when two people fall into sync. It can almost feel like you're reading each other's minds . . . which, as it happens, is partly true. Research shows that when two people are in communicative harmony, their brains actually start interpreting the environment around them in the same way, something called *neuro coupling*. They begin mentally experiencing their social setting at a deeper level than they would have if they were by themselves or in a group but not speaking. It's the difference between engaging in meaningful conversations at a party versus being a wallflower.

When you have rapport, the person you're speaking to begins to like you. They also become more willing to trust you with what they say. Trust and rapport work hand in hand when it comes to influencing behavior.

Building trust actually creates a chemical change in the body. When someone trusts you, a hormone in their body called *oxytocin* is released. Oxytocin is produced in the hypothalamus and interacts with receptors in the amygdala, which are responsible for our bonding behaviors, such as recognizing people socially, creating group memories, and building relationships. It's also referred to as the *love hormone*. This is why we are more likely to see the positive qualities in someone that we form an easy connection with rather than their flaws. It's only later, when that connection is broken, that we are able to take on a more objective view and see their faults more clearly.

All of this means that when it comes to persuading others, building rapport is the secret sauce. However, once rapport is built, you have to work just as hard to sustain it because rapport can leave a conversation just as quickly as it arrives.

Empathy Is Queen

The word *empathy* is defined as the ability to emotionally understand another person by assuming their point of view. However, a lot of people think of empathy as being synonymous with weakness. They see an empathetic person as someone who is gullible and easy to manipulate psychologically. In my experience, this is the furthest thing from the truth. Empathy, in fact, is a strength. It utilizes your discernment and powers of observation. By being empathetic, you become a better negotiator, which is why empathy should be your weapon of choice in your arsenal of communication strategies.

One quick distinction: Being empathetic is different than being sympathetic. Empathy is another important part of rapport in making people feel understood: "It sounds like the loss of your mother was really difficult for you." Sympathy, on the other hand, is sharing in the pain and suffering of another person: "Losing a mother is a really hard thing to go through." The problem with sympathy is if you haven't directly experienced what the speaker has expressed to you—say, in this example, that you haven't lost your mother—your comment comes across as disingenuous and your sincerity seems fake. When that happens, you will almost instantly lose your connection to the person.

Or imagine a situation in which your significant other slams their laptop shut after sending an email to a client. You might see this and respond, "Wow, someone's in a bad mood." Rest assured that if they weren't in a bad mood before you said this, they are now! Why? Because you just passed judgment on their behavior rather than using empathy to discover what was really wrong. It would have been much wiser to say, "It seems like the email you just sent to your client was frustrating." By saying it this way, you're not labeling them or judging their response, but using empathy to understand their behavior.

Because most people just want to feel understood, expressing empathy toward someone can have a cascading effect on that person's emotions. The more empathetic you are, the more people will be drawn to you. They will want to be your friend, your coworker, maybe even your spouse. You gain the ability to connect with them on an entirely different level because you radiate a sense of understanding, compassion, and respect. In return, people will begin to trust and value your opinion.

Your ability to empathize opens the lines of communication. People would tell me their darkest secrets and deepest sources of shame in interrogation rooms because they believed I could understand their perspective—even when they knew that telling me these things could land them in jail. Despite this, by empathizing I was able to get them to put down their defenses and give me what I needed: The truth.

Now, it isn't always possible to feel genuine empathy for everyone. In fact, there are times when I feel the exact opposite and all I want to do is to point out someone's flaws, or how distorted their way of thinking is—but I don't. I hold my tongue, because in the end I know that this type of behavior will only sabotage my efforts to gain influence over them. In those times when your empathy isn't genuine, you should at least give the illusion that it is—especially in those situations where it will serve your interests the most.

Author and educator Stephen Covey said of empathy, "When you show deep empathy towards others, their defensive energy goes down, and positive energy replaces it. That's when you can get more creative in solving problems." Just as empathy was a foundational practice in my career as a Special Agent, it has become equally essential in my current career and personal life. I know that when I'm able to forge an easy connection with someone sitting across from me, they will be more receptive to my needs. You want to be able to get into people's heads and into their hearts, to get them to see that you understand where they're coming from. Once you're able to get beyond their barriers and throw off their defenses, people will reveal themselves to you in ways that they normally wouldn't to anyone.

Looking in the Mirror

The next time you're in a social gathering where two people are actively involved in a conversation, such as a restaurant, coffee shop, or a friend's party, pay attention to the way they're standing or sitting. If they're thoroughly enjoying each other's company, many times you'll see their body positioning looks exactly alike. They may both be standing with a hand on one hip as they lean toward each other or they might be sitting with their elbows resting on the table. They may even take a drink at the same time. And if you're close enough to eavesdrop on what they're chatting about, you'll often hear their speech patterns and voice volume match as well.

What you've just witnessed is called *mirroring*, or sometimes known as *mimicry*. When two people fall into communicative sync, their verbal and nonverbal behaviors will align and mirror one another. For the most part, this process occurs unconsciously, such that if you bring it to someone's attention, they're usually unaware it even happened. Mirroring takes place through speech, paralinguistics, and body language, and multiple research studies show that it can play a big role in facilitating rapport. In one particular experiment, waitresses either intentionally echoed their customers' orders by repeating back what they said ("Two eggs over easy and a side of bacon.") versus simply responding with an "Okay!" or "Coming right up." In those instances where verbal mirroring took place, the waitresses received larger tips. Verbal mirroring is a strategy I use on a daily basis. If a person I'm speaking with tends to use the same word repeatedly, such as *cool* or *awesome*, I use those words to create more of a connection. The same is true when I send emails or texts. If I want to establish rapport in writing, I'll pay attention to how the sender opens and ends their email. If they start with *Dear*, I'll start with *Dear*. If they end with *Sincerely* or *Kind regards*, I'll mirror their response. So much can be lost in written language, since you can't see the person you're communicating with, so mirroring small details like this can go a long way toward establishing a connection.

If you're in an important meeting and want to use your influence to create a positive outcome, a great strategy would be to mirror the body language of the person sitting across from you. If they have a hand cupped under their chin, you might do the same. If they lean in toward you, you should lean in as well. This will physically signal that you're on the same page.

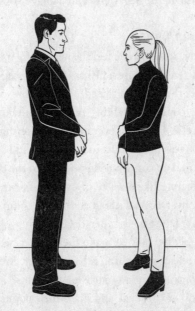

Mirroring

One of the best ways to put mirroring to the test is in situations like speed dating, which is exactly what a group of researchers did. In a speed dating experiment, two groups of women were studied to determine which had the most success. In one group, the women mirrored the body language and speech patterns of the men they met. The women in the other group didn't. When the men were later asked to describe which of the women they felt most attracted to, the women in the mirroring group won hands down.

All this said, you should be mindful that if you're ever "caught" intentionally mirroring someone, all bets are off. You'll be regarded as untrustworthy and whatever rapport you built up to that point will likely be lost. Mirroring is an effective influencer, but like all persuasion skills, it must be subtle and works best when it goes unnoticed. Also be mindful of mimicking negative body and verbal language. Mirroring defensive postures, such as crossed arms and legs, will not help you establish rapport and will be more likely to harm the connection. If someone is using insulting or degrading language, attempting to copy them will only escalate the negativity and damage your own demeanor.

Keep Your Ego in Check

As discussed earlier, some people feel the need to fill up silence in a conversation with scattered thoughts. Others feel the need to express every opinion that passes through their head. We all know someone who prefers to be the one constantly talking rather than taking a moment to listen to someone else. Have you ever been in a meeting when you could tell that the person was talking just to hear the sound of her own voice? Not only do they end up contributing nothing to the conversation, but it often ends up feeling like a waste of everyone's time. When people monopolize the conversation without adding anything of substance, it's a sign of insecurity. Don't be that person.

When people ask me how to make their voices heard, the best advice I can give is to have something relevant to say. Are you adding any value? Are you contributing any ideas or thoughts? More important, are you allowing others to speak and share their points of view? Or are you trying to dominate the conversation simply to show everyone how smart you think you are? Sometimes knowing when to shut up is just as important to knowing when to speak up.

In one child abuse case I worked, a little boy was brought in with a broken arm. Once again, the nanny was a prime suspect, but in this case the nanny was actually guilty. The nanny had been interviewed four times by the state police, and each time she was completely adamant that she hadn't harmed the infant.

I had been asked to interview the nanny alongside a fellow Special Agent who was also a trained polygrapher. Within minutes of the interview starting, I established rapport with the nanny. I asked her to tell me everything that happened on the day of the injury, from when she woke up to the time she went to bed. My partner remained silent as we both listened.

The nanny started telling me about her day, and what I noticed right away was that she kept explaining in a variety of ways what a difficult day it had been. It had been stressful. She had been trying to rush to work with her own young children. She described how the infant had been fussy, crying all the time.

Some people might have dismissed these tangents as venting and tried to get her to focus back on the story of what happened to the baby, but I knew what she was telling me was important. She was walking me through her frustrations and allowing me to see what was going on in her mind on that day. In short, she was giving me the motive for why she had broken the baby's arm.

I nodded my understanding as she told me how difficult it had been to watch over a baby who wouldn't stop crying, how she had tried shushing and holding him, everything she could think of to get him to sleep. "So then I put him down in his bed and he went quiet," she said. As soon as she said "he went quiet," I realized that was the moment she had broken his arm and caused the baby to pass out. She had already told me all the reasons why she'd done it before I even asked. It wasn't difficult for her to offer a confession after that.

Later, when I asked her why she had confessed this time and not during her prior interviews, she replied, "Because you were nice to me."

But more important, here's what was also happening in that

room: While I established rapport with the nanny, offering her a judgment-free space to vent her feelings and frustrations, my partner stayed silent. Why? Because he knew that the best way for us to obtain a confession was to sit back and allow me to steer the conversation. Our training and experience had taught us to never allow our egos to dictate how we interviewed someone. I had established good rapport with our suspect, which meant that she was speaking openly and honestly with me. Periodically throughout the interview I checked in with my partner to see if there was anything he wanted to ask, but he knew that we were getting all of the information we needed, and so he would simply shake his head, letting me resume my line of questioning. Had he inserted himself into the conversation out of a desire to be helpful or to hear the sound of his own voice, chances are he could have done much more harm than good. But he kept our larger goal in mind—getting at the truth—and knew that the most helpful thing he could do was to stay quiet.

There were plenty of times in my career when the roles were reversed, when I knew to sit back and allow my partner to get the information needed because we always had the larger objective in mind. Our goal in those interview rooms wasn't to prove our cleverness with a barrage of cunning questions or to dominate the conversation—our goal was discovering the truth using all of the skills, training, and knowledge we had at our disposal. So we kept our egos in check in service of the greater good.

This checking of the ego can be hard for many of us, especially for someone like me. We New Yorkers tend to believe that we are the mecca of everything and that nothing worth knowing could possibly exist outside of the five boroughs. Plus, I'm Greek, so of course I was groomed from birth to believe that everything in the world originated from Greece. We created civilization, philosophy, the Olympic Games, medicine, drama, the arts, sculpting, the gods, democracy—I mean, c'mon. Even the word *ego* is Greek. It actually means *self*.

That said, one of the most common ways for communication to fall apart is when we get wrapped up in our egos. We make everything about us and fail to look at a situation from another person's perspective, not taking their values and feelings and circumstances into account. But if you want to communicate well and influence behavior, you need to tap into your humility. Because it's not always about you. In fact, getting out of your own way is the only way you're going to get what you want, which brings me to the next strategy . . .

Do You Like Me? ☐ Yes ☐ No ☐ Maybe

Let me pose a question to you: Do you care whether people like you or not? When I ask a large audience the same question, there's usually a fair number that say "No." We've entered an era in which being likable is no longer a popular quest. It's almost cooler to be hated than to be liked. Think about the sorts of clichés we've gotten used to seeing on reality TV ("I'm not here to make friends!") or on social media when people brag about having haters. In fact, not caring about whether people like you has almost become a badge of honor. Some supervisors might say that they don't care if their employees like them, so long as they're doing their job. If you're one of those people who don't care whether people like you—well, you should. Your likability affects all of your relationships, both professional and personal. And science shows that people are more likely to work well and listen to people they like.

Consider the story with the nanny who confessed to me simply because I had been nice to her—that was by no means an isolated incident. In fact, anytime I got a confession from someone, I would always end the interview by asking the person if they thought I had treated them well. Without exception, every person answered "Yes." Some even hugged me before leaving the interview room, telling me how much better they felt after our conversation. Many of these were people who might face jail time as a result of having talked to me. That's the power of likability.

I remember one woman in particular I brought in for an interview. I had been investigating her on suspicion of Treasury fraud. She was a property manager and single mom, and she had been collecting the Social Security checks of several tenants who had passed away on the properties she managed, which was a felony. This had been going on for years and she had accumulated a lot of money, so after compiling all the evidence, there was enough to charge her.

When I arrested her, I did everything I could to treat her respect-fully. I didn't put handcuffs on her in front of her two little children and kept everything low-key until she accompanied me outside her home. Before the interview, I could see that she was hungry, so I brought her something to eat.

One of my fellow agents was confused when he saw me bringing her a burger and fries. "Why are you feeding her?" he asked.

"Because she's hungry," I replied.

As a result, she opened up and told me about the scam and how others had been a part of it—even her own family members. It wasn't difficult getting her to talk. After we had finished she hugged me and, through her tears, asked me to be by her side when she went before the judge.

I was the case agent in the investigation. I had personally investi-gated this woman, gathered all the evidence against her, and was now sending her to jail. And because she felt that I cared, she wanted me with her every step of the way.

People are more willing to talk and say "Yes" to those they like. Even if you don't think that your likability plays much of a role in your life, answer this: Do you enjoy being around people you dislike? I'm guessing no. No one does. Do you want to be the person that people avoid at a party, or the person people can't wait to talk to? Do you want people to come to you with their great ideas because they know you'll be excited to hear them, or do you want to be someone they're too afraid to approach?

Here's the thing: You can't dismiss the importance of likability. If you're likable, people will gravitate toward you, opportunities will open up, and life will become easier in myriad ways. However, the sort of superficial liking that takes place on social media isn't genuine likabil-ity. When people feel that you're listening to them and taking them seriously, when they feel that you're empathetic to their struggles and willing to understand them—that is genuine likability. There is value in people liking you, both for them and for you.

Now, I'm not saying you should go around trying to please people all the time. We tend to equate likability with being a people pleaser, and that is definitely not what I'm advocating here. This isn't about being a pushover or overly polite. Just as I would maintain my rapport with a suspect I was interviewing while pointing out holes in their story, I could still be likable and hold people accountable. You can still say "No" when you need to. In fact, if you care about your likability, these sorts of boundaries will probably be better received if others like you.

You Sound Just Like Me

Listen to the way people speak. Take into consideration who they are—their age, culture, intellect, emotional intelligence, etc.—and speak to them in a way they can relate to.

Getting a baseline on my interviewees' paralinguistics was so important that I would ask them to read a consent form aloud before the interview began, just to gather information based on how they spoke. Everyone I interviewed came from different backgrounds, and so they had drastically different ways of expressing themselves. I wouldn't use the same style of speech with a corporate executive as I would with a terrorist sympathizer or teenager suspected of a crime. I would adapt in order to form a better connection with each person.

At the same time, I didn't want to profile the people I spoke to or make assumptions based on what I saw. I paid close attention and used active listening to understand who was across from me. I would try to match their speech style as best I could within reason. If someone had a softer tone, I would use my softer tone. If they spoke in a more affluent manner, then I did the same. It's not about copying someone, because that would be inauthentic and people can read through bullshit a lot faster and better than you might imagine. But I found the version of me that I thought would work best with that person, which allowed me to more effectively build rapport with them.

As you probably know, New Yorkers are known for being fast and loud talkers (I can attest to this). My brother-in-law, Aidan, is from Missouri, where people are known for being a little more laid-back and relaxed in their speech. I love my brother-in-law, but on occasion it can take him forty minutes to explain something that took only ten minutes to happen! So, us having a conversation is kind of like the tortoise and hare running around the same track. We're both going in the same direction, but it's a bit of a one-sided race. And as much as he might wear me down waiting for the next word to fall out of his mouth, I'm sure he's as easily worn out with my loud mile-a-minute chatter. We're not really in sync. But what's important here is that I know we're not in sync. If needed to, however, I could put us there.

If Aidan were someone I wanted to influence, I would start by slowing down the rate of my words considerably. I would also lower the volume of my voice to match his. So however loudly or softly he was speaking, I would start speaking that way as well. Once I matched his linguistic output, I would watch to see if he'd start mirroring anything I'm doing: The way I'm sitting or standing, how my feet or arms are positioned, even whether his body alignment matches mine. If and when it does, I know that he's now communicating with me on a deeper level—remember neuro coupling? Once we're in sync, it makes him unconsciously like me even more.

One of the things you don't want to do, however, is try to match a person's accent. So when my brother-in-law's midwestern drawl comes out, I wouldn't want to start throwing in a few "Y'alls" for good measure. Research shows that when we try to match the accent of the person we're talking to (British, Australian, etc.), it comes across as disingenuous and ruins whatever rapport was previously built.

It's important to note that the way you can influence people with paralinguistics is the same way they can influence you. So if Aidan started speaking louder and faster within the first few minutes of our conversation, I would consider the possibility that he might actually be trying to influence me! Paralinguistic influence, like the other principles discussed in this book, is a two-way street. So pay attention and always ask yourself, "Do I like this person a little more now than I did a few minutes ago?" If the answer is "Yes," then you're also now a little more susceptible to being influenced by them.

Chapter 21

The Tactics of Influence

Let us conduct ourselves so that all men wish to be our friends and all fear to be our enemies.
—Alexander the Great

But First, Let Me Prime You

When you hear the word *priming*, what comes to mind? A body shop specialist might imagine the *priming coat* that goes onto the car before it's painted. A gun enthusiast may envision the *priming charge* used to ignite the propellant that fires the bullet. And a financial advisor may think about the government's effort to stimulate the economy called *priming the pump*. No matter what context it's used in, the word *priming* always means the same thing—something that's done first to make whatever follows better. Better paint job, better firepower, better economic growth.

In the world of everyday communication, marketing strategies, and police interrogations, priming is a strategy used to mentally sway people toward a direction you want their minds to go. It often occurs with such subtlety that recipients are unaware it even happened. Take this, for example: You're seated in the reception waiting area of a large technology firm for a 9 a.m. business meeting pitch. If all goes well, there could be a significant financial upside for both you and your five-person start-up company. Precisely on time, an older gentleman whom you've never met strolls into the front office, carrying a stainless-steel cup in one hand and a folder full of papers in the other. He calls out your name and as you stand, he nods politely and turns back toward the lobby doors. You follow him out. While standing together at the elevator bank, he introduces himself as Jim and asks you to hold his cup so he can swipe his ID into the card reader. The cup feels warm in your hands. Although it's covered with a lid, the fact that it's only 9 a.m. makes you assume it's coffee. The elevator doors open and you step into the empty car with Jim while handing him back his cup. He presses 15. As you ride up the floors in silence, you have a slight smile on your face. You like Jim. This is going to be a good interview.

. . . and you've just been primed.

Do you know how?

In a study that looked at how physical temperature affects people's perception of others, researchers found that when someone experiences the feeling of warmth, such as holding a warm cup of coffee, they will subconsciously judge the originator of that warmth as more trustworthy, friendly, and likable. Interestingly enough, the opposite is also true. If Jim had handed you a cold glass of iced tea, for example, you would have seen him as less friendly and more likely to interfere with your plans for success.

Priming comes in many forms. Whether through our use of specific words, the way in which furniture is arranged, even the lighting in the room—these can all affect the way in which the person being primed (the primee) feels about their environment, themselves, and the person priming them (the primer).

Keeping with our above scenario, imagine yourself and Jim getting off on the fifteenth floor and walking into an immense well-lit corner office with overstuffed couches and floor-to-ceiling windows overlooking the cityscape. Sitting on the conference table is a large pitcher of coffee, two uncapped bottles of water, and a few magazines, one of which is opened to an article about your start-up company.

Seeing the magazine article opened to your spotlight story may seem a bit over-the-top, but that's not the prime. It's the magazine that is laid open on the table, rather than closed. Remember, it's the subtle things you wouldn't consider or even report back later as influencing your perceptions. But they do.

The lighting in the room, for example, will extenuate whatever mood you're already in. If the lights are bright, your mood is enhanced, while dimmer lighting will cause you to be less stimulated. And being as you were already in a good mood and liking Jim during the elevator ride up, you're probably liking him even more now without him having done anything new to earn your amiability. The open bottle of water, open magazine, and multiple open windows all display what? Yes, a sense of openness. These primers have been shown to nudge you to be more open with your thoughts and your willingness to consider other people's perspectives, which could have an interesting effect on your negotiating power.

Now Jim sits down at the conference room table, gestures for you to have a seat, and begins by saying, "Thank you for accepting our invitation and agreeing to meet with us. We feel there is a real opportunity here. If you're open to working together and sharing ideas, I'm positive we can make this partnership extremely lucrative for both our team and yours."

Seems like a really good start to a conversation on top of an already good day, wouldn't you think? Does Jim have your attention? He should, because his opening lines are packed with priming words. Before reading on for the answers, reread what he said and see if you can pick them out. There are nine.

Accepting, agreeing, opportunity, open, together, sharing, positive, partnership, and *team*. All these words focus the listener's attention around three things: Positivity, openness, and a sense of collaboration. In a nutshell, you're now more open to hearing what Jim has to say and liking the idea of working with him.

Research shows that when people are exposed to words that carry a certain meaning, they'll adopt the persona of those words. In a fascinating study regarding this phenomenon, two groups of participants were asked to unscramble words in a sentence. One group was given words that, unbeknownst to them, all described elderly stereotypes, such as: *Old, forgetful, wrinkle, Florida, dependent, helpless, gullible*, and *bingo.* The second group was given neutral words that had no associated stereotype, such as: *Thirsty, clean,* and *private.* After the participants finished unscrambling the sentences and left the experiment, researchers surreptitiously timed how long it took them to walk down the hallway. The participants who had the elderly scrambled sentences walked slower! That's the power of priming.

Now that you're aware of how priming works, there are several things you can do to make it work in your favor . . . besides walking around all day asking people to hold your warm cup of coffee. The next time you're in an important business meeting, consider having it in a place where there are windows to the outside world, which promotes openness. If that's not possible, then have an open pitcher of water or some open books. Lighting is obviously important; just make sure the person you're meeting with is in a good mood. Also, much like Jim, it really helps to plan your opening lines ahead of time. Those first few sentences prime the direction the entire conversation will go. Write them out and rehearse them. Think of it like a book. The deciding factor to why most people will or will not buy a book is the introduction. A lot of high-level negotiators I know will actually write out their opening lines and practice them with colleagues to make sure they contain enough priming words, ensuring that their delivery comes off naturally.

Know What You're Talking About

When we talk about authority in the context of influence, we're not talking about imposing your authority on other people. This principle is about being an authority on what you're talking about. More than anything, this means preparation. It means doing your due diligence so that you can speak cogently and thoughtfully on a subject, which will inspire everyone who listens to you to defer to your expertise. In short, know what the fuck you're saying. People are influenced by those they perceive to be the authority of the topic at hand.

Something to bear in mind is that this isn't about showing off or being arrogant—no one wants to hear you recite your resumé or CV. In fact, that sort of conceit can be perceived as overcompensating for a lack of knowledge or experience, so you want to be careful about overstating your qualifications. This isn't about convincing others that you're the authority on a subject; this is about *showing* them that you're the authority.

When you can speak deeply and intelligently on a topic people are more willing to give you their trust.

But be careful—using authority as an influence strategy goes both ways.

I've seen this happen when people hire financial advisors. After spending years painstakingly counting their pennies and saving their money, they'll then hand it over to an investor with almost no questions asked—because they assume that person is an expert. Maybe he told them that he knew exactly what he was doing and they should "trust him" (*red flag*), rather than questioning him about his investment process. This is common in financial scams. When I'd ask victims of fraud whether they had asked their so-called financial expert about his credentials or strategies, most said "No." They blindly deferred to the advisor on all decisions because he carried himself as the authority— expert—when it came to investing. This is also common with other perceived authority figures—such as doctors and lawyers. People take their word as gospel and rarely seek second opinions.

Do your homework and make smart decisions about whom you choose to trust and why.

You're in My Space

Imagine that you had to get up early for a work meeting. You're still a bit groggy from the night before, and the inside of your local coffee spot is busier than usual. As you patiently wait in line to order, you *feel* the person standing behind you is a little too close. Although they haven't physically touched you in any way, you sense your personal space is being violated. *Maybe I'm just cranky and need caffeine*, you think as you step forward, hoping to put some distance between you and the space intruder. But just as you do, they seem to follow. Either they're oblivious to the unwritten distance rule or they're intentionally up to something. Internally, you feel your blood pressure rising along with your annoyance . . . and it's not even 7 a.m. yet. The internal stress you're feeling, however, is not from a lack of caffeine. It's normal—in fact, it's biological. Humans are hardwired to feel increasing amounts of anxiety and discomfort when someone unknown or unwelcome gets too close. How close is too close? That all depends on how we feel about them personally. According to cultural anthropologist Edward Hall, there are four socially acceptable distances that correspond with those feelings.

1. **Intimate space:** Direct contact up to 18 inches. This distance is reserved for only those we're most intimate with, such as lovers, close family members, and children.
2. **Personal space:** 18 inches to 4 feet. This distance is shared with our close friends and family members.
3. **Social space:** 4 feet to 12 feet. This distance is for strangers, people we just met, and acquaintances.
4. **Public space:** 12 feet+. This distance is best for giving public speeches or interacting with an audience.

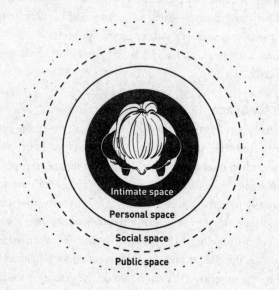

Proxemics, which is the study of space between people, is critical to understand. Because we psychologically own the immediate space around us, it's okay to confront someone who has entered into it without an invitation. Although I'm not telling you to be a jerk about it, I am telling you that you shouldn't feel wrong for pointing out the obvious, especially as a preemptive way to protect yourself (refer back to Part 1 of this book if you need some helpful pointers). There are exceptions to the rule, though, such as when you're on a crowded subway train, walking through a busy airport, or moshing at a concert. There are also cultural differences as well, so pay attention to your surroundings and respond accordingly.

Now that you understand how most people—at least in Western cultures—associate physical distance with intimacy, I'm going to show you how to use, and in some cases override, those buffer zones to influence your situation.

The inside of most police interrogation rooms looks the same. There are usually a few chairs, a table, a two-way mirror, and not much else. This is where the use of proxemics comes into play. Most interviews begin with the investigator sitting directly across from the person being questioned. Sometimes there's a table between them; sometimes not. Based on proxemics, how far away should the investigator sit in order to make the interviewee feel most comfortable? Assuming they've never met, about four feet, which places them firmly in *social space*. As the interview continues, what oftentimes happens is the interviewer will move closer to and farther from the person they're talking to. Why?

Influence.

Remember our discussion on the use of *authority* as an influencer? In this example, the police investigator is the authority in the room, so what he or she does mentally impacts the interviewee. When the interviewer moves closer, let's say within 12 inches (*personal space*), it gives the impression that their relationship has progressed from a social affair to a more personal one. And when someone is in our personal space, we consider them to be a close friend or family member. Why is this important? Because these are the people with whom we're more likely to speak openly and share intimate details. Being a highly skilled negotiator means being capable of getting into a person's *intimate space*—it can be as simple as putting a hand on their shoulder as a sign of assurance or briefly touching their arm to redirect their attention forward. These professionals know the value of touch and the effect it can have on people talking. Of course, physical contact should be made only with consent from both parties.

Conversely, when a good negotiator moves away from the person, oftentimes rolling back in their chair, it's to give the impression that what's being said is either not important or they disagree with it. Now, this isn't to suggest that every time you close the gap between yourself and the person that it automatically strengthens your emotional bond—it doesn't. In fact, I've seen instances when the person will actually lean back in their chair trying to reclaim some of that lost space. If that happens, rather than forcing your way into a person's personal space, try to wait for a nonverbal invitation (eye contact, body alignment, forward posture). You don't want whatever rapport you've established to get lost due to the invasion of personal space. Just like with mirroring, you need to be subtle about using proxemics to influence someone.

This very same "proximity tactic" can be used with great success in your everyday life. The next time you're starting a conversation with someone you just met, pay attention to the space that naturally forms between you. As the dialogue continues, if the person you're speaking with seems engaged, and you're interested in getting to know them better, slowly start to close the gap between you two. This will subtly give off the vibe that the relationship is turning from an acquaintance into a friendship, and that you're a trustworthy person they can chat with candidly. If, however, when you move in, they seem to step away or their nonverbal behavior changes for the worse, consider retreating just a bit to allow the space to open back up. Determining the proxemics in any new relationship takes time, but when used correctly, its influence can create a stronger, deeper bond.

Here's another scenario. Imagine you're new to the neighborhood and attending your very first neighborhood social gathering. Your plan is to get onto the community board of directors so you can have a say in the new zoning laws that may affect your school district. Knowing the board's president would be in attendance, you did a bit of homework and found out he's passionate about golf, St. Louis Cardinals baseball, and waterskiing. You notice he just finished a phone call and is now standing by himself in the corner. Using proxemics, how best would you approach him?

The strategic move would be to introduce yourself with a handshake, which naturally establishes a social distance of about four feet, and then start off with the fact that you're new to the area and ask him where he's from, best places to eat, discussions that will help you build rapport. As the conversation progresses, using the reading people section in this book, simply judge his reception to you. If he seems engaged, continue. At some point, I would bring up one of the topics he's passionate about—whichever you may know most about, all the while trying to close the gap between you two. Now, remember, when you walked up to him, he was standing in the corner, so all of the proxemics adjustments are based on you. Because of his passion about baseball, for example, he's more likely to speak openly and excitedly, giving you a segue into a bit of his personal life. Assuming the conversation stays on the positive track, it's likely the next time you two meet, he'll remember you as the friend who shared his love of America's pastime. You'll have earned his trust, and possibly his vote in the upcoming board of directors election.

At times, we may misjudge the distance that goes best with each relationship. Some people are quick to come in for the hug and remain close talkers, while others like to keep an arm's-length distance. Remember, because you're trying to influence them, pay attention to their nonverbal behavior, eye contact, and body alignment as indications on how close or far you should stand. Using the proxemics diagram is a good place to start, but also pay attention to how they move as the conversation continues. The closer they come into your space, the more personally connected they're feeling toward you. Conversely, if they start to back away, either you're too close or they're losing interest in what you have to say.

Oh My God!

Imagine that you're on a first date, and your date mentions that they are a huge fan of the YouTube series *Cobra Kai*. And you immediately jump out of your chair saying, "Oh my God! I love that show, I love *Cobra Kai*!"

And you think, *Wow—that's so cool*. At least that's what I thought when one of my colleagues admitted it to me. I instantly felt more connected to her.

How often is it that we get excited when we meet someone with the same birthday, or who shares the same favorite sports team or town where we grew up? And why do those sorts of commonalities feel like such a big deal?

Because we like people who are like us.

Look at your friends. Chances are you probably share a lot of similarities with them. Similar foods, similar values. You probably like to hang out at similar places or do similar activities. We gravitate and feel comfortable with people who we think are like us. We also tend to be uncomfortable with the unknown, or with those we perceive as "different." We have a harder time connecting with people whose tastes and interests are unfamiliar from our own.

One way to bridge the gap is to try to find things in common with the people you interact with, especially those whom you want to impress. Perhaps it's a favorite kind of food or music—it can be anything. We like people who remind us of, well, us. Trying to find "common" ground with people is important. And even when there isn't any, you can create it in subtle ways.

When I go to important business lunches or dinners, depending on the circumstances, I may order the same meal as the person I'm with. Even the same drink. When I'm having lunch with a group of media executives in Los Angeles, I'll order a salad or a veggie wrap, just like everyone else (even though I usually like burgers). By creating common ground with someone, I'm signaling that we're on the same page, that we're in sync in more ways than one, which means we're more likely to connect on important topics like an idea I want to pitch or how I hope a business arrangement will shake out.

During one interview I did with a local police detective, we were investigating a young man who had been an accessory to murder. I was trying to find some common ground with our suspect, but we had none. We all came from very different worlds—but I knew the value of creating commonality, so I was determined to find it. After being in the interview room for a while, I asked the young man if he was thirsty. He admitted he was and asked for a Pepsi. I got up, left the room, and returned with three Pepsis—one for the young man, one for myself, and one for the detective.

I remember the detective glancing up at me with an inquisitive look. "I drink Coke," he mumbled.

"Not today," I said. "Today you're drinking Pepsi."

And so we all three sat in the room together and drank our Pepsis. An hour later we had a confession.

This isn't to say that you have to pretend to be something that you're not. You shouldn't have to fundamentally change your personality in order to adapt to someone else. But if you're struggling to find connection where there seems to be none, extending yourself in these small, subtle ways can go far in creating common ground when you need it.

Own Your Mistakes

As a Special Agent, accountability played a huge role in how people perceived one another in the Service. On one occasion, I was the lead agent in charge of security for one of President Obama's public speaking events at American University. Basically, I was responsible for everything—how the president got to the venue, how we were supposed to get him in and out of the event, how many agents would be stationed where, the number of ingress and egress points, the rope lines, crowd management, communicating with the White House and support staff. All of it. Given the magnitude of responsibilities, I was also given a site agent to carry out on-the-ground security at the venue.

"There needs to be two ingress and egress points," I told him at a site visit two days prior to the president's speech. "Two ways in and two ways out—minimum."

"Well, the staff told me that could be problematic for them."

"They'll have to figure it out," I said. "Two ways in and two ways out. No matter what."

"Okay."

The next evening, I went to visit one last time as the stage and venue were being built out. "Did you make sure to integrate the two egress and ingress points?" I asked. "You made sure to build it in, yes?"

"Yeah, it's all figured out."

So you can imagine that when I arrived the following morning with the president's motorcade and saw only one way into the venue, I nearly lost my shit.

Fortunately, the event went off without any problems, but I knew I was in for the reaming of my life when it was over. Sure enough, as soon as the president was on his way back to the White House, I received a call from my supervisor ordering me to come to his office—and to bring my site agent.

We arrived back at the White House, where my boss proceeded to tear into and lecture me. He didn't say a single word to my colleague—every bit of his dressing down was directed to me, and rightfully so. I had been in charge. I was responsible for everything that had happened, and I wasn't about to shirk that responsibility. The only words I spoke for the duration of the lecture were "Yes, sir."

Meanwhile, the site agent stood beside me in silence. He didn't interject once. He didn't explain that I had ordered him on multiple occasions to create the entry and exit points and that he had failed to do so. Now this may seem unfair—but it doesn't matter.

In the Service we were taught to take responsibility not just for ourselves, but for others as well. Almost every agent I knew faced the fire head-on, as I did. The ones who didn't quickly fell out of favor with everyone else.

We all make mistakes. Some are small and some not so small, but the fact remains that they happen. We've all been taught that mistakes are terrible, a source of shame that will tarnish us forever. Frankly, that's true only if you don't take accountability for them. Here's the thing—many mistakes are inevitable and forgivable. Yet, no mistake is worse than failing to own up to it. It's a matter of character and integrity. There is truly nothing more inspiring than when people make an honest and thorough appraisal of a mistake and take full responsibility for their own errors or lapses in judgment.

The same is true of your accomplishments. Take ownership of the things you do, whether they're good or bad. And remember that no one wants to follow anyone who shirks or cowers away from taking responsibility. We all fuck up. But how we recover from our fuckups is how we differentiate ourselves.

Be Able to Adapt

During a pre-fight interview, then heavyweight boxing champion Mike Tyson was asked if he was worried about his opponent who was preparing for the fight against him. Tyson's response to this question was: "Everyone has a plan till they get punched in the face." This is one of my favorite quotes because it reminds me of the reality that I can plan, prep, lay everything out perfectly, and then . . . *whack* . . . right in the fucking face. Life will check me.

At some point, everyone has experienced what happens when things don't go according to plan. Say you're preparing for a meeting or a negotiation. You've got it all laid out. You know all your talking points, what you're going to say and when, how the room will be laid out, where you'll stand, everything. But then on the actual day, nothing goes as planned. Your car stalls in the driveway and won't start. You call a car service and they're twenty minutes later than they said they would be. You arrive late to the meeting and can't get the projector to work. Then your slides are out of order and the one person you were counting on being there to support you called in sick. How would you fare under these circumstances? Would you roll with the punches, or would you be so caught off guard that you'd stumble through the presentation and forget all of your talking points?

We all try to make a best-guess assessment of how we think things will go, and sometimes they don't work out in our favor. When we go into a situation with rigid reliance on a certain outcome or a predictable order of events, we become ineffective. We struggle to problem-solve and cannot shift our thought process because we're stuck in a non-negotiable plan we laid out for ourselves.

In the Service, everything we did was well choreographed when it came to protection. Yet we understood that no matter how carefully things were laid out, anything could break bad at a moment's notice, which meant that we had to be able to quickly adapt. That's why we had contingency plans for contingency plans. We planned for it all. A bomb. A fire. A riot. A biochemical agent. A radioactive agent. We'd have a plan A, a plan B, a plan C, and more if needed. That way, when things went wrong—which inevitably they did—we could swiftly adapt to the new environment or new situation.

Rigid people are the most dangerous people. Because they don't know how to adapt, they become tethered to the one narrative they have created in their minds. They become unable to pivot so when life delivers a blow, it's almost impossible for them to recover. A breakup or the loss of a job could send them into a tailspin because they haven't worked to develop their adaptability. Don't let a bad five minutes in your day—a traffic incident, disagreement with a friend, anything—ruin your entire day or week. You have power in how you react to setbacks, and being able to move on is a skill worth cultivating.

Give People a Choice

One of the things we desire as individuals is the ability to choose for ourselves. We call this *autonomy*. Autonomy is being able to have a personal choice, which gives you a sense of control and independence. In an interview room, those choices were pretty limited, but they still existed. "Which chair would you like to sit in?" Or "Would you like something to drink?" In our personal lives, autonomy may come in the form of "Where would you like to eat?" Or "What movie would you like to see?" Although these may not seem like much, when it comes to influence, having a personal choice pays dividends.

When I meet with production companies to pitch ideas, there's usually something specific that I'm after—meaning I'm not willing to negotiate or compromise on certain aspects. But when it comes to things I don't care about, such as the location or timing of the meeting, I'll give all of the autonomy to the other party. I'll drive an hour out of my way or clear my schedule in order to give people the flexibility they need. Once we're sitting across from each other in the same room, however, I'll use all of my influence to get them excited and supportive of what matters to me.

The next time you're at a meeting with a colleague or a new client, if it's appropriate, give them a choice:

"What would you like to drink?"

"Sit anywhere you like."

"Where do you want to eat?"

"When works best for you to meet?"

Remember: People will be more willing to compromise and work with you if they feel that you've already extended courtesy and flexibility toward them, so offer autonomy wherever you're willing to give up control so you don't have to surrender it for those things you truly care about. Give when you can so you don't have to give when you don't want to.

Chapter 22

How Others Influence You

Know how to listen and you will profit even from those who talk badly.
—PLUTARCH

Everyone Is Your Mentor

The word *mentor* brings to mind different things for different people. For some, it might be a teacher who encouraged and supported you in high school. Or it may be that hippie uncle who always seemed to give the right advice at the right time, or a generous boss who took you under their wing.

The word *mentor* actually originates from ancient Greece (shocker, I know). In Homer's epic poem *Odyssey*, the main character, Odysseus, leaves his young son, Telemachus, in the care of his faithful friend Mentor while away fighting the Trojan War for ten years. In the English language, *mentor* has come to mean an experienced and trusted advisor who willingly imparts knowledge onto the less knowledgeable.

There are two prevailing myths about mentorship. The first is that seeking out a mentor is the key to our success—that we need someone to guide us, give us advice, and keep us focused. For anyone who has access to someone like this, consider yourself lucky. But what about the rest of us who don't? If we never cross paths with someone of this caliber who is willing to help us reach our full potential, are we screwed?

The problem with this notion of mentorship is that it fosters a psychological sense of dependence on another. It tells us that in order to be successful in life, we need somebody else to get us there.

The truth is, you don't need a helpful teacher, a witty uncle, or a supportive boss to help you reach your goals. In some ways, it's better if you don't. By relying on that one person to steer you clear of life's pitfalls, how will you ever learn from your mistakes? How will you become resilient when faced with rejection, or confident in your decisions after your mentor is gone? Worse yet, how will you ever know whether the thoughts in your head are organic to you or a mere carbon copy of someone else's?

So, instead of seeking the counsel of just one person, why not seek the counsel of many? Everyone around you can be your mentor in some form or fashion as long as you're willing to observe and absorb their lessons. These teaching points in life don't need to come only from those you consider admirable. You can learn just as much from an asshole as you can from a role model. Some people possess qualities you admire most while others show you what you should carefully avoid. A great supervisor, for example, can show you the kind of leader you want to be, while a bad parent can help you see how *not* to raise a child. Think of mentoring as a buffet—there are plenty of options to choose from. You don't have to try everything on the menu; just load up on what you want.

The second myth when it comes to mentoring is that we need direct access to that person. Just like the first myth, this too is untrue. Maybe it was true in a time long before the Internet or the library, when communities were small and the primary source of wisdom was the town elder. But today, we have access to whomever and whatever we want. And by access, I don't mean personal direct access—I mean we have the ability to watch, listen, and learn from everyone, whether they live next door, the next state over, or on the other side of the world.

In all my years of working at the White House, I never privately sat down with any of my protectees to seek out their advice. I was there to protect them, not to seek counsel—plus they were already pretty busy running the country. President Obama never pulled up a chair next to me on *Air Force One* to share his personal thoughts on what it meant to be "presidential"—but I can assure you that, after watching the way he carried himself through the constant chaos around him, I understand the true definition of the word. In the next chapter, I will share with you some of the mentoring lessons I learned from him as well as other leaders I protected.

There has never been any *one* person in my life that I called my personal mentor. As is the case for so many people, that simply wasn't a luxury that I had access to growing up. I had to figure out a lot of things on my own. At times it was difficult and beyond frustrating. Looking back now, however, I realize what a critical part it played in building who I am today. It taught me how to be independently driven, a self-thinker, and an efficient problem solver. Better yet, it taught me to look for important lessons in everyone around me so that I could continue building my character and diligently discard those qualities I found unappealing.

So, the next time you see someone you admire or even despise, ask yourself, "What is it about this person I can learn from?" Perhaps it's the confident way they enter a room or their friendly smile. Or it might be the unflattering way they speak to their wife or how they seem to complain about everything. Each observation, both good and bad, can become your guidepost.

There's Power in Solitude

Being alone has gotten a bad rap in our culture. There's an assumption that the more friends we have, the better we'll feel about ourselves, and so many of us do everything we can to constantly surround ourselves with other people. The problem is that those other voices can start drowning out our own. It's important to be able to hear ourselves, to tune in to the things we need and want in life. For these reasons, we need to take regular breaks from the noise of the world in our daily lives and seek out time alone.

Humans are social creatures by necessity. Our survival as a species is a result of having formed tribes that fostered cooperation and collaboration. Today, however, we often feel that in order to be most productive, we need to be in the presence of others. That may be true if the task is a cognitive one where collective brainpower is being harnessed to generate a vast number of ideas. But when it comes to our personal productivity, we're actually better alone, away from the distractions of others. Studies show that being by ourselves enables us to tap more deeply into the creative side of our brains, allowing our thoughts to flow freely without limitations. Simply put, solitude gives us the ability to cut through the clamor of external voices and opinions, to focus on our personal truth, and to find the clarity to think for ourselves.

Spending time alone also boosts personal effort. When we're part of a group, the amount of effort we exert actually decreases compared to when we're working on the same task solo. This is referred to as *social loafing*. In a study called the *Ringelmann Effect*, a group of individuals were blindfolded and tasked with pulling on a rope as hard as they could. The amount of effort they exerted was then recorded. The same subjects were then told to pull on the rope again, and advised that this time they would be pulling as a member of a group ranging from two to six people. During their second "group" pull, the subjects pulled with less force. At times when we're relying on others to help us meet a goal, we actually end up putting out less energy than we would in going at it alone.

Influence is knowing when taking a break from others is in your best interest. There are moments in our lives when we're more vulnerable or susceptible to the opinions of others. People can confuse us, make us second-guess ourselves, or completely derail us from achieving our goals. At times we unknowingly allow ourselves to be influenced by those we're closest to. Judgments and attitudes held by parents, spouses, siblings, or good friends can weigh heavily on the choices we make, even if we aren't fully aware of it. The antidote is solitude and self-reflection. Spending time alone will help you determine whether the thoughts and emotions you carry are truly yours, or if you've taken on the attitudes, beliefs, and biases of the people or culture surrounding you.

Remember: Even Superman had his Fortress of Solitude, so consider how you might create your own version of that. Take a walk by yourself. Wake up before anyone else and spend time journaling or sipping on a cup of coffee while the house is quiet. Find a secluded place to meditate. Sit on a park bench and people watch. Take a weekend trip alone. The point is to find moments in your day, even if just for a few minutes, to step away from the chatter of the world and find quiet clarity within.

Be Careful Not to Self-Edit

Once you begin to see how others may be influencing you, the next step is to look for the ways in which you may be influencing yourself. Negative self-beliefs can easily prevent us from taking chances or pursuing the things we want.

I recently had a conversation with one of the designers of the training curriculum for the US Army's Special Operations branch in Fort Bragg, North Carolina. When I asked how they managed to turn average people into elite warriors, she simply said, "We don't."

"What do you mean?" I asked.

"The average person doesn't apply. People self-select themselves out of the running. So we get only the strongest candidates who already believe they can do the job."

The concept of self-editing is often dictated by our fear of failure. We choose not to be part of a group because we feel we are inadequate. But sometimes it goes beyond that. We can also begin to edit the choices we make in other areas of our lives. We allow our beliefs about what we are and are not capable of to determine what paths we pursue. We can be so terrified of taking risks that we don't even make the attempt to go after something we want, and something that we may indeed be very good at if we could just give ourselves the chance to try. Instead, we'll create a dream and kill it in the same moment. We convince ourselves that we lack the skill, talent, or self-worth, assuming that others are infinitely more qualified. We identify why it can't be done rather than focus on how it *can* be done.

Just like the US Army's special operators, those who apply to be Secret Service Special Agents go through the same self-selection process. Only those who have unwavering confidence and mental toughness put themselves forward as potential candidates. Those who doubt themselves never even bother to apply, which means they will never know what could have been. This notion of self-editing stays with us every step of the way through our lives and careers. You don't just over-come it once—it is a lifelong process, and fortunately it's one that gets easier with practice.

When it comes to taking a leap, the first obstacle to push past will always be yourself. First look at the tone and attitude of your thoughts—are they self-limiting? Do you sabotage a goal by convincing yourself there are too many obstacles in your way? Do you focus on all of the reasons why you can't pursue something rather than how you can? There will always be that voice of doubt that crops up when you're considering taking a risk. There will always be an inner critic lurking in the wings, willing to point out all of your flaws and inadequacies. If you turn every obstacle into a wall you can't get over, you let yourself become the cause of your failures. Knowing how to notice and navigate the self-editing process is the difference between trying or not, achieving or not. The first "No" you hear should never come from you.

The Problem with Comparing

In 1954, Englishman Roger Bannister and Australia's John Landy were considered two of the world's fastest runners. Earlier that year, Bannis-ter was the first man to run the mile in under four minutes, with a time of 3:59:04. Less than two months later, Landy eclipsed Bannister's mile time by 1.4 seconds to become the new record holder. Later that summer, both men met for the first time to compete in the British Empire and Commonwealth Games in a race that became known as the *Miracle Mile*.

During much of the race, Landy held a commanding lead, but even-tually Bannister closed the gap. As both men dashed toward the finish line, Landy, who was in first, did the unthinkable. He temporarily lost focus of his goal, turned his attention away from the finish line and toward Bannister. As Landy looked over his shoulder in search of his opponent, Bannister sprinted past him to win the race. In the heat of battle, Landy was so concerned with his competitor that he became distracted. And lost.

Whether we admit it or not, many of us define our place in this world by comparing ourselves to others. We base our accomplishments on someone else's failures and compare our shortcomings to another person's success. We use others as barometers to assess our strength and beauty as well as our wisdom and wit. There is nothing unjust about being a competitive person. In fact, individual rivalry has been ingrained in our character throughout our childhood, beginning with grammar school grades, homecoming votes, and SAT scores. Competition is what motivates us, but it's how we compete that drives us to become better—or unhinged.

During practice at the shooting range with the Secret Service, our instructors would always tell us to stay focused on our own target. We would line up, side by side, standing just a couple of feet apart. This made it pretty tempting to glance over at my neighbors' targets to see how well they were shooting. Without fail, whenever I let my eyes wander, my shooting deteriorated significantly. My bullets became a smattering around the bull's-eye rather than the tight grouping it was only moments before. If you think about it, it's a little ridiculous that someone else's shooting proficiency could affect where my bullets landed—but it did. I knew how to shoot well—strong stance, sight alignment, and smooth trigger pull—but once I began comparing my shot placement to someone else's, my accuracy suffered. That's because I became distracted by what the person next to me was doing, taking focus away from the task in front of me.

Landy's lifelong quest to become the world's fastest man was the healthy competition that drove him, but his immediate need to know what his competition was doing cost him that title. Every ounce of energy you waste worrying about someone else's progress or performance is one less ounce of energy you can spend on yourself, on building your skills and making your own strides forward.

No Fucks to Give

There is an incredible opportunity for growth when you're willing to invest time and energy on learning a new skill from square one. You do this by focusing not on what others think of you, but exclusively on your goal of learning and improving.

My husband and I signed up to learn Brazilian jiujitsu and muay thai at one of the best schools in New York, Renzo Gracie. While my husband had practiced the art many years before and was eager to get back into it, I was a total novice.

Before you go on thinking that learning jiujitsu might be easy for me because I had training as a US Secret Service agent, you couldn't be more wrong. We aren't taught this kind of fighting in the Academy. Instead, we learned techniques centered on safety and survival. Getting into hand-to-hand combat with a potential assailant was not only dangerous for them, but for me as well. You never knew if an assailant was armed, mentally unstable, intoxicated, or homicidal. You can't place yourself on an equal playing field with an adversary like that, nor should you. In law enforcement, we are trained to resolve an issue as quickly and efficiently as possible using only the level of force necessary—no more, and no less.

So grappling on a mat with an unarmed training partner who's not trying to kill me the first chance he gets is uniquely different. Jiujitsu is a martial art that focuses on ground fighting and grappling techniques used to force an opponent into submission. Currently, my belt is so white it's nearly transparent. When I go to class, I'm often lost and confused. I forget a move thirty seconds after the professor shows it (in jiujitsu, instructors are referred to as *professors*). I try to outmuscle my opponent rather than outwit him. In other words, I suck . . . a lot.

Regardless, whenever I find the time to take a class, I go. No matter how out of sorts I am. No matter how disheveled I feel.

You know why?

Because I don't give a fuck.

I don't care that I have no makeup on or that my hair looks like a wild rat's nest. I don't care that I make primitive animal faces when rolling around, or that my gi is two sizes too big and looks unflattering on my small frame. I suppose I could spend more money to get a sharper-looking one, but that would defeat the purpose of why I go.

Because if I cared about how I looked or what others thought of me in class, I would never go. I'd be racked with feelings of inadequacy, worrying if I was lowering the bar for the other, more experienced fighters. If I was constantly comparing myself to the most talented people on the mat, I'd be too embarrassed to ever return. For that reason, I don't tell anyone that I was a Special Agent, because I don't want the pressure of feeling like I need to prove something to them.

I go for myself alone. To become strong. To learn a different art of fighting. To protect myself. To move and work my body in a new way. To become comfortable with being uncomfortable so that I can continue the never-ending quest of building my resilience. I am there for me, and no one else.

There are few times in my life where I don't think about or calculate my outward appearance and how I present myself to the world. When I work out or go to jiujitsu, it's not about the world—it is about me and my own inward focus. It's about tuning in to the movements of my body, mind, and soul. I am there to find the strongest version of me. Frankly, I live for these moments, when I go in so deep that I no longer care who or what others see and center entirely on my own growth. Finding an area of my life in which I give no fucks is the greatest gift I have given to myself.

I know that with time and practice, I will get better. I know I will learn more and grow more confident. And eventually I will move up in rank, if I choose to. I don't go hoping to get the approval of others, or even that of my husband, as much as I love him. When I go, I compete with no one but myself.

Creating a Bulletproof Mind

Our mental state of mind influences how we interact with the world. You can nurture either a strong mind or a weak one. But even for those of us who invest energy into maintaining a strong mind, there will be flux and flow. Everyone has highs and lows—there's no avoiding them, and unfortunately there is no way to always be and feel strong. Like being in the ocean, no matter how strong a swimmer you are, there will be times when the current will pull you under. And that's okay.

When you find yourself struggling with the weight of everything and desperately needing to come up for air, there are some simple things you can do to help. Whether you use them for a daily pick-me-up or something right before a big event, these "influencers" can give you the strength and courage you're looking for.

THE BULLETPROOF MOVIE

Is there a particular movie that really amps you up? Research shows that watching a movie can set complex processes in your brain to work toward shifting your psychological mindset. This is what allows us to get swept up in a movie, to internalize the struggles of a protagonist we relate to and rejoice in their victories. Personally, *Gladiator* and the *Rocky* movies are my go-tos. Every time I watch them, I feel mentally inspired and physically stronger. My internal supply of resilience gets replenished, allowing me to charge into any of the challenging situations I'm facing.

Birgit Wolz, a psychologist focusing on movies as therapy and author of *E-motion Picture Magic*, explains, "Because many films transmit ideas through emotion rather than intellect, they can neutralize the instinct to suppress feelings and trigger emotional release. . . . By eliciting emotions, watching movies can open doors that otherwise might stay closed." When we watch movies that uplift and inspire us, those sensations linger long after the movie is over. Pick a movie that mirrors a current problem you are struggling with in your life—hopefully it's not *Titanic*. Not only will it offer an emotional release, it will also motivate you to take action.

THE BULLETPROOF SONG

Music is another tool you can use to influence your mind in a more positive direction. A study came out recently that adds another important piece of information as to how our brains process music. When we satisfy our desire to eat, sleep, or reproduce, our brain releases dopamine—the "feel-good" neurochemical that elicits experiences of pleasure and reward. It turns out that this same chemical is released when listening to music as well.

I once worked with a fellow polygrapher who listened to the same song before every interrogation he did. While I was diligently reviewing my questions and strategically arranging the room, he would sit in the corner and listen to whatever it was that amped him up. We were often working on important, nerve-racking cases, and he knew that he would be a better interviewer if he felt powerful and confident from the get-go.

Find a song that makes you feel invincible. Try listening to it every morning, either on your way to work or school or before a significant event. If you're typically nervous or self-conscious before presenting at a meeting, the right song might give you just the lift you need to walk in with your head high.

PHYSICAL FITNESS

Another great resource for influencing your mindset is a regular work-out routine. Working out will make you not only physically strong, but mentally as well. Plus, working out releases endorphins, which positively influence your mood. Try setting aside time in your daily schedule to devote to your fitness and boost your mindset.

Additionally, our posture affects our mood. If you spend your day slumped over, you'll likely end up in a bit of a mental slump as well. Posture checks are a useful way to make sure that you're standing or sitting up straight, shoulders back, chest open. The mind follows the body, which means that shifting how we physically carry ourselves can shift our mindset just as much. I wear a bracelet that has POSTURE CHECK written on it. Every time I look at it, it reminds me to adjust my posture—which turns out to be dozens of times a day. Research shows that certain kinds of "power postures" can make us feel stronger. If you want to give this a go, try the Superman or Wonder Woman pose: Feet apart, firmly planted on the floor. Hands on hips. Chin up.

EXTREME EXPERIENCES

Now, for those really daunting situations, like quitting a job or leaving a bad relationship or anything that feels terrifying or overwhelming, there is another tier of tools you can try.

Odd as it might sound, extreme experiences like skydiving, bungee jumping, or race car driving are a great way to help you overcome other fears in your life. Jumping out of a plane prompts a spike of fear no matter how many times you do it. At the same time, it is empowering as hell to deliberately defy that F3 response. Even if the obstacle you need to overcome has nothing to do with planes or a fear of falling, research shows that facing one kind of fear can make others feel less overwhelming. These experiences can also help you feel more proactive and creative about solving your problems.

Chapter 23

Being Presidential

The greatest virtues are those which are most useful to other persons.
—ARISTOTLE

Virtues of a President and First Lady

There is no finer example of virtues than those embodied by our nation's presidents and First Ladies. During my time in the Secret Service, I witnessed these men and women become targets of unrelenting ridicule and insults. Neither their words nor actions were ever safe from public scrutiny. Every decision they made was picked apart, analyzed, and openly criticized for the entire world to see. To say that the president of the United States and the First Lady have to be resilient is an understatement.

The public tends to overlook the fact that they are people, like the rest of us, with a heart that can be broken, a mind that can be tormented, and a spirit that can despair. They endure the same amount of pain and suffering as anyone else. Yet none of the presidents or First Ladies I protected ever retaliated to cruelty with similar behavior. They have always tried to act honorably, with both class and composure. They have remained, in essence, "presidential."

My first introduction to the concept of distinct virtues came from the ancient Greek philosopher Aristotle. He described twelve virtues to be the embodiment of good moral character: Courage, Temperance, Liberality, Magnificence, Magnanimity, Ambition, Patience, Friendliness, Truthfulness, Wit, Modesty, and Justice. I later learned of a similar but slightly different set of virtues as a Secret Service recruit. The five points of the Secret Service star represent a virtue that each agent is meant to embody: Justice. Duty. Courage. Honesty. Loyalty.

Loyalty is where I want to begin. As an agent, I was given access to remarkable people and places. I've protected presidents and their families, foreign heads of state, and emirs. I have witnessed history in the making, and I've been privileged to see what transpires behind the scenes.

People often ask me questions like "Who was your favorite president?" Or "What was Michelle Obama really like?" I've been asked to confirm gossip or rumors. Spill secrets or dirt. Reveal the intimate details about people I swore to protect.

When I became an agent, I took an oath to uphold the virtues of the star. It is an oath I still keep today.

Besides, their stories are not mine to tell. When people want to know intimate stories about First Lady Obama, I tell them to ask her. The people I protected were, well, people. My people. People I vowed to protect, and not just in the physical sense. They placed a great deal of trust in me as an agent to let me in and be around them. So if you're after the gritty details of a particular administration, look elsewhere. You will not find those stories within these pages or within me.

But what I can and do want to share are the virtues I have learned from these remarkable men and women. Because they are all each remarkable in their own way. No matter what your political stance—left, right, upside down, or sideways—it takes an extraordinary person to be the president or First Lady of the United States. It is by no means an easy feat.

Over the years of standing in the shadows, I have observed and absorbed everything from them. I've noted the strengths and qualities my protectees embodied and done my best to emulate those I most admire. For that reason, among many others, I am forever grateful for my time with them. Unbeknownst to them, they were all my mentors.

Bill Clinton: GENEROSITY

If I had to put together a band made up of all the US presidents I protected, President Clinton would be the front man. And not just because he plays a mean saxophone, but because he was by far the rock star of the group. People loved him—and he loved people. Wherever he went, droves of adoring fans clamored around, seeking his attention. He was genuinely curious about them, which meant he never missed an opportunity to stop and talk. For a Clinton admirer, getting the president's personal attention, if only for a moment, was a memorable experience. As a Secret Service agent assigned to protect him, however, his impromptu chats caused more than a few gray hairs.

I can point out the location of a couple of wrinkles that exist thanks to President Clinton.

During one such occasion, I was the site agent at the New York City Hilton hotel, where he was speaking at an annual teacher's conference. To be clear, the New York Hilton in Midtown is the largest hotel in the city, with more than 1,900 guest rooms, 150,000 square feet of meeting space, and three full-service restaurants. This means it's busy—all the time. So not only did I have to find the safest path to get the president from his armored limo to the podium and back, but I had to do it without completely disrupting the hotel's services. Not an easy task.

For this particular event, to get the president inside the building I used an unmarked side door, which led through the kitchen—not the most ideal route, thanks to sharp knives, heavy pots, and people everywhere, but it made the most sense at the time. Part of our security agreement with the hotel was their promise to keep their employees out of the president's path and my promise to move through the hotel as quickly as possible. Once we passed through an area, the hotel workers could get back to doing whatever it was they were doing.

When President Clinton's motorcade arrived, I met the lead detail agent at the door and led the entourage of agents, the president, and support staff through the labyrinth of secure corridors to the backstage entrance. Just like clockwork. He entered, the crowd cheered, my security plan up to this point was flawless . . . and then he finished his speech early.

As the president made his way along the rope line, shaking hands with his guests, I sprinted back through the hallways, clearing the route and locking things down. Then I got to the kitchen. Scurrying about in front of me were line cooks, dishwashers, and chefs, all tending to the dietary needs of the hotel guests. I knew if the president saw these workers, he'd stop and talk, which was not part of our streamlined security plan. Nor were they cleared or vetted properly for a close interaction with him. I scrambled to get them all together, but it was like herding cats.

"Coming your way, Poumpouras," I heard the detail leader bark into my earpiece. "Make sure the route is secure."

"You guys are going to have to hold in here," I said while pointing to the large walk-in storage closet along the wall to my left. "Just a minute or two. As soon as he walks by, I'll let you out."

With smiles on their faces and not a shred of resistance, all fifteen of them filed inside. I had the sense they were happy just knowing the president would be passing by, even if only a few feet away—never mind the stainless steel barrier between them. After the last worker stepped in, I quickly closed the door behind them and locked it. Immediately, I heard commotion from within. I looked up only to see all their grinning faces smashed up against the glass looking back at me. Somehow, they had managed to cram nearly all their heads into the door's little circular window, hoping to get a glimpse of the rock star.

I frantically looked around for something to cover the hole. A piece of paper, aluminum foil, maybe even a pot lid. Nothing and no time. At that moment, the kitchen doors swung open and in walked President Clinton, smiling and happy as ever. As a last-ditch effort, I positioned myself directly in front of the door and made myself as big as possible. My body splayed out like a starfish. I hoped that my head would cover the porthole, but it didn't even reach the bottom of the window frame. The door was too large.

Please don't look, please don't look, please don't look, I kept repeating to myself. And then—*Shit!* He looked.

"Hey!" President Clinton said as he stopped in front of me. "Who's in there?"

The detail leader walking with the president gave me a look like he wanted to string me up next to the rib roast. Sure enough, President Clinton reached out and opened the closet door. The kitchen workers all stumbled out, as if they'd been piled into a clown car, each grinning with excitement to meet the president.

Quickly, I organized everyone into a makeshift line, which gave the president some room to maneuver and us the chance to set up a security bubble around him. President Clinton paused to greet each of them. Their faces beamed. He asked them their names, where they were from, and what their jobs were at the hotel. His questions weren't rushed, nor were they simple pleasantries he was exchanging.

His generosity toward others never ceased to amaze me. Too often in life, we can become distracted by our personal interests or time constraints, but President Clinton taught me how to slow down. Through watching him, I realized that my time is never too valuable to offer to the people I meet every day. Genuine curiosity about others, and learning about experiences and lives that are different from our own is how we build empathy and compassion. Generosity is often attributed to money, but the generosity I learned from President Bill Clinton is the generosity of time.

Hillary Clinton: FORTITUDE

We were all gathered on a secluded New York City side street—the Secret Service, NYPD, and Hillary Clinton's staff—briefing for the upcoming movement. A "movement" is when a Secret Service protectee physically moves from one place to another, such as walking from their residence to the motorcade, going from the East Wing to the West Wing, or working their way through a rope line. This movement, however, was a bit different—and exceptional. The former First Lady of the United States, Hillary Clinton, was going to march in New York City's Gay Pride Parade. She was the only Secret Service protectee I had known to do so. We were reviewing our security plan one last time before entering the parade route. I was assigned to be the follow-up driver. My job was to cover her six o'clock—literally her back—by following closely behind her with one of the Service's trucks. Should anything happen, I would use the vehicle to shield us from an attack, get Mrs. Clinton into the car, and hightail us out of the danger area.

We all looked at each other uneasily. Were we really about to put her into the middle of a parade route? In New York City? Surrounded by thousands—no, tens of thousands of people? With no way of knowing where a threat might come from, who was carrying a weapon, and how we would control all those spectators if things went wrong? We were only a handful of agents and we were relying heavily on the NYPD, as we so often did. We had Mrs. Clinton's back and the NYPD had ours.

But as much as we all frowned at the idea of even trying to talk her out of it, we knew there was no use. She was marching.

Dear God, I thought. *This is gonna be a doozy.*

I strapped on my bulletproof vest, hopped into the driver's seat of the large black Chevy Suburban, and started the engine. "Here we go," I murmured under my breath.

While she walked in the parade, I tailed right behind her. My eyes scanning the crowds, looking for anything that could cause her harm. I was hypervigilant and on edge the entire time. But Mrs. Clinton was, as ever, calm, cool, and collected.

As she walked in the parade, smiling and waving at everyone she saw in that sea of fun and flamboyance, people were shouting and waving back. Drag queens adorned in sparkling dresses and glamorous wigs were hollering, "You go, Miss Thing!" punctuated by frequent exclamations of "Queen!" It was clear that Hillary was having the time of her life, and so was the crowd. This was back in the early 2000s, when it wasn't the "popular" thing for a politician to do. Being gay was something many still criticized or shied away from. The Gay Pride Parade hadn't yet become a part of mainstream culture.

But the former First Lady was a woman who did what she believed in.

She was there because she wanted to be. Because it was important to her to show support and solidarity for a community of people that needed it.

As terrified as I was to be amid an unpredictable sea of people, it was one of the coolest assignments I've ever had. After she passed, the spectators saw me trailing behind her and quickly diverted their hoots and hollers my way.

"Ooooooh, girl! You go with your bad self!"

"You go, Miss Secret Service thing!"

"You keep our girl Hillary safe!"

I kept my face stoic, but couldn't help smiling on the inside. I was proud to be there, to be part of what she was doing and the message she was conveying by marching in that parade.

It took fortitude to do what she did. And I don't just mean showing up that day. I mean *everything* she did.

She went from being First Lady to senator to secretary of state to presidential candidate, all the while enduring the harshness of politics and a world that took aim at a woman who had the nerve to try. Over the course of my career, I have never seen anyone take as much mistreatment as Mrs. Clinton endured in the public eye.

While most of us would want to go home, hide under the covers, and soothe our pains by shoveling down a pint of ice cream, Hillary did the opposite. Hell, she'd get up on a stage in front of thousands and give a speech. Her unwavering defiance is unlike anything I have ever known.

When I am faced with ridicule, criticism, or judgment from others I think of her.

She is one of the most prevailing women—no, human beings—I've seen, and this wasn't just demonstrated once or twice in my years of protecting her. In every situation, she was like a mountain standing tall and strong in a blizzard. I know the sorts of insults and slander that world leaders receive can't help but penetrate their hearts, yet Mrs. Clinton seemingly had an ability to govern herself that made her impermeable. Her resilience wasn't a matter of getting back up after being knocked down. With Hillary, it was like "I never fell."

President George H. W. Bush: GRATITUDE

It was August 2004 and the Summer Olympics in Greece were coming to a close. For the past month, I'd been in Athens working alongside Greek officials as part of the security team for President Bush's visit to the Games. "Forty-One" was how we in the Service referred to President George H. W. Bush—the forty-first president of the United States. We did this to make sure we didn't confuse him with his son George W. Bush, the forty-third president of the United States.

One of the last formal events 41 was attending before heading back to the United States was taking place on a large private yacht docked in the port of Piraeus, the country's chief seaport, located along the western coastline of the Aegean Sea. The guest list was composed of a who's who of celebrities, wealthy Greek businessmen, government officials, and athletes.

The gathering was uneventful, which by Secret Service standards was a good thing. Because of the exclusivity of the attendees along with the limited access to the boat, the concerns for 41's safety were minimal. As the party started to wind down, President Bush went on a stroll along the yacht deck and toward the galley where the food had been prepared. As we walked, he paused to greet each person who had made his evening enjoyable. And I'm not talking about the other VIPs whom he'd been mingling with during the event. I'm talking about the crewmen and waitstaff, the bosun and bartenders. A woman in a maid's uniform was on the floor, organizing the towels in the pantry closet. When President Bush stopped to say hello, she paused as though not quite sure why he was speaking to her, before shyly returning a smile. We walked by the stewards, the deckhands, and the kitchen crew. At each passing, 41 stopped and expressed his utmost appreciation, letting them know they were the ones responsible for the event's success.

This was the nature of President George H. W. Bush. No matter where he was or who he was with, he always made it his business to show his gratitude for others. And when I say others, I mean the ones that most people of influence tend to ignore or overlook. But not 41. He'd let you know he was thankful, not only through his words, but his actions as well. Every Christmas Eve, President Bush stayed put at the White House so the agents assigned to his protective detail could spend the day with their families before accompanying him home to Kennebunkport, Maine, for the holidays. This was a tradition that his son, George W. Bush, carried on during his presidency.

And after finding out the two-year-old son of one of his detail agents had been diagnosed with leukemia, 41 shaved his head along with all the other agents as a sign of solidarity.

Over the years I have worked hard to embody this level of thoughtfulness. I am always searching for ways to express my gratitude to the people around me who make my world better.

George W. Bush: AUTHENTICITY

For some people, Waco, Texas, is known as the home of Baylor University; for others, it's the once small town now popularized by the television show *Fixer Upper*. For the Secret Service, Waco is considered the second home of President George W. Bush.

Officially called *Prairie Chapel Ranch*, or just *the Ranch*, by the agents who spent time there, it served as the Western White House for George W. during his eight years as the nation's forty-third president. It's where he spent nearly every vacation and holiday. This meant that when he was in Waco, we were in Waco, keeping the perimeter of his nearly 1,600-acre property and everything within it secure.

I'll be honest—I didn't like the Ranch the first time I went. Part of our overnight protection assignments meant standing for twelve-hour shifts alongside one of the shacks that encircled the property. At my particular post, however, I was forced to stand inside the shabby wooden box all night when a wildcat and her cubs decided to take up residence in the brush right outside. I'll take New York City subway rats any day.

Once the sun came up, the Ranch was a different story. It was beautiful, peaceful, and quiet. As was typical of mid-Texas terrain, the grounds were smattered with mature oaks and elm trees, waves of thick Buffalo grass, white prickly poppies, and more than forty miles of bike trails crisscrossing the landscape. Just the kind of place where George W. felt at home. And a far cry from the concrete and steel I'd grown accustomed to living with in Queens.

The president's time at the Ranch was anything but relaxing—for the agents, specifically. He was a constant outdoor enthusiast, which was why his Secret Service code name was *Trailblazer*. When he wasn't hacking new walking paths into the countryside, he was pulling fish out of the Brazos River. But I believe his favorite pastime was trying to outpace his Secret Service detail agents during his "leisurely" trail rides around the property. I saw only the bravest agents volunteer for this assignment, because not only was the president agile on a mountain bike, he was fast. Like, really fast. It wasn't uncommon to see former college athletes turned Secret Service agents fall out during the middle of these impromptu races. Reduced to jumping into the back of the follow-up vehicle and forcing the remaining "pedaling protectors" to pedal even harder always gave him a chuckle. That is why I never volunteered—I knew my limits. And mountain biking with 43 was one of them.

Regardless of whether he was trekking through a newly cut trail at the Ranch or strolling through the South Lawn of the White House, the greatest thing about President Bush was that he was the same man. In the world of politics, where artifice and pretentiousness ruled the stage, I never saw his character change once. Not in Waco, not in the White House. Not when the cameras were rolling or when they stopped. He remained authentic to who he was. He was true, he was consistent, and he was genuine—something you rarely see among the upper echelons of Washington, where everyone is trying to impress you by projecting a fabricated version of themselves.

I've thought a lot about President Bush's authenticity. Being a female agent in a male-dominated profession tested my willingness to conform on more than a few occasions. Sure, there were certain job requirements we all had to abide by regardless of gender, such as the clothing we wore, the protection equipment and gear we carried, and where and when we stood post. But beyond that, I chose to be my authentic self. I chose to read *Vogue* rather than *Guns & Ammo* while flying on *Air Force One*. I wore makeup, kept my hair long and in a ponytail, and had my nails manicured at least once a week—although I think some of the male agents did, too. The point is that it would have been easy to mold myself into the typical male agent stereotype. I had seen other female agents do it. But I knew that by doing so, I would lose a part of who I was.

Being a Secret Service agent was *what* I did for a living; it wasn't *who* I was as a person.

President George W. Bush's job was being the leader of the nation, an eight-year assignment. He was sixty-three years old when he left office. That's a mere 13 percent of his life. He was something else the other 87 percent of the time—a governor, Texas baseball team owner, husband, son, father, and now a painter. He knew exactly who he was, and he never let anyone alter his authenticity.

Laura Bush: GRACE

The town of Kennebunkport sits on the Atlantic coastline of Maine about thirty miles south of Portland. Within the town of about 3,600 residents lies a rocky outcropping called *Walker's Point*—home to President George H. W. Bush since the 1970s. This was the Bushes' second home outside their official residence in Washington, DC; it was a coveted spot where they'd go to take a pause from the demands of running the free world.

On this particular Memorial Day weekend, I was at Walker's Point with the Bush family—the entire Bush family: President George H. W. Bush and his wife, Barbara; their son President George W. Bush and his wife, Laura, their twin daughters Barbara and Jenna, their cousins, uncles, aunts . . . pretty much the whole family tree.

Because secondary presidential homes are nearly as secure as the White House, we make an effort to hang a bit more in the shadows, giving our protectees as much private time as safely possible. Plus, with so many high-level dignitaries in one place, the compound was swarming with sunglasses-clad agents. It honestly looked like a Ray-Ban fashion convention.

I was sitting in the command post, a separate structure on the compound that served as our headquarters, when my BlackBerry pinged. It was Barbara letting me know she was going for a walk with her mom, Laura. "Turquoise is going for a walk with her mom," I announced to the other agents. (As I mentioned previously, Turquoise was Barbara's code name.)

I grabbed my gear, adjusted the straps on my bulletproof vest, and headed out the door with Mrs. Bush's detail leader. As was typical for these types of unplanned movements, detail leaders would walk a few paces behind our protectees while a team of agents both led and followed on foot and in support vehicles.

"We just want to go out for a speed walk," Mrs. Bush said as we met the two women near the front steps to the house.

"Of course, ma'am," her Detail Leader replied.

As Barbara and the First Lady strolled along Walker's Point, they would have looked like any other mother and daughter duo out for a bit of exercise . . . But Kennebunkport was a small town. Everyone knew who they were, a fact further exemplified by their two armed escorts and slow-rolling black Suburbans only a few yards away.

"Mrs. Bush! Mrs. Bush! A picture please!"

It hadn't been more than a few minutes since we left the compound gates, and Mrs. Bush was already being swarmed by the locals—another mother-daughter pair who just happened to be walking toward us on the same side of the street. As I stepped in to say something, Mrs. Bush gave me the "It's okay" look.

"Of course," she said.

As Barbara walked over to me, Mrs. Bush stood smiling next to the woman while her daughter snapped away. The photo op ended, but the woman quickly careened into a lengthy monologue, excitedly chatting away. Barbara finally grabbed her mother's arm in a gesture to quickly end her talk and move on. "Thank you," Mrs. Bush said, and we continued down the sidewalk . . . for about three more minutes.

This time it was another woman with a few small children in tow. "Mrs. Bush! Mrs. Bush!" she yelled. Again, the Detail Leader and I looked at Tranquility—Mrs. Bush's code name. It was common practice for us to physically step in between our protectees and anything or anyone that was unwelcome at the time.

"It's okay," she said again.

As before, she greeted them all, took another photo, and we went on our way. Until it happened again . . . and again. There were cars honking, people waving. Even I was getting annoyed.

But if the First Lady was, she never showed it. Despite being unable to share just a few moments of peace with her daughter, she showed the same amount of patience and kindness to the first mother-daughter team as she did to the ones long after I stopped counting. She never appeared flustered or irritated. *Tranquility* was the perfect code name for her.

Finally, after the attention began turning into a bit of a spectacle, she looked at us and said, "I don't think this speed-walking thing is going to work. Let's head back."

As a result of becoming Barbara's Assistant Detail Leader, I ended up spending a great deal of time with Mrs. Bush. There was something special about her—a uniqueness to her mannerisms and speech. The way she moved and spoke to others. Her warmth and openness.

I never saw her refuse anyone a few minutes of her time, a smile, or a photo opportunity. While most other protectees used us agents (understandably) as buffers from overeager spectators, Tranquility did not. She understood how important it was to the person asking for her attention, and she was completely willing to offer it.

When people ask me to describe Mrs. Bush, only one word comes to mind: Grace. It embodied everything she did and every word she spoke.

Evy is short for Evyenia—my real name. Ironically it means *grace* in Greek. I always thought it was the worst possible way to describe me. Growing up, I wasn't graceful in any way. Not in my movements or my mannerisms. The most graceful thing I ever did as a child was body-slam my brother onto the couch, WWE style.

Yet, after years of watching Mrs. Bush interact with the public, her family, staff, the agents, I began to understand its true definition. It means treating each person you meet with kindness, being thoughtful in your words, and thankful in your heart. I didn't know what grace looked like, until I met Mrs. Bush.

Whenever I find myself flustered or overwhelmed by the demands of too many people, too many questions, or too many emails, I think of Tranquility. I try to exemplify the patience and eloquence she exuded that made her such a pleasure to know. She was the type of person you always wanted to be around. Whenever I left her presence, I left a better person.

Michelle Obama: SELF-WORTH

The morning shift at the White House was probably my least favorite assignment. I would wake up at 3:30 a.m. to get dressed and ready so I could be at the White House on post by 5 a.m. Shift work was difficult in that it changed every two weeks. In other words, you'd work two weeks of day shifts, two weeks of afternoon shifts, two weeks of night shifts, two weeks of training or travel, and then start the rotation all over again. Aside from working in freezing temperatures, for me this was the hardest part of the "job."

When you page through lifestyle magazines like *Forbes* or *Inc.*, you'll likely come across an article or two about how many of the most successful people in the world have a steady morning routine to jumpstart their day. I learned the truth of this firsthand from First Lady Michelle Obama.

Her mornings were perfectly choreographed. She would wake up early, get her daughters, Malia and Sasha, ready for school, send them off, and then start her day. First, there was her morning workout. Every day, without fail, she would spend an hour focused entirely on her physical fitness. This was followed by her morning prep of hair and makeup, where I observed the thoughtfulness she put into how she presented herself and prepared for the day's events.

Mrs. Obama—a girl from the South Side of Chicago—understood what it meant to take pride in herself. She put a great deal of care in making her body strong, in her appearance and eloquence. Her morning rituals weren't about vanity, rather self-respect and self-worth. And as a result, there was an undeniable splendor to her—a glow and a magnificence that radiated from how she spoke and carried herself. When she entered a room, everyone took notice.

Mrs. Obama has a formidable kind of strength and poise that was expressed in everything she did. As the first black First Lady of the United States, Mrs. Obama had to withstand certain kinds of disparagement that none of her predecessors ever faced. I was on her protective detail when we were driving to a school to deliver a speech; we passed someone on a bridge holding up a shockingly racist sign directed at her. I remember feeling outraged—after all, it was part of our jobs to protect the first family mentally as well as physically. But if the First Lady saw the sign, she gave no indication of it. We arrived at the school and she walked out with her head held high, ready to inspire all of the students eagerly waiting for her.

Mrs. Obama taught me that self-worth does not depend on the opinion of others. It isn't something you stumble upon. It is something you cultivate. It is something you prioritize and practice every single day. Her daily routine was a part of that and it was nonnegotiable. She prioritized her time as a mother and she prioritized her self-care.

It reminded me of the safety instructions you get on an airplane— put on your own oxygen mask before helping someone else put on theirs. Taking care of ourselves is how we are fortified and able to care for others.

From her I have discovered that self-worth, magnificence even, comes from the small things we do every day to show that we value ourselves.

Barack Obama: MAGNANIMITY

One day I was escorting President Obama through the Oval Colonnade on his way to the East Wing when a congressman approached us with his wife and children in tow. They were at the White House attending the Congressional Picnic, an annual event hosted on the South Grounds for all the members of Congress and their families. President Obama had just finished a full day at the Oval Office and was hurriedly making his way to the residence so that he and the First Lady could appear at the event together. The congressman walked up to President Obama with an enthusiastic handshake and a huge smile. The president responded in kind and the congressman quickly ushered in and introduced each of his family members. He then asked the president for a group photo, which he politely obliged. As the congressman engaged the president further in what appeared to be a heartfelt, rather animated conversation, I couldn't help notice that the congressman's behavior seemed odd, more like a teenage groupie rather than an elected official. Throughout the interaction, the president remained courteous and amiable, as though they were old friends. And despite the need to return to his residence to meet the First Lady, President Obama opted instead to chat with the man's children about school and their visit to the White House.

Finally, after a pause in the conversation, the president politely excused himself and we continued our walk to the East Wing, eventually entering the elevator manned by the White House butler.

When the doors closed, the president looked at the butler and me and said, "That man who we just met, the one who was so eager to introduce me to his family? That's the same man who has been publicly berating me since my first day in office." I watched a disheartened expression cross the president's face as he recalled each and every insult the congressman had subjected him to.

This is one of the moments I always recall when I contemplate the qualities that make a person truly "presidential." Facing one of his fiercest critics, with every reason to avoid the congressman's engagement let alone deny his family photo request, President Obama instead extended nothing but magnanimity to his critic.

Regardless of the pressures put upon these leaders, time and again I have seen them exhibit tremendous self-control. Just as we expect no less from those who lead our great nation, we should also expect the same of ourselves. Acting "presidential" is not predicated on holding a position of professional power or public notoriety. That day on the Oval Colonnade was about the president's personal virtue, not political authority. He could have reacted in kind to the ridicule he had endured. That response, by all accounts, would have been justified. But that immediate gratification, that fleeting bit of payback, would have only lessened his character. So in that very instance, he made a choice. Instead of settling the score, he settled his sentiments.

There are times when we find ourselves mocked, embarrassed, or even publicly humiliated. Though our first and strongest inclination may be to "hit back," that doesn't mean it's the best choice for *our* character. Defending our honor is not the same as defending our ego.

Conclusion: Becoming Bulletproof

In the end, when it's over, all that matters is what you've done.
—ALEXANDER THE GREAT

"I have something to show you," my father said as he parked the car. We had just driven up a long, winding road through the mountainous terrain of the island of Chios in Greece. It was burning hot in midsummer, and somewhere back where we had come from, there were dozens of kids playing in the clear blue Aegean waters, peeling clams from rock beds, eating ice cream. I was nine years old and wanted nothing more than to be doing those things with the other kids, but instead we had just arrived at an ancient-looking monastery at the top of the mountains.

"Why are we here?" I asked. My father didn't answer. Instead, he got out and walked toward the walled courtyard.

I followed.

As I caught up to him, the hill leveled off into a plateau of sorts. A large stone compound spread out before us, its building and high walls painted stark white, outlined against the blue sky and rustic tiles that covered the roof. The entrance was a large steel door embedded with black crosses.

I tried a different tack. "What is this place?" I asked as we walked through the open gate.

Almost in answer to my question, a nun approached us. She exchanged simple pleasantries with my father, then gestured us to follow her toward the centermost building—a small church. As we followed, I couldn't help but feel this place was unlike anywhere I had ever been. I was quiet and reverent as we walked inside. The nun approached the altar and then pointed to a large spot on the white marble floor that was stained a dark hue of brownish red. "This is where they killed them," she said.

The Agios Minas Monastery overlooks the small village of Neocori on the island of Chios, where my father grew up. Built in the fifteenth century, the convent is famous for its place in the Massacre of 1822, when thousands of fleeing Greeks sought refuge within the walls of the convent and were cornered by the invading Turkish army. Over the course of days, more than three thousand Greeks were slaughtered or burned alive here.

I looked down to the ground beneath my feet and then back to my father, who simply nodded. From a distance the nun watched the revelation take hold on my face. She then slowly turned and led us into a small room adjacent to the altar. As we walked inside, a strange scent clung to the walls, something I couldn't place. The chamber was cavelike—a cold and dank cavern built into the stone. My eyes slowly adjusted, and then I saw them. Their sallow holes staring back. Hundreds and hundreds of skulls stacked among thousands of bones. That's when I realized it wasn't a cave, but a coffin.

"These are the skulls of the men, women, children, and babies the Turks killed," the nun said. Her voice was neither filled with rage or anguish. It was as if she had come to peace with the unthinkable long ago and was now merely reciting the facts.

As a little girl, I struggled to make sense of it all. *Why would anyone want to kill babies? Or Greeks? What had the Greeks done to cause so much hate? To perpetuate the annihilation of an entire culture?*

We were seeing the result of a slaughter. After almost four hundred years under Turkish rule of the Ottoman Empire, the Greeks had grown weary of their persecution. So in 1821, Greece revolted and declared its independence from Turkey's rule. In retaliation, the Turks punished the Greeks severely for their defiance. Turkey sent more than 40,000 of its troops to the island.

We followed the nun out of the church, back into the startling sunshine. She came to pause next to an old drinking well in the courtyard and took me by the hand, leading me toward it. "Inside is where they hid the children," she said. "Their parents put them inside the well to try to save them."

"What happened to them?" I asked.

"The Turks set the well on fire."

I looked down into the darkness of the well and then back at the church. I remember thinking, *I hope they fought back. I hope they fought back to the end.*

The island of Chios had a population of 120,000 Greeks. By the end of the massacre, only 2,000 remained.

I understood why my father had taken me there. And why he had taken my brother and me to many other places like it—to teach us the history of our ancestors. My father made it a point to expose us to as much as he could to the world, its injustices, and the importance of fighting back. He was preparing us for the realities of what life had in store. While most kids might have been afraid of what they saw, I wasn't. By now, these sorts of stories were already familiar to me. That's because my father wanted to teach us not to fear death, but to embrace it for what it is—part of life.

We are never done with fear. Whenever you think you've conquered one fear, there will always be another to take its place. There is no end point, no ultimate state of fearlessness that you can eventually achieve. This is as true for me as anyone else, because even now, as the final pages of this book are being written, I'm facing one of the worst fears of my life: Watching someone I love die.

Invasive adenocarcinoma of the pancreas is incurable. My father's diagnosis came with the news that he has only weeks, maybe months to live. Enough time, they told us, to settle his affairs and say good-bye. Sitting by his bedside, I've watched him diminish, both physically and cognitively. He's no longer the 165-pound, fierce-hearted man whose knee I sat atop while listening to stories of our ancestors. Instead, I now hold the frail hand of a man I hardly recognize, a shadow of his former self, unable to do anything. To eat anything. To understand anything, other than his pain and imminent death, which I cannot stop. There is only one other moment in my life when I felt this helpless—the day the Twin Towers fell, when all those people around me died and I could do nothing to save them.

Bulletproof though I may be, I am deeply afraid. I'm afraid of watching my father die. I'm afraid of seeing him suffer. I'm afraid to go to sleep at night in case something happens to him. I'm afraid of making the wrong decisions for his care. I'm afraid to say good-bye. I'm afraid of burying him. I'm afraid of what life will be like after he is gone. I've dedicated so much of my life to protecting people. There is no worse feeling than being unable to protect my father from the disease that is ravaging him.

Something else my father taught me, perhaps without meaning to, is that fear isn't always fear. My father disguised his love for me in the fear he expressed about the many unorthodox choices I've made in my life, from pursuing a career in law enforcement, to putting myself in harm's way and defending others, to pushing myself as far as I could in every part of life. I remember the way my father tried to warn me when I was growing up, his desire to make life simple and safe for his daughter, who did nothing the easy way. And I remember the day that he found the Secret Service's Valor Award I had been given for my actions on 9/11, which I had stashed haphazardly underneath my bed, and which he proudly displayed on the wall of our family home for everyone to see. It's still there now.

So often love and fear are two sides of the same coin. Which means that if we're willing and able to love, fear is inevitable. In this very moment, every single person you meet is dealing with something they're afraid of. But while fear can be the cause of so much hatred and hardship in the world, it doesn't have to be an isolating or limiting influence. We've all lost things to fear. We've all heard fear whispering in our ears, shivering across our skin, quickening our heartbeats. Yet, if you can learn to step away and see it for what it is, fear can be that singular thread woven deep through our shared humanity, our biological connection to one another.

Life has proven this to me again and again. It was proven to me on 9/11, when the building super cleared away the ash from my eyes and that little boy offered me his Snapple to rinse my mouth. And it's being proven to me again in the nights I spend at my father's bedside, when the woman at the front desk comes in to see if there is anything she can do to help us; when the police officer standing post by the emergency room entrance asks us if we are okay; when the people we pass in the hallway meet our eyes with compassion in recognition and understanding of the pain we are going through.

Each of these seemingly small acts of care and kindness has shown me that, even when we're at the mercy of circumstances, there is always a choice. Sometimes it's a choice that you never want to make, like the men and women who jumped from the towers on 9/11; each of those people knew that they were going to die—and they chose to fall rather than to burn. The choice I made to face my death head-on when the tower fell. The choice my father made not to prolong his life and his pain by undergoing chemotherapy. And the choice I'm making now to be here with him, to honor his last wishes to die on his terms.

All these choices are both terrible and terribly important. Yet simple, too, because they are all about having courage in the face of fear. Even in the most hopeless situations, this is one of the most meaningful acts of power you can claim for yourself. When the worst is happening, we can still face it honestly, humbly, courageously.

This, to me, is what it truly means to be bulletproof. To find the strength to bear the unbearable.

As you learn to use the knowledge I've shared with you in these pages to build your own Kevlar-like layers of resiliency, I hope you'll gain the confidence and perseverance to live your life fearlessly. To become someone who steps up—not just for yourself, but for others, too. We are all capable of making the world a safer place—to protect and defend others in their moment of need. You don't have to be a Secret Service agent to be courageous in a crisis. All of the experience, knowledge, and strength already exist within you, waiting to be unleashed.

No one told me what to do if I found myself in the midst of a massive terrorist attack, or if a 110-story building collapsed on top of me. I was twenty-five years old on September 11. I was five feet, two inches tall, 100 pounds, and just three months out of Secret Service training. I had no knowledge. No experience. No real wisdom. All I had was who I was as a human being. I still remember that moment vividly—me crouching under that metal table after the first tower fell, covered in toxic ash and debris, blinded and choking, so certain that my life was about to end at any moment. And the one thought foremost in my mind was, *Had I done enough? Had I helped enough?* Because, at my core, that is who I want to be. That is why I put myself through the rigors of training with the NYPD and Secret Service. It wasn't so that I could feel tough or invincible. It was because protecting and serving others is what I care about most—I always have and I hope I always will. Those strengths and skills are meaningful only if they're in service of something greater than yourself. My actions on September 11 had nothing to do with my training; they were a result of who I was as a person.

This is my hope for you as well. I want you to be governed not by your fear, but by the deeper elements of who you are—your innate strengths, your resilience, your genuine compassion. Once you build the skills to face your fears head-on, my true hope is that you will use those gifts to look out not just for yourself but also the world around you. In order to become the best and strongest humans we can be, we need to stay anchored to our humanity, to be willing to help those in need.

In all my years of protecting and serving a higher calling, this is what I've learned: Heroism is quiet. It isn't about bravado or being the biggest or the strongest. It isn't about firing guns or being awarded medals. It's about what's in your heart and mind and spirit. In a world full of unknown and unpredictable perils, most of us have been taught that it's someone else's job to protect us and keep us safe. It isn't. If you have the courage to take ownership of your own well-being, you will begin to see the world differently. You will begin to live differently. You will become rooted by your own strength and power in every situation, no matter how big or small. At the end of the day, the one person you should be able to fully rely upon to save you is you.

You are the hero you've been waiting for.

You are the hero the world has been waiting for.

Afterword: Fear and Courage

This book published in hardcover on April 21, 2020. In the year leading up to its release, a number of plans were made for the book launch—television appearances, interviews, a book tour. But a month before pub date, the world shut down in a way that was unprecedented. Canceling a book launch was a small thing compared to schools and offices shutting down, travel restrictions, and the fear that spread and touched every corner of the globe. How could it be that life could change so drastically in an instant for so many? Because we had not collectively gone through a global pandemic like this before, there was both fear and panic that grew week after week in a 24-hour news cycle of increasing numbers of infected, increasing deaths, and often conflicting information on what to do. On how to stay safe.

As weeks stretched to months, every single person had to practice the strategies in this book: resilience, mental toughness, and courage in the face of the unknown. What made it harder was we had no way of knowing when it would end. And without a timeframe to measure against, it felt impossible to pace ourselves.

Fear of the unknown has always been one of the hardest fears to overcome.

As of October 2023, there have been close to seven million deaths attributed to the pandemic. And within that number are the individual names of a person who had a life and a family who lost them. Like feeling helpless to watch my father die of cancer, many felt helpless as their loved ones passed away. I was able to be at my father's side as he passed, many could not be with their loved ones as they passed. Collectively we mourned. Collectively we are still in mourning.

The other side of this is the same as it was on September 11th: First responders doing what they do because not only is it in their training, but it is in their very nature, to help others in need. To run toward danger rather than away. And we saw ordinary people become heroes, stepping in to help others, to show us the best of what it means to be human. We sang together, we cried together, and even in isolation, we found a way to face our fear of the unknown together.

People weren't trained to deal with a pandemic, but they did. They found their courage in a million small and big ways. Humanity is resilient. You are resilient.

So while my book launched in a way unlike anything I had planned for, another thing happened after its release—people began reaching out asking for my help with a number of unique issues. They ranged from trying to manage a difficult boss to recovering from an unfulfilling career to ending an abusive relationship or overcoming a traumatic experience. I think the isolation of the pandemic was a time for people to reflect on the areas of their lives that they wanted to change. Survival sometimes means reevaluating our lives and searching for what matters most.

The requests came from all over the world via emails, direct messages, and social media posts. As much as I tried to respond to everyone and attempt to offer sage advice, it became nearly impossible to respond to them in the way they deserved. And because each person is as unique as their story there was no simple or quick response I could give. It also felt inauthentic and wrong to offer life changing advice in a mere one or two sentence reply. To better understand the full context of every dilemma that was shared with me, I needed to get clearer insight into who was reaching out and what was really going on. To do this right,

I needed to invest time and effort to ask the appropriate questions and thoughtfully give guidance.

So, I began mentoring people. I started off just doing a few at first, mostly for those who had already asked for help. I set some time aside which we'd spend together talking through whatever it was that was ailing them. Although I never directly asked, most told me they specifically sought out my counsel because they knew I would be honest and tell them the truth.

As my mentoring continued, I soon found I was doing multiple sessions for the same people, being referred to others, and even in talks with large corporations seeking personnel management strategies. What started out as a few requests, had now morphed into a massive undertaking.

Whether it was the head of the Human Resource Division within a Fortune 500 company or a stay-at-home mother of three, everyone received the same amount of care. As was my mission while a special agent, to serve and protect—I now considered each person I mentored my protectee; someone whose well-being was my responsibility—at least for the time we were together.

Over the last couple of years and after doing hundreds of sessions, I began to see a pattern emerge. It was vague at first, seemingly innocuous as though it was always there but not a noticeable player in my mentee's decision-making process. But the deeper I probed into the "why" of their problem, the more prominent it became.

Fear.

But not the obvious fear—what I call *overt fears*—like being afraid of heights or spiders.

I'm talking about fears that are concealed deep within us. Those we don't want to talk about. Those we suppress. Those we pretend aren't there—what I call *covert fears*.

These are the fears we intentionally—or unintentionally—hide away because we don't want to face them head on. Because doing so would mean two things: First, recognizing that we are responsible over the trajectory of our lives. And second, we don't yet have the nerve or courage to make the changes that need to be made.

And so, we make fear-based decisions. Meaning we make our choices based on fear. Based on what we are afraid of.

For example:

I am not going to leave my unhealthy relationship because I might not meet anyone else.

I am not going to leave my tyrant of a boss because I may not find another job.

If you look at the decision-making process in the above examples, they are both based on fear. Fear of not meeting someone else. Fear of not finding another job.

The problem with fear-based decisions is that they keep us locked in a hidden life of chronic stress and pain. Because we will do everything but deal with the real problem at hand. We will even look to create new problems elsewhere in order to distract and revert our focus from where it truly needs to be.

Fear-based decisions were the bedrock for nearly every important choice my mentees were making, or in most cases, not making. Their choices were all created from, weighed against, and executed through fear. To put it another way, they weren't making decisions based on what was BEST for them, they were making choices based on what they were AFRAID of.

Fear is an emotion. And it can be a confusing one. More times than not, we surrender too much power to it. To the point where it rules our lives. We become so accustomed to asking for its input, that we eventually allow it to control everything we do. It's now in the driver's seat. And we're in the passenger's seat, strapped in and holding on for dear life as fear completely wreaks havoc.

Fear-based decisions also often lead to inaction. We are so overwhelmed and confused by fear that we don't know what to do. When we don't know what to do, we usually do nothing. Doing nothing keeps us locked into more fear. More pain. More disappointment.

When we decide not to act, there is comfort in making that decision—

our mind is quick to justify that choice, finding reasons—mostly made up—as to why not doing something was the better option. But in truth, our self-talk is strategically designed to limit feelings of personal inadequacy and guilt. Unfortunately, when we buy into our own deception it not only makes us feel better, but it makes it easier to do it again, and again, and again. It's the inertia of staying in the same place.

I've had many sessions where my mentees failed to take personal action for their circumstances. Instead, they focused all of their attention on fixing someone or something else. For example, telling me how much they despised their boss. How underappreciated they felt. Often blatantly disrespected. And they will ask me how best to deal with this person. To get her to see things clearly. To change her behavior for the better.

"Evy, tell me how to change the way my boss treats me."

When I tell them I can't change their boss, they're confused. Seemingly lost. They quickly become silent as if imagining what the rest of their career will look like working under the oppression of a tyrant. I see it time and again. So I do my best to explain to them there is a whole other human being we are dealing with here. Someone who has a value and belief system fully ingrained in them based on so many intricate and long term factors—their genetic makeup, parents, siblings, whether they had parents or siblings, socioeconomic background, culture, geographical upbringing, level of education, their past and ongoing drama or trauma.

Here's the thing I also explain, we cannot change people who do not seek out change on their own. There is no magic formula, secret strategy, or time-proven tactic. What I can guide them through is how to create change for themselves—shifting the conversation away from the other person.

Me: *"It sounds like your boss is difficult."*

Them: *"Yes, she's beyond what I ever imagined I'd have to deal with in the workplace."*

Me: *"Why are you still working for her?"*

Them: *"Well, I can't leave."*

Me: "*Tell me why you can't leave?*"

Them: "*I don't have another job to go to and I have bills to pay.*"

Me: "*Have you looked for another job with comparable pay?*"

Them: "*No.*"

Me: "*Have you looked for another job at all?*"

Them: "*No.*"

Me: "*Have you tried transferring to a different division within the company?*"

Them: "*No.*"

Me: "*Have you done anything to better your situation rather than focusing on your boss?*"

Them: "*No*"

Me: "*Why?*"

Them: *Silence.*

They want the easy answer. For me to tell them it's their boss, that if we can fix her then . . . all will be perfect. But that's not the reality. And that's really not why they came to me. They came to me because they wanted to change their circumstances. To be encouraged—toward a better way of living. To not be placated. Or told everything was someone else's fault.

I am not in any way suggesting that how her boss is treating her is acceptable. It certainly isn't. A lot of my corporate consultations end up focusing not on employee problems, but on the way their management team is leading their staff.

What I am suggesting is that when we are able to unmask our fear and honestly answer what's holding us back—well that changes everything. We now have ownership over our life and the direction it is going. And if we don't like our supervisor or job, then we can make decisions to resolve this issue.

Moving beyond our personal fear of . . . fill in the blank, starts with peeling back the layers of *why*. Why are we not doing something? Why are we waiting?

Why are you waiting?

I have known fear and I have known courage and I have known fear again. There are things my special agent training prepared me for and things no amount of training can ever prepare me for. Just like with a pandemic, it's hard to prepare for something you haven't imagined. But the one thing we can train is our minds. Our agency. Our ability to face the things we want to turn away from.

Since my book published I have also become a mother for the first time. I didn't share my family's years of fear and frustration and devastation that my personal fertility journey entailed. But it's the story of so many parents struggling to conceive. Becoming a mother was the thing I wanted most in my life, but it felt like something too difficult to share publicly. There were times when I felt like a failure. Times when I wanted to give up. Times when I thought no matter how hard I tried, it was never going to happen.

And then it did. In the middle of a global pandemic I had a high-risk pregnancy, and my daughter was born. I also almost died during the delivery. I remember hovering above my own body thinking there was so much I wanted to teach my daughter about how to be strong in this world. How to face her fear. How to find courage. How to be a good human. There was so much love I wanted to share with her, so much joy I wanted to experience alongside her. But I could feel myself fading away, and I knew there was a choice to make.

But that is a story for my next book. As are the lessons I knew I wanted to share with her, and with all of you.

Life is hard and beautiful and wonderful and devastating. It is precious and fragile. We can train and prepare and fight for ourselves and others, but in the end, we are given the time we are given to honor each other, to learn from each other, and still, as always, to protect each other.

Challenges are a given, fear is a given, but so is courage. I know that whatever happens next in life, you are brave enough and strong enough to face it.

My wish for my daughter is the same as my wish for you: Trust in yourself. Have faith in yourself. Respect yourself. Love yourself.

This is how you survive hard times. This is how you lessen the energy of fear.

May you always be strong. May you always be fierce.

May you always own your existence.

May you know courage.

May you know love.

May you know that no matter what, you are never, ever, alone.

Acknowledgments

I am not self-made. I didn't get anywhere in life alone. I have been able to do the things I've done because others have helped me along the way. The same holds true with this book. I was able to write it because there were people who supported me, guided me, trusted in me, and had faith in me. Either through their words or actions, this book came to be because of them.

There are so many people in my life both past and present whom I am thankful for. Although your name may not appear here, please know you are not forgotten and I am forever in your debt.

I would like to thank my father—Ioannis Poumpouras—for passing his F3 response to me. Without it, I would not have had the nerve to stand up, speak up, and fight. Your spirit and fire live on within me.

I love you, Dad.

Σε αγαπώ μπαμπά.

There are so many others to thank who have made this journey possible:

My mother—Parthena Poumpouras—who, despite my wild and unorthodox ways and all the sleepless nights I caused her, still loves me unconditionally. Thank you for teaching me how to quiet the fight within me, and to be patient and thoughtful in my words and actions.

My brother—Theodoros "Teddy" Poumpouras—for letting me body slam you, put you in headlocks, and pick on you throughout our childhood. Despite it all, you still shared your toys and crayons with me even when I wouldn't share mine. You are the most giving person I know.

My husband—Desmond O'Neill—babe, you have been my True North. My constant and my rock. Thank you for challenging me and always believing in me. I was able to do this because of you.

My grandmother—Penelope Poursanidou—for pushing me to get an education and study hard. Yiayia—I hope you are proud of me.

My childhood friend—Fotini Marcopoulos—this idea all began with you. Thank you for being there for me when I had no clue how I was going to do this. I'll never forget how much you supported me.

My literary agent—Doug Abrams—I am honored to know and work with you. Thank you for letting me be a part of the Idea Architects family. I am humbled.

To Lara Love—my other literary agent/editor/travel companion/ collaborator/psychotherapist—Lara, this book would not exist were it not for you. Thank you for taking a chance on me. Not only did I get to write a book, but more important, I gained a lifelong friend.

To my manager, Pam Kohl—you've stuck by me all these years. Guiding me through a career I knew absolutely nothing about. Thank you for being my filter and keeping my F3 in check so I didn't piss off everyone in Hollywood.

To my friend Maria Menounos, who somehow inherited the same F3 response I did. (Must be a Greek thing). You, my sister, are a fighter. And to Keven Undergaro, thank you for always being there. You've inspired and taught me so much. You are one of a kind.

To Annie Wylde, for helping me organize all the chaos in my head into cohesive thoughts so people could actually read them. I still owe you a keg.

To my editors, Matthew Benjamin and Sarah Pelz, and the entire Atria team, for your unwavering support and guidance. Thank you for your counsel and sticking by me.

To my team across the pond, Kiera Jamison and the team at Icon—Caspian Dennis, Sandy Violette, Camilla Ferrier, and Jemma McDonagh—thank you so much for jumping on board and helping me share this book with the world.

To my attorney, David Schulz, for guiding and advising me through the pre-publication review process with the Secret Service. Thank you for making sure I didn't inadvertently spill any national security secrets.

To my publicist, Jill Fritzo, and her extraordinary team. Your hustle, work ethic, and expertise rival that of the Chief of Staff. I've never seen anyone work so hard. Thank you for helping me get this book out there.

To Robbin Mangano—my other publicist/deal maker/collaborator/social media guru. Thank you for being with me all these years. Explaining, guiding, advising, and showing me how to get shit done in this business.

And of course I must not forget to thank all those people who over the course of my life have confused, derailed, manipulated, tormented, and challenged me. Thank you for helping me to become bulletproof.

Index

About the Author

Evy Poumpouras is a former Special Agent of the United States Secret Service and on-air national TV contributor who frequently appears on NBC, MSNBC, CNN, and HLN. She holds a Master of Arts in forensic psychology and a Master of Science from Columbia University Graduate School of Journalism. She is also the recipient of the United States Secret Service Valor Award for her heroism on 9/11 and has been part of the protective details for former presidents Barack Obama, George W. Bush, William J. Clinton, and George H. W. Bush. She is also an adjunct professor for the City University of New York, where she teaches criminal justice and criminology. To learn more, visit EvyPoumpouras.com.